"We kinda hedge"

EMPOWER
SECOND EDITION
STUDENT'S BOOK
WITH EBOOK

• we left for the airport

• Linguahouse.com

B2 UPPER INTERMEDIATE

Adrian Doff, Craig Thaine
Herbert Puchta, Jeff Stranks, Peter Lewis-Jones

EMPOWER SECOND EDITION is a six-level general English course for adult and young adult learners, taking students from beginner to advanced level (CEFR A1 to C1). *Empower* combines course content from Cambridge University Press with validated assessment from the experts at Cambridge Assessment English.

Empower's unique mix of engaging classroom materials and reliable assessment enables learners to make consistent and measurable progress.

Content you love.

Assessment you can trust.

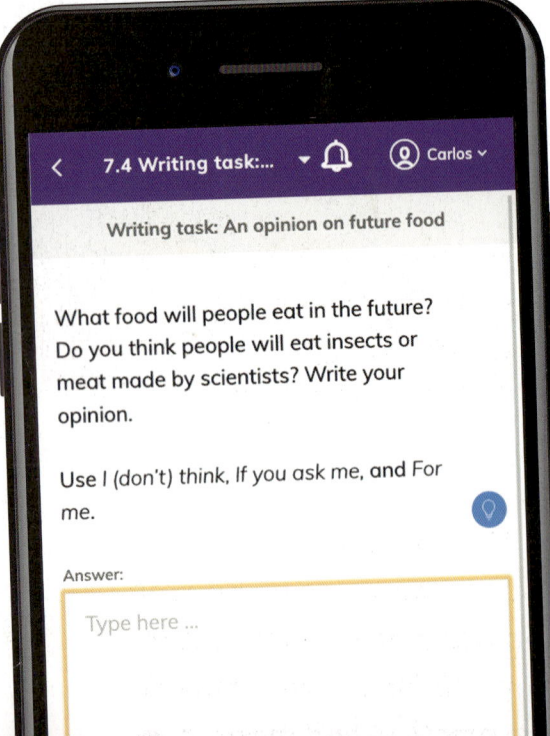

Better Learning with *Empower*

Better Learning is our simple approach where insights we've gained from research have helped shape content that drives results.

Learner engagement

1 Content that informs and motivates

Insights
Sustained motivation is key to successful language learning and skills development.

Content
Clear learning goals, thought-provoking images, texts and speaking activities, plus video content to arouse curiosity.

Results
Content that surprises, entertains and provokes an emotional response, helping teachers to deliver motivating and memorable lessons.

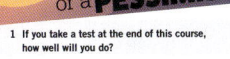

2 Personalised and relevant

Insights
Language learners benefit from frequent opportunities to personalise their responses.

Content
Personalisation tasks in every unit make the target language more meaningful to the individual learner.

Results
Personal responses make learning more memorable and inclusive, with all students participating in spontaneous spoken interaction.

> "There are so many adjectives to describe such a wonderful series, but in my opinion it's very reliable, practical and modern."
>
> **Zenaide Brianez, Director of Studies, Instituto da Língua Inglesa, Brazil**

Measurable progress

1 Assessment you can trust

Insights
Tests developed and validated by Cambridge Assessment English, the world leaders in language assessment, to ensure they are accurate and meaningful.

Content
End-of-unit tests, mid- and end-of-course competency tests, and personalised CEFR test report forms provide reliable information on progress with language skills.

Results
Teachers can see learners' progress at a glance, and learners can see measurable progress, which leads to greater motivation.

Results of an impact study showing % improvement of Reading levels, based on global *Empower* students' scores over one year.

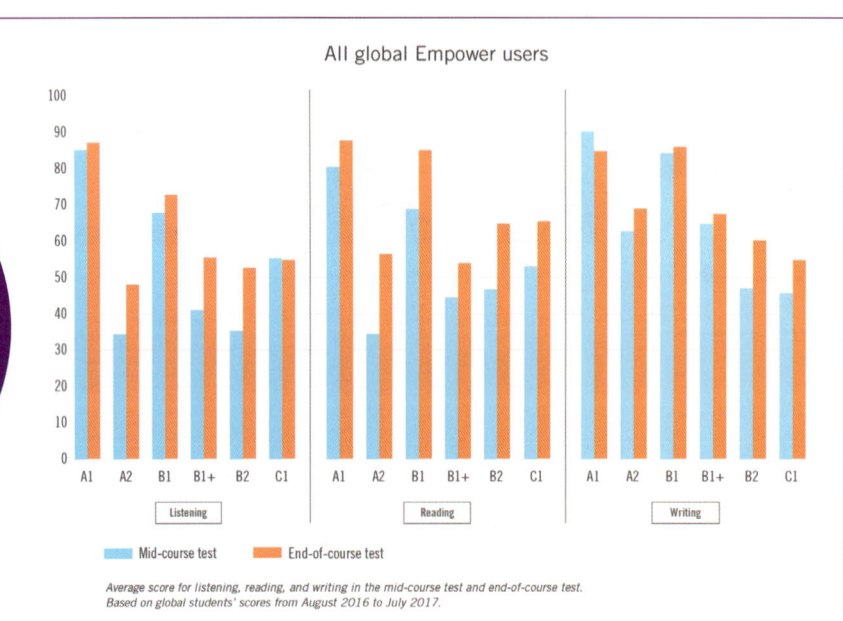

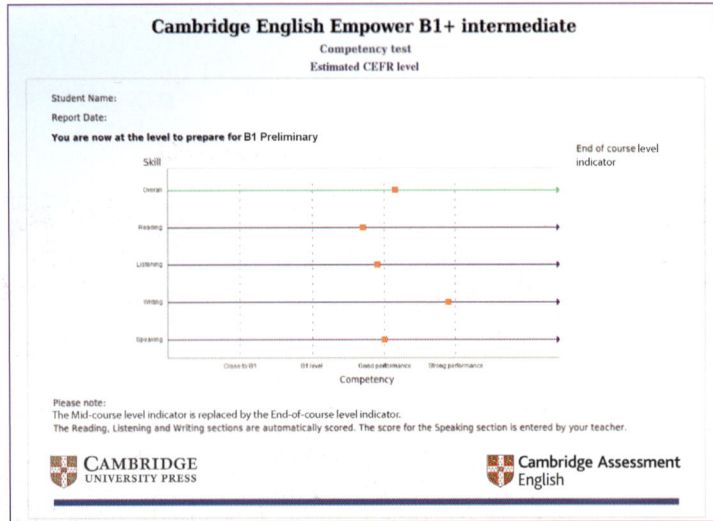

> "We started using the tests provided with Empower and our students started showing better results from this point until now."

Kristina Ivanova, Director of Foreign Language Training Centre, ITMO University, Saint Petersburg, Russia

2 Evidence of impact

Insights
Schools and universities need to show that they are evaluating the effectiveness of their language programmes.

Content
Empower (British English) impact studies have been carried out in various countries, including Russia, Brazil, Turkey and the UK, to provide evidence of positive impact and progress.

Results
Colleges and universities have demonstrated a significant improvement in language level between the mid- and end-of-course tests, as well as a high level of teacher satisfaction with *Empower*.

Manageable learning

1 Mobile friendly

Insights
Learners expect online content to be mobile friendly but also flexible and easy to use on any digital device.

Content
Empower provides easy access to Digital Workbook content that works on any device and includes practice activities with audio.

Results
Digital Workbook content is easy to access anywhere, and produces meaningful and actionable data so teachers can track their students' progress and adapt their lesson accordingly.

> *I had been studying English for ten years before university, and I didn't succeed. But now with Empower I know my level of English has changed.*

Nikita, *Empower* Student, ITMO University, Saint Petersburg, Russia

2 Corpus-informed

Insights
Corpora can provide valuable information about the language items learners are able to learn successfully at each CEFR level.

Content
Two powerful resources – Cambridge Corpus and English Profile – informed the development of the *Empower* course syllabus and the writing of the materials.

Results
Learners are presented with the target language they are able to incorporate and use at the right point in their learning journey. They are not overwhelmed with unrealistic learning expectations.

Rich in practice

1 Language in use

Insights
It is essential that learners are offered frequent and manageable opportunities to practise the language they have been focusing on.

Content
Throughout the *Empower* Student's Book, learners are offered a wide variety of practice activities, plenty of controlled practice and frequent opportunities for communicative spoken practice.

Results
Meaningful practice makes new language more memorable and leads to more efficient progress in language acquisition.

2 Beyond the classroom

"There are plenty of opportunities for personalisation."

Elena Pro, Teacher, EOI de San Fernando de Henares, Spain

Insights
Progress with language learning often requires work outside of the classroom, and different teaching models require different approaches.

Content
Empower is available with a print workbook, online practice, documentary-style videos that expose learners to real-world English, plus additional resources with extra ideas and fun activities.

Results
This choice of additional resources helps teachers to find the most effective ways to motivate their students both inside and outside the classroom.

Unit overview

Unit Opener
Getting started page – Clear learning objectives to give an immediate sense of purpose.

↓

Lessons A and B
Grammar and Vocabulary – Input and practice of core grammar and vocabulary, plus a mix of skills.

— **Digital Workbook (online, mobile):** Grammar and Vocabulary

↓

Lesson C
Everyday English – Functional language in common, everyday situations.

— **Digital Workbook (online, mobile):** Listening and Speaking

↓

Unit Progress Test

↓

Lesson D
Integrated Skills – Practice of all four skills, with a special emphasis on writing.

— **Digital Workbook (online, mobile):** Reading and Writing

↓

Review
Extra practice of grammar, vocabulary and pronunciation. Also a 'Review your progress' section for students to reflect on the unit.

↓

Mid- / End-of-course test

↓

Additional practice
Further practice is available for outside of the class with these components.
Digital Workbook (online, mobile)
Workbook (print)

Components

Resources – Available on cambridgeone.org

- Audio
- Video
- Unit Progress Tests (print)
- Unit Progress Tests (online)
- Mid- and end-of-course assessment (print)
- Mid- and end-of-course assessment (online)
- Digital Workbook (online)
- Photocopiable Grammar, Vocabulary and Pronunciation worksheets

CONTENTS

Lesson and objective	Grammar	Vocabulary	Pronunciation	Everyday English
Unit 1 Outstanding people				
Getting started Discuss meeting famous people				
1A Discuss people you admire	Review of tenses	Character adjectives	The letter *e*; Word stress	
1B Discuss a challenge	Questions	Trying and succeeding		
1C Explain what to do and check understanding			Rapid speech	Breaking off a conversation; Explaining and checking understanding
1D Write an article				
Review and extension More practice		WORDPOWER *make*		
Unit 2 Survival				
Getting started Discuss coping with natural disasters				
2A Discuss dangerous situations	Narrative tenses	Expressions with *get*	Sound and spelling: *g*	
2B Give advice on avoiding danger	Future time clauses and conditionals	Animals and the environment		
2C Give and respond to compliments			Intonation in question tags	Agreeing using question tags; Giving compliments and responding
2D Write guidelines in a leaflet				
Review and extension More practice		WORDPOWER *face*		
Unit 3 Talent				
Getting started Discuss what makes something a work of art				
3A Discuss ability and achievement	Multi-word verbs	Ability and achievement		
3B Discuss sports activities and issues	Present perfect and present perfect continuous	Words connected with sport	Word stress	
3C Make careful suggestions			Sound and spelling: Consonant sounds	Keeping to the topic of the conversation; Making careful suggestions
3D Write a description of data				
Review and extension More practice		WORDPOWER *up*		
Unit 4 Life lessons				
Getting started Discuss childhood experiences				
4A Discuss events that changed your life	*used to* and *would*	Cause and result		
4B Discuss and describe rules	Obligation and permission	Talking about difficulty	Sound and spelling: *u*	
4C Describe photos			Contrastive stress	Describing photos; Expressing careful disagreement
4D Write an email to apply for work				
Review and extension More practice		WORDPOWER *as*		
Unit 5 Chance				
Getting started Discuss attitudes to risk				
5A Discuss possible future events	Future probability	Adjectives describing attitude	Sound and spelling: *th*	
5B Prepare for a job interview	Future perfect and future continuous	The natural world		
5C Discuss advantages and disadvantages			Intonation groups	Responding to an idea; Discussing advantages and disadvantages
5D Write an argument for and against an idea				
Review and extension More practice		WORDPOWER *side*		

Contents

Listening	Reading	Speaking	Writing
Conversation about Jocelyn Bell-Burnell	Articles: *Protector of the sea* and *The woman who reinvented children's TV*	Discussing inspiring people	
Podcast: *The 30-day challenge*	Interviews: *30-day challenge*	Asking and answering questions about challenges	
Starting a new job		Explaining a process; Checking understanding	✓ Unit Progress Test
Conversation about technology	Article: *Tech free!*	Discussing technology	Article Organising an article
Conversation about a survival situation	Article: *Lost at sea*	Telling a survival story	
Interview: *The Tiger*	Leaflet: *How to survive … an animal attack*	Giving advice; Asking questions	
Cooking for a friend		Giving compliments and responding	✓ Unit Progress Test
Talking about getting lost	Leaflet: *Be wise and survive*	Discussing the natural environment	Guidelines Organising guidelines in a leaflet
Conversation: learning experiences	Text about learning: *Learning to learn*	Talking about something you have put a lot of effort into	
Radio programme: *The sports gene*	Article: *Born to be the best*; Three articles about athletes	Discussing sport and ways to improve performance	
Making wedding plans		Planning a party	✓ Unit Progress Test
Interviews about sport	Article: *Fitness: Seattle snapshot*	Talking about popular sports	Article describing data Describing data
Interview: Psychology of money; Two monologues: Life-changing events	Two texts about life-changing events that helped people become rich	Talking about how your life has changed	
Two monologues: training for a job	Article: *Training for the emergency frontline*	Discuss experiences of training and rules	
Presenting photos		Describing photos; Expressing careful disagreement	✓ Unit Progress Test
Three monologues: living in different places	Advert for being an international student 'buddy'	Discussing living in a different country	Job application Giving a positive impression
Monologue: What are your chances?	Quiz: *Are you an optimist or a pessimist?*; Article: *Why we think we're going to have a long and happy life*	Discussing possible future events	
Conversation: talking about work	Quiz: *The unknown continent*; Article: *Cooking in Antarctica*	Role play: a job interview	
Money problems		Explaining and responding to an idea for a café	✓ Unit Progress Test
News reports: environmental problems	Essay about protecting the environment	Giving opinions on environmental problems	For and against essay Arguing for and against an idea

3

Lesson and objective	Grammar	Vocabulary	Pronunciation	Everyday English
Unit 6 Around the globe				
Getting started Discuss travelling				
6A Discuss choices	Infinitives and -ing forms	Travel and tourism	Consonant clusters	
6B Discuss changes	The passive	Describing changes		
6C Introduce requests and say you are grateful			Consonant sounds	Introducing requests; Showing you are grateful
6D Write a travel blog				
Review and extension More practice		**WORDPOWER** *out*		
Unit 7 City living				
Getting started Discuss the design of new buildings				
7A Discuss living in cities	*too / enough*; *so / such*	Describing life in cities		
7B Discuss changes to a home	Causative *have / get*	Film and TV; Houses	Sound and spelling: *o*	
7C Imagine how things could be			Stress in compound nouns	Imagining how things could be; Using vague language
7D Write an email to complain				
Review and extension More practice		**WORDPOWER** *down*		
Unit 8 Dilemmas				
Getting started Discuss attitudes to money				
8A Discuss personal finance	First and second conditionals	Money and finance		
8B Discuss moral dilemmas and crime	Third conditional; *should have* + past participle	Crime	Stressed and unstressed words; Sound and spelling: *I*	
8C Be encouraging			Word groups	Being encouraging; Showing you have things in common
8D Write a review				
Review and extension More practice		**WORDPOWER** *take*		
Unit 9 Discoveries				
Getting started Discuss the impact of new inventions				
9A Discuss new inventions	Relative clauses	Health	Sound and spelling: *ui*	
9B Discuss people's lives and achievements	Reported speech; Reporting verbs	Verbs describing thought and knowledge		
9C Express uncertainty			Linking and intrusion	Expressing uncertainty; Clarifying a misunderstanding
9D Write an essay expressing a point of view				
Review and extension More practice		**WORDPOWER** *come*		
Unit 10 Possibilities				
Getting started Discuss ambitions and expectations				
10A Speculate about the past	Past modals of deduction	Adjectives with prefixes	Word stress	
10B Discuss life achievements	Wishes and regrets	Verbs of effort	Linking	
10C Describe how you felt			Consonant clusters	Describing how you felt; Interrupting and announcing news
10D Write a narrative				
Review and extension More practice		**WORDPOWER** *way*		
Communication Plus p.127	**Grammar Focus** p.134		**Vocabulary Focus** p.154	

Contents

Listening	Reading	Speaking	Writing
Two monologues about sightseeing tours	Website about four tourist destinations; Website: *Where to go?*	Comparing different tourist destinations	
Interview: disappearing languages	Article: *Danger! Dying languages*	Agreeing and disagreeing	
Asking for a favour		Asking for a favour	**Unit Progress Test**
Conversation: a trip to the Grand Canyon	Travel blog: *Around the Grand Canyon*	Discussing local tourist destinations	Travel blog Using descriptive language
Interview: 'Smart' cities; Two monologues talking about 'smart' cities	Article: *Quick – slow down!*	Discussing good and bad points about a city	
Two monologues: house renovations	Article: *Who puts the 'real' in reality TV?*	Planning a home renovation	
Flat hunting		Designing and describing a new room	**Unit Progress Test**
Interviews about a new shopping centre	Email: complaining about an important issue		Email of complaint Using formal language
Radio programme: personal finance	Article: *Is it time to give up on cash?*	Giving opinions on financial matters	
Three monologues about honesty	Newspaper article: *The honesty experiment*	Discussing moral dilemmas	
Going to the bank		Talking about hopes and worries	**Unit Progress Test**
Conversation about a TV programme	Review: *Crime with a smile*	Discussing programmes about crime	Review Organising a review
Conversation about inventions	Article: *Too good to be true?*	Talking about inventions	
Conversation about an email hoax	Article: *The rise and fall of Barry Minkow*	Describing a hoax or a scam or a case of fraud	
Finding the perfect flat		Giving and receiving surprises	**Unit Progress Test**
Four monologues about alternative medicine	Essay: *The value of alternative medicine*		Opinion essay Presenting a series of arguments
Interview about Dan Cooper	Story: *The man who disappeared*; Blog: *The Wreck of the Titan*	Telling stories about coincidences	
Two monologues: pursuing a dream	Article: *Dream to help*	Describing and comparing brave or amazing people	
Celebrating good news		Telling an important piece of news	**Unit Progress Test**
Conversation about goals	Story: *Rosa's diary: The ultimate goal*	Talking about performing	Story Making a story interesting

Phonemic symbols and Irregular verbs p.164

This page is intentionally left blank.

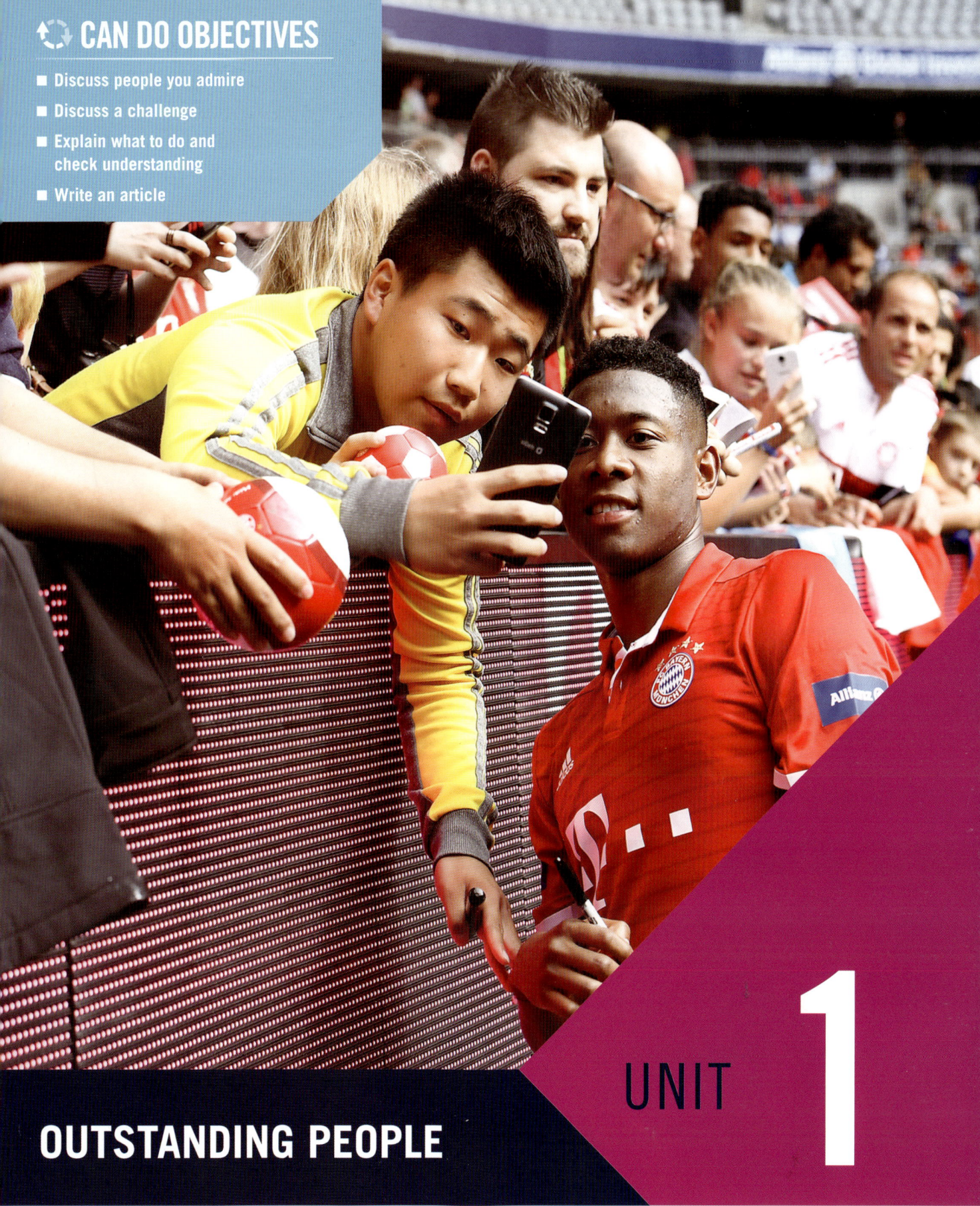

CAN DO OBJECTIVES

- Discuss people you admire
- Discuss a challenge
- Explain what to do and check understanding
- Write an article

OUTSTANDING PEOPLE

UNIT 1

GETTING STARTED

a Look at the picture and answer the questions.
  1 Who do you think the people taking a selfie are? Where are they?
  2 What are the people around them doing?
  3 What do you think they have just said to each other? What's going to happen next?

b Discuss the questions.
  1 On what occasions do you normally take photos?
  2 If you could take a selfie with a famous person, who would you choose and why?
  3 What role do you think famous people play in society? Should they be good role models? Should they inspire other people?

7

1A SHE IS AN INSPIRING WOMAN

Learn to discuss people you admire
- G Review of tenses
- V Character adjectives

1 READING

a What kinds of people do you admire most? Why?

b Look at photos a and b. What do you think these people have done to make others admire them?

c Read *Protector of the sea* and *The woman who reinvented children's TV* quickly and check your answers.

d Read the texts again and answer the questions. Write Swietenia Lestari (*SL*), Joan Ganz Cooney (*JC*) or both (*B*).
Who … ?
1. ☐ had training in their area of work
2. ☐ carried out some research
3. ☐ set up her own company/organisation
4. ☐ was one of the first people in their role
5. ☐ was encouraged by a family member
6. ☐ was interested in other people's learning
7. ☐ trained the public to be more aware of an issue
8. ☐ helped to raise money

e Who do you think is more inspiring, Swietenia Lestari or Joan Ganz Cooney? Why?

Protector of the sea

Like most people these days, I'm really concerned about the state of our planet – but it sometimes seems really difficult to know what to do about it. I really admire people who just do something and make a difference. That's why I think diver and environmentalist Swietenia Puspa Lestari is an inspiration to us all.

In the time you're reading this article, about one lorryload of plastic will go into the sea. And ¹**it's getting** worse. By the year 2050 some scientists predict there will be more plastic than fish in our oceans.

Since primary school, Swietenia Pupsa Lestari (known by the name Swietenia) ²**has been** a keen diver. She was born and brought up on Pramuka Island, which is part of the Thousand Islands chain north of Jakarta in Indonesia. When she was 13 years old, she realised just how much the sea ³**had changed** since she was a little girl. She could no longer see beautiful marine life and the seabed was covered with rubbish. She continued to worry about the state of the marine environment and this motivated her to study environmental engineering.

While she ⁴**was studying** at university, Swietenia ⁵**tried** to find an organisation that was doing something to protect the marine environment around Thousand Islands. But there was nothing. So, with two friends, she set up a community of about 100 divers who began cleaning up the rubbish they found in the sea. Two years later, the community became a foundation known as Divers Clean Action (DCA).

They collected data on marine waste and began to run workshops and training sessions to raise public awareness of marine rubbish. They have also worked with people living in coastal communities and showed them how they can recycle a lot of marine waste.

From being just a group of people who collected rubbish, DCA now employs 12 full-time staff and has a network of 1,500 volunteers. Swietenia's work in marine conservation has been recognised internationally.

Swietenia ⁶**believes** in the ability of young people to get out and do things in order to make a change. So, if I want to save the world, it's up to me.

8

THE WOMAN WHO REINVENTED CHILDREN'S TV

I've always felt passionate about television's ability to entertain and educate. I grew up watching what I consider to be a masterclass in how you can combine these two aspects of television: *Sesame Street*. This is the programme that brought us Big Bird, Elmo, Cookie Monster and more. These characters were brought to TV thanks to a woman I consider a genius: Joan Ganz Cooney.

In the mid-1960s, Ganz Cooney was working as a producer of television documentary programmes in America. She realised television could play an important role in the education of preschool children. She researched this idea and in 1967, she wrote an outline for *Sesame Street*.

Ganz Cooney presented her ideas to the TV network she was working for at the time. However, the network rejected her proposal, saying that they thought she didn't have the right experience to produce a TV programme for children. As a result, she set up Children's Television Workshop with a colleague, and two years later they had managed to raise $8 million to finance production. Even so, many people working in the television industry questioned her ability to manage such a project. This was during the 1960s, when the industry was largely controlled by men.

At first, Ganz Cooney didn't want to fight to keep her role as the director of the production company and the producer of the programme. However, her husband and a colleague encouraged her to do so because they knew the project would fail without her involvement. This meant she became one of the first female television executives in the United States.

In 1969, two years after her initial research, *Sesame Street* went on the air, and today it's still going strong. However, Joan Ganz Cooney didn't stop there. She continued to take an interest in early childhood education and in 2007, the Joan Ganz Cooney Center was founded to help improve children's digital literacy. I really admire the way she continued helping young children. She's not a household name like Big Bird, but she's won many awards for her work and had a huge impact on the education of millions of children around the world.

Sesame Street Facts
- more than 150 million viewers worldwide
- shown in more than 150 different countries
- now has a production budget of around $17 million a year

UNIT 1

2 GRAMMAR Review of tenses

a Match the verbs 1–6 in **bold** in *Protector of the sea* with the tenses below.
- ☐ present simple
- ☐ past simple
- ☐ present continuous
- ☐ past continuous
- ☐ present perfect
- ☐ past perfect

b Complete the sentences with the tenses in 2a.
We use the:
1 _____ to refer to an event that takes place at a specific time in the past.
2 _____ to refer to a temporary event in progress in the present.
3 _____ to refer to a state or action that began in the past and has continued until now.
4 _____ to refer to something that's generally true.
5 _____ to refer to an action that was in progress in the past when something else happened.
6 _____ to refer to a past action that occurred before another past action.

c <u>Underline</u> examples of the six tenses in the second text.

d ≫ Now go to Grammar Focus 1A on p. 134.

e Read the text about Susmita Mohanty and <u>underline</u> the correct answers.

f ▶ 01.02 Listen and check your answers.

SUSMITA MOHANTY

Not many people can answer the question 'What do you do?' with the answer 'spaceship designer'. But Indian-born Susmita Mohanty can. A space entrepreneur, she [1]*was setting up / has set up* three companies in three different continents. Since 2008, EARTH2ORBIT (E2O) [2]*helped / has helped* companies outside India take part in launches of the Indian PSLV rocket. Before that, Susmita [3]*had established / was establishing* LIQUIFER, an aerospace design firm in Vienna. And while she [4]*was living / has lived* in San Francisco in 2001, she [5]*set up / has set up* MOONFRONT, an aerospace consulting firm. Susmita has always loved space flight. She [6]*has / is having*  numerous degrees in engineering, design and space studies that allow her to make connections between the worlds of technology, business and architecture. Today she [7]*made / is making* science fiction become reality. Susmita is also a climate activist who makes satellite data on our planet available so that we can fight climate change. In the past few years, she [8]*receives / has received* recognition and awards from around the world. Susmita [9]*believes / is believing* that in this century, space travel will be as important as air travel was last century.

9

UNIT 1

3 LISTENING

a ▶ 01.03 Listen to two colleagues, Amelia and Chloe, talking about the scientist, Jocelyn Bell-Burnell. Tick (✓) the correct sentences.

1 She's always been famous. ☐
2 She isn't very well known. ☐
3 She made an amazing discovery. ☐
4 She created a new mathematical theory. ☐

b ▶ 01.03 Listen again. Are the sentences true or false?

1 Amelia's reading a nonfiction book about planets and stars.
2 Jocelyn Bell-Burnell discovered a kind of star.
3 Bell-Burnell won a Nobel Prize for her discovery.
4 Bell-Burnell did badly when studying science at high school.
5 Life wasn't easy for her when she made her discovery.
6 The press didn't treat Bell-Burnell seriously.
7 Amelia has been inspired by Jocelyn Bell-Burnell.

c 💬 Discuss the questions.

1 Could Jocelyn Bell-Burnell's story have happened in your country? Do you know any similar examples?
2 How popular is science in your country? Is it popular with both men and women?
3 Is it important what gender a scientist is? Why do you think it was important in the case of Jocelyn Bell-Burnell?

4 VOCABULARY
Character adjectives

a Underline the five adjectives that describe people's character in sentences 1–4. Which two adjectives have a similar meaning, and what's the difference between them?

1 She's a respected physicist.
2 She is an inspiring woman.
3 She was really determined, but in a quiet way.
4 Well, you've always been motivated, that's for sure. And stubborn.

b ▶ 01.04 **Pronunciation** Listen to the pronunciation of the letter *e* in these words. Which two sounds are the same? What are the other two sounds?

r**e**sp**e**cted   d**e**t**e**rmined

c ▶ 01.05 Look at the words in the box and decide how the underlined letter *e* is pronounced. Add the words to the table, then listen and check. Practise saying the words.

sl**e**pt   r**e**vise   h**e**lpful   s**e**rve   d**e**sire
pref**e**r   id**e**ntity   univ**e**rsity   wom**e**n

Sound 1 /ɪ/	Sound 2 /e/	Sound 3 /ɜː/

d Complete the sentences with the character adjectives in 4a.

1 Once Dan gets an idea in his head, nothing will change his mind. He's the most _____ person I know, and it's really annoying.
2 I'm not the sort of person who gives up easily – I'm very _____ to achieve new goals.
3 He's worked hard and has done some very interesting research. He's a highly _____ chemist who's known around the world.
4 Doing a PhD is hard work, so you have to be really _____ if you want to complete one.
5 In my last year of high school, we had a really _____ biology teacher. Her lessons were so interesting that we all worked very hard for her.

e ≫ Now go to Vocabulary Focus 1A on p. 154.

5 SPEAKING

a Think of an inspiring person who has influenced you in some way. It can be someone you know or someone famous. Make notes about the person. Use the questions to help you.

- What is this person's background?
- What important things has this person done in their life?
- Why are they inspiring?
- How have they changed or influenced your life?

b 💬 Tell other students about your person. Ask questions.

> My cousin Vera is an athlete. She trains really hard every day – she's very determined.

> How does she stay motivated?

10

1B ARE YOU FINDING IT DIFFICULT?

Learn to discuss a challenge
- G Questions
- V Trying and succeeding

The 30-day challenge

Have you ever started a new hobby but given up after only a couple of weeks? Or started a course and stopped after the first few lessons? Most of us have tried to learn something new, but very few of us ever really get any good at it – it's just too difficult to continue doing something new.

But now there's some good news: did you know that if you can keep up your new hobby for just 30 days, you have a much better chance of succeeding? And you may learn something new about yourself, too.

1 SPEAKING AND LISTENING

a 💬 Look at photos a–c and read *The 30-day challenge*. Then discuss the questions.
1 What are the people in the photos doing? Have you ever taken up similar activities? If so, how successful were you?
2 Do you think doing something for 30 days gives you a better chance of succeeding? Why / Why not?

b ▶01.09 Listen to a podcast about the 30-day challenge. Tick (✓) the main point that Alison makes.
1 The 30-day challenge is the only way to give up bad habits.
2 It's too difficult for the brain to adapt to new habits.
3 If you try something new for 30 days, you're more likely to keep to it afterwards.

c ▶01.09 Alison made some notes at the seminar. Complete her notes with one or two words in each gap. Listen again and check.

Seminar notes
- It takes the brain 30 days to adapt to a new ¹_____.
- 30 days isn't a ²_____ time, so it's fun to do something new.
- Also a chance to try something ³_____ – not just giving up bad habits.
- Two ways to do it:
  1 do something that doesn't get in the way of your ⁴_____
  2 take time out to do something you've always ⁵_____ do
- You need to make an ⁶_____ !

d What examples of 30-day challenges did you hear? Use words from both boxes for each challenge.

Cycle everywhere, even if it rains.

| ~~cycle~~   drink   climb   get up   eat   paint   write |

| rise   poem   coffee   meal   picture   mountain   ~~everywhere~~ |

e What do you think of the ideas Alison talks about? Make notes.

f 💬 Compare your ideas.

11

UNIT 1

2 VOCABULARY
Trying and succeeding

a ▶ 01.10 Complete the sentences with the phrases in the box. Listen and check your answers.

> give up   have a go at   keep it up   keep to
> make an effort   manage to   drop out
> try out   work out

1. Often if we try something new, we _____ after about a week or two because our brain hasn't adapted.
2. So if you _____ do something new for a month, you'll probably _____ it.
3. Maybe you wouldn't want to _____ for your whole life, but it might be fun to do it just for 30 days.
4. If you're successful it's great, but if it doesn't _____, it doesn't matter too much.
5. It's not just about giving up bad habits. The idea is really that you _____ something new.
6. You can be motivated and _____ something you've always wanted to do.
7. You must _____ to complete your goal.
8. Don't _____ of the challenge! Keep going and you will succeed.

b Match words and phrases from 2a with the meanings.

1. succeed _____, _____
2. stop trying _____, _____
3. not stop trying _____, _____
4. try hard _____
5. try to see if it works _____, _____

c Complete the sentences below about 30-day challenges. Use the words and phrases in 2a and your own ideas. There is more than one possible answer.

1. He tried giving up coffee for 30 days. It wasn't easy, but he …
2. You've woken up at 5:30 every morning for three weeks now. You only have one week to go, so …
3. 30-day challenges sound fun. I want to do something different, so I think I'll …

d 💬 Work in small groups. Tell the group about a time when you:
- found something difficult but didn't give up
- made a real effort to succeed
- had a go at something unusual
- managed to do something that worked out successfully
- tried to do something that didn't work out.

3 READING

a Look at challenges 1–3. Who do you think will find it easy, and who will find it difficult? Why?

b Read the interviews and check your ideas.

30-DAY CHALLENGE

Challenge 1: Sofia decided to go vegan.

What made you decide to become a vegan, Sofia?

Well, for quite a long time now I've been trying to eat less meat, partly for health reasons. I think a plant-based diet is better for you.

1 _____

Yes, but I always thought I'd miss meat too much. The idea of going vegan for 30 days was really good because I could give it a try and then see how I feel.

2 _____

No, I feel really good. Actually, I don't miss meat or dairy at all, so I think I'll easily manage the 30 days, and I might try to keep going longer.

Challenge 2: Carla decided to draw something every day.

Carla, why did you decide to draw something every day?

Well, I've never been very good at drawing, but I've always thought I'd like to start drawing things around me. It's one of those things that you think about doing, but you never get round to.

3 _____

All kinds of things. At the beginning, I drew objects around me at home. Then I went out in my lunch break and started drawing things outdoors, like yesterday I drew a duck in the park – that was really difficult!

So do you feel like it's been worthwhile?

Oh yes, definitely. I'm still not very good at drawing, but it's been a lot of fun and it's very relaxing.

12

UNIT 1

c Complete the interviews with the missing questions.
   a And who do you practise with? Or are you just studying alone?
   b Didn't you ever think of going vegan before?
   c And how do you feel? Are you finding it difficult?
   d And do you think you'll keep going after the 30 days?
   e What have you drawn pictures of so far?

d ▶ 01.11 Listen and check your answers.

4 GRAMMAR Questions

a Read the rules about questions. Find examples of each type of question in the interviews and 3c.

> 1 In questions, we usually put the auxiliary verb before the subject. If there is no auxiliary verb, we add *do* or *did*.
> **Are you** making dinner? **Have you** eaten?
> What **did you** eat?
> 2 If the question word (*who*, *what* or *which*) is the subject, we keep normal word order.
> **Who spoke** to you? **What happened** next?
> 3 If a question has a preposition, it usually comes at the end:
> You were talking to someone. → Who were you talking **to**?
> 4 To ask an opinion, we often ask questions starting with a phrase like *Do you think ... ?*
> The second part of the sentence has normal word order.
> Is it a good idea? → **Do you think** it's a good idea?
> NOT *Do you think **is it** a good idea?*

b Compare examples a and b.
   a Did you see her at the party?   b Didn't you see her at the party?
   Which example ... ?
   1 is a neutral question (= maybe she was there, maybe not)
   2 expresses surprise (= I'm sure she was there)

c Compare examples c and d.
   c Which colour do you want?   d What colour do you want?
   Which example ... ?
   1 asks about an open choice (there may be a lot of colours to choose from)
   2 asks about a limited range (e.g., black, red or green)

d ≫ Now go to Grammar Focus 1B on p. 134.

e 💬 Work in pairs. You are going to role-play two of the interviews in 3b and continue with your own questions.
   1 Choose one of the interviews.
      Student A: Interview Student B. Add your own questions.
      Student B: Answer Student A's questions using your own ideas.
   2 Choose a second interview. This time Student B interviews Student A.

5 SPEAKING

a Work in pairs.
   1 Write a short poem every day
   2 Get up at dawn
   3 Go running

   1 Write down three challenges you might do in the next three months.
   2 Look at your partner's challenges. Write some questions to ask about each one. Ask about:
      • reasons for doing the challenge
      • details of what they plan to do
      • how they about it.

   Are you planning to ... ?   Do you think it will be ... ?
   How are you going to ... ?

b 💬 Interview your partner about his/her three challenges. Do you think they will be successful?

Challenge 3: Steve decided to learn Italian.

Steve, what language did you decide to learn?

Well, I thought I'd choose a language that isn't too different from English, so I decided to try Italian.

Isn't it difficult to keep it up?

Yes, it is. I've had to be very strict with myself. I'm using a book with online support, so I usually try to cover one lesson a night.

4 _____

Well, there's an Italian restaurant nearby and I'm friends with the owner, so I go there and chat to him. That's another reason I chose Italian.

5 _____

Maybe, or I might try a different language every month. I'm thinking of trying Japanese next.

1C EVERYDAY ENGLISH
Don't touch the food!

Learn to explain what to do and check understanding
- S Breaking off a conversation
- P Rapid speech

1 LISTENING

a Discuss the questions.
1 In your country, how do students manage financially? Do they … ?
   - rely on their parents
   - get a part-time job
   - use student loans
2 What do you think is the best way? Why?
3 If you had to do a part-time job to earn some money as a student, what job would you choose and why?

b Look at the photo of Tessa and Becky from Part 1. Who do you think they are?
1 tourists visiting a famous building
2 university students doing a course
3 journalists who have just done an interview

c 01.14 Watch or listen to Part 1 and check your ideas.

d 01.14 Watch or listen again. Answer the questions.
1 Are Becky and Tessa friends? How do you know?
2 Why does Becky have to go?

e 01.15 Watch or listen to Part 2. Are these sentences true or false?
1 Becky and Tom are married.
2 Becky is free this evening.
3 Becky is in a hurry.

2 CONVERSATION SKILLS
Breaking off a conversation

a 01.16 Look at these ways to break off a conversation and say goodbye.
1 I really must go now.
2 I must run.
3 I've got no time to talk now.
4 I'll see you tomorrow.

Listen to the speaker. Which words does she not use in 1–4?

b Look at some more ways to break off a conversation. Which words has the speaker not included?
1 Must be off now.
2 Talk to you later.
3 Can't talk just now.
4 Nice talking to you.

3 PRONUNCIATION
Rapid speech

a 01.17 In rapid speech we often leave out sounds. Listen to the phrases below. Which sound is left out? Is it a consonant sound or a vowel sound?
1 must go
2 must run
3 got to go
4 can't talk

b Read the conversation. Put B's replies in order. Is more than one order possible?
A So how was your holiday?
B Got to go. / Sorry. / Can't talk now. / It was great.
A OK, well, have a nice evening.
B Bye. / See you tomorrow. / Yeah, thanks. / Must be off now.

c Work in pairs. Have short conversations.
Student A: Tell Student B about what you did last weekend. Continue until he/she stops you.
Student B: You're in a hurry. Use expressions in 2b and 3b to break off the conversation.
Then swap roles.

4 LISTENING

a ▶ 01.18 Watch or listen to Part 3. What happens to Becky? Choose the correct answer.
1 Becky meets Sam and learns how to make coffee.
2 Becky learns how to handle food and meets a café customer.

b ▶ 01.18 Watch or listen again. Answer the questions.
1 Sam explains three things to Becky. What are they?
2 What does Phil do in the café?
3 Why do they call him 'JK'?
4 Who is Emma?

c 💬 Discuss the questions with other students. Give reasons for your answers.
1 Do you think the others like Phil coming to the café?
2 Do you think Becky will be good at her new job?

d ▶ 01.19 Watch or listen to Part 4. Which of these topics do Tom and Becky mention?

coffee   food   Becky's new job   the reason Tom is here
Phil's book   their wedding plans

e ▶ 01.19 Watch or listen again. What do Tom and Becky say about each topic?

Becky and Sam

Becky and Emma   Phil

5 USEFUL LANGUAGE
Explaining and checking understanding

a Look at the expressions Sam uses to explain what to do. Put the words in *italics* in the correct order.
1 *most / thing / is, / the / important* don't touch the food.
2 *to / always / remember* use these tongs.
3 *is, / remember / thing / to / another* the tables are all numbered.

b ▶ 01.20 Listen and check your answers.

c Why does Sam use these expressions?
1 because he needs time to think
2 because he's not sure
3 to emphasise important points

d Look at these ways to check that someone has understood an explanation. Complete the questions with the endings in the box.

the idea?   got that?   clear?   I mean?

1 Is that …   3 Have you …
2 Do you understand 4 Do you get …
  what …

e ▶ 01.21 **Pronunciation** Listen to each question in 5d said in two ways. Which way sounds … ?
• friendly and polite
• unfriendly and not so polite

To sound friendly, does the speaker's voice go up (↗) or down (↘) at the end?

f Practise asking the questions in 5d in a friendly and polite way.

g Here are some other things Sam could explain to Becky. Imagine what he could say using language in 5a and 5d. What could Becky say to show she has understood?
1 how to clear and arrange a table when a customer leaves
2 what to do with the coffee machine at closing time
3 what to do if customers leave something behind

h 💬 Practise the conversation in 5g. Swap roles.

6 SPEAKING

a Choose a process you are familiar with or something you know how to do. It could be:
• something connected with a sport or a hobby
• how to use a machine or an electronic device
• how to make or cook something.

b You are going to explain the process to your partner. Prepare what you will say. Think how to emphasise the important points and check that your partner understands. Use expressions from 5a and 5d.

c 💬 Work in pairs. Take turns to explain the process to your partner and ask each other questions to check understanding.

✓ UNIT PROGRESS TEST

→ CHECK YOUR PROGRESS

You can now do the Unit Progress Test.

1D SKILLS FOR WRITING
I really missed my phone all day

Learn to write an article
G Organising an article

1 SPEAKING AND LISTENING

a Discuss the questions.
1 In your daily life, how much do you depend on technology?
2 What aspects of technology make your daily life easier?

b Look at the research results below and discuss the questions.
1 Do you think people you know would agree with these results?
2 Do you agree with the results? Is there anything you would add to the list?

IT anxiety!
Recent research has revealed the things that make people the most anxious about information technology (IT). Here are the top five:
1 There is less face-to-face social contact.
2 IT companies know too much about us.
3 Artificial intelligence could mean job losses.
4 Too much time is wasted online.
5 Information online is often unreliable.

c 01.22 Listen to Gina and Derek talking about technology. What aspect of technology do they talk about? Are they describing positive or negative experiences?

d 01.22 Listen again. What's the speaker's relationship with the other person in the story? What made the experience positive or negative? Why?

e Discuss the questions.
1 Do you agree with Gina's reaction to her boss? Why / Why not?
2 Do you know people like Derek? Do you think they should try to change? Why / Why not?

f Work on your own. Think about the questions below and make notes.
- When has technology created a problem for you?
- When has technology helped you solve a problem of some kind?

g Discuss your experiences in 1f.

2 READING

a Read *Tech free!* Did Sam have a really difficult day or some nice surprises?

b Read the text again. Are the sentences true or false?
1 Before the experiment, Sam was a bit worried by the idea.
2 Sam was annoyed that he had to chat to someone in the bank.
3 The bank clerk was surprised that Sam wanted to withdraw money.
4 Sam was able to work better when he wrote by hand.
5 As the day progressed, Sam thought less about using his phone.
6 The book he read made him fall asleep.
7 Sam learned something about the way we depend on technology.

c How would you feel if you had to live without using technology for one day? Discuss what you would and would not enjoy.

3 WRITING SKILLS
Organising an article

a How does Sam organise his article? Choose the correct summary.
1 He explains his attitude towards technology, describes his day, requests readers to do the same thing.
2 He explains his level of dependency on technology, describes his day, finishes with an evaluation of the experience.
3 He explains his feelings about technology, describes his day, finishes by promising to repeat the experience.

b How does Sam get the reader's attention at the beginning of the article?

16

UNIT 1

TECH FREE!

by Sam Winton

🏠 HOME ✏ BLOG 👤 FOLLOW ME

[1] Have you ever wondered what it would be like to give up technology? I'm a freelance marketing consultant and I spend a lot of my working life in front of a computer. I've been working on a marketing campaign for this nature resort where any kind of digital device is banned. I wanted to know what it's like, so I decided to conduct my own private experiment: Spend a day without technological devices – scary!

[2] The first thing I usually do every day is reach for my smartphone to check the time and read any messages, but I'd locked it in a drawer the night before. Already I was feeling very cut off from the world, and it was only … actually, I had no idea what time it was!

[3] After breakfast, I needed to get some cash. Inevitably, this meant a trip to the bank because I couldn't use my card or a cash machine. I had to queue at the bank, but I had a very nice conversation with a woman while I was waiting. She told me how they're going to upgrade the local park with a new playground and a running track. Not surprisingly, the bank clerk thought I was a bit strange to be making a cash withdrawal in person. Most people use machines.

[4] Afterwards, I came home to try writing my marketing plan by hand. Interestingly, I found it easier to concentrate on my writing. But my hand got really sore from writing with a pen! And I have to confess – by this stage, I was having to make a real effort not to get my phone out and check my messages.

[5] Then, I wanted to relax and watch the next episode in a series that I'm streaming. Naturally, that was out – I had to read a book. It's a crime story a friend recommended to me and it's great. I couldn't put it down and I ended up going to bed late.

[6] All in all, I wouldn't say I could live without technology. Predictably, I really missed my phone all day. However, I kept to my promise of a tech-free day and had more face-to-face interaction by avoiding machines. Undoubtedly, it has made me realise just how addicted to technology we all are.

c Complete the tasks.
1. In paragraphs 2–5, underline the linking word or phrase that sequences the events in Sam's day. The first one has been done for you.
2. In paragraph 6, what linking phrase shows that Sam is going to summarise his experience?

d Look at the example sentence from the article.

Inevitably, this meant a trip to the bank because I couldn't use my card or a cash machine.

The adverb *Inevitably* shows the writer's attitude. Find five other comment adverbs in the article.

e Add the adverbs in the box to the sentences. There is more than one possible answer.

amazingly   naturally   inevitably
(not) surprisingly

1. Why do some websites ask you to change passwords so often? _____, after changing the password for my bank, I was asked to change it again just a week later.
2. I usually hate anything to do with technology. _____, I like using the self-service check-out at my local supermarket.
3. I always expect digital devices to be expensive. _____, the tablet I bought last week cost very little.
4. I find it very difficult to install new software. _____, I've downloaded the new version of a program, and now my computer is frozen.

f Which piece of advice is not correct for writing an article? Why?
1. Begin the article with a question to get the reader's attention.
2. Use direct questions to connect with the reader of your article.
3. Think about how you can structure the main part of the article. You can use a sequence of events or you could compare and contrast ideas.
4. Use linking words to guide the reader.
5. Be as objective as possible.
6. Use comment adverbs to show your opinions.
7. Summarise your experience or ideas and evaluate them.

4 WRITING

a Imagine you had to live for a week without a technological device you use in your daily life. Choose a device from the article or use your own idea. Make notes about what the experience might be like.

b 💬 Discuss your notes.

c Write an article about your experience. Organise your article to follow the structure in 3a. Use the linking phrases and adverbs from 3c–e to help you.

d Swap articles with another student. Does the article follow the advice in 3f? Is the article interesting to read? Why / Why not? What could make it more interesting?

17

UNIT 1
Review and extension

1 GRAMMAR

a Write the correct tense of the verbs in brackets.
My wife Anna and I first ¹_met_ (meet) at a party while I ²_living_ (live) in London in the 1970s. When I ³_arrived_ (arrive) most people ⁴_____ (already/leave). I ⁵_____ (notice) Anna immediately. She ⁶_____ (wear) a blue dress, and she ⁷_____ (chat) with a group of people on the balcony. I ⁸_____ (go) up to her and we ⁹_____ (start) talking. We both ¹⁰_____ (feel) as if we ¹¹_____ (know) each other all our lives. Now we ¹²_____ (be) both in our 70s. We ¹³_____ (know) each other for 44 years.

b Read an interview with a famous actor about his life. Correct the mistakes in the questions.

1 *Where you grew up?*
   In San Diego, California. I left when I was 18.
2 *Did not you like living in San Diego?*
   Yes, but there were more opportunities in San Francisco.
3 *How long for did you stay there?*
   About eight years. Then I moved to New York.
4 *What did make you decide to move?*
   I got an offer to act at the Apollo Theater in New York.
5 *Do you think was it a good decision?*
   Oh, yes. It was a chance to work with some great people.
6 *Did you work with who?*
   Oh, a lot of good actors – Terence Newby, for example.

2 VOCABULARY

a Add an adjective to complete each gap.

1 The students are all keen to learn English. They're very m_____.
2 All Sophie's family and friends have warned her about marrying Fred, but she's going to anyway. She's so s_____.
3 Everyone agrees the new president is a good leader. She's highly r_____.
4 My brother used to be very shy, but he's become much more s_____ since he left home.
5 I've always loved acting more than anything else. I'm p_____ about it.
6 Five thousand people came to hear him talk. He's a very i_____ speaker.
7 Try not to criticise his work. He can be very s_____ about it.
8 Just because they're rich, they think they're better than everyone else. I hate a_____ people like that.

b Choose the correct answers.

1 I ¹*took / had* a go at running a café, but it didn't work ²*up / out*. I didn't make enough money, so I had to ³*give / stop* up.
2 He's really ⁴*doing / making* an effort to lose weight. He's on a diet, and he's ⁵*kept / held* it up for six weeks now. But I don't know if he'll ⁶*make / keep* to it for much longer.
3 He saw a poster for a pottery class and decided to try it ⁷*out / on*. After two classes he managed ⁸*to / for* make a vase.

3 WORDPOWER *make*

a Match the statements with the pictures.

a 'I can't make up my mind.'
b 'It really makes a difference to the room.'
c 'I can't make out what it is.'
d 'We'll just have to make the best of it.'
e 'This is to make up for last night.'
f 'That doesn't make sense.'
g 'It wants to make friends with us.'

b ▶01.23 Listen to the conversations and check your answers.

c Add a word or phrase from **a** after *make* in these sentences.

1 What was that? I can't make _____ what you're saying.
2 Why don't you drive faster? We need to make _____ lost time, or we'll be late.
3 So, do you want to come with us? You need to make _____.
4 When the sun shines, it makes _____ to the way I feel.
5 I didn't buy any more food. You'll just have to make _____ of it.
6 He gave a long explanation, but it didn't make _____ to me. I still don't understand.
7 Don't sit in front of the computer all day. You should go out and make _____ with people.

d 💬 What kind of person are you? Discuss these questions.

1 If you upset a friend, how would you make up for it? Would you buy a present, buy flowers, apologise …?
2 When you buy clothes, do you make up your mind quickly or do you need a long time to decide?
3 You have to spend the night at an airport. Would you stay there and make the best of it or would you pay money for a hotel?
4 You see a dog in the street. Would you try to make friends with it or would you keep out of its way?

⟳ REVIEW YOUR PROGRESS

How well did you do in this unit? Write 3, 2 or 1 for each objective.
3 = very well   2 = well   1 = not so well

I CAN …	
discuss people I admire	☐
discuss a challenge	☐
explain what to do and check understanding	☐
write an article.	☐

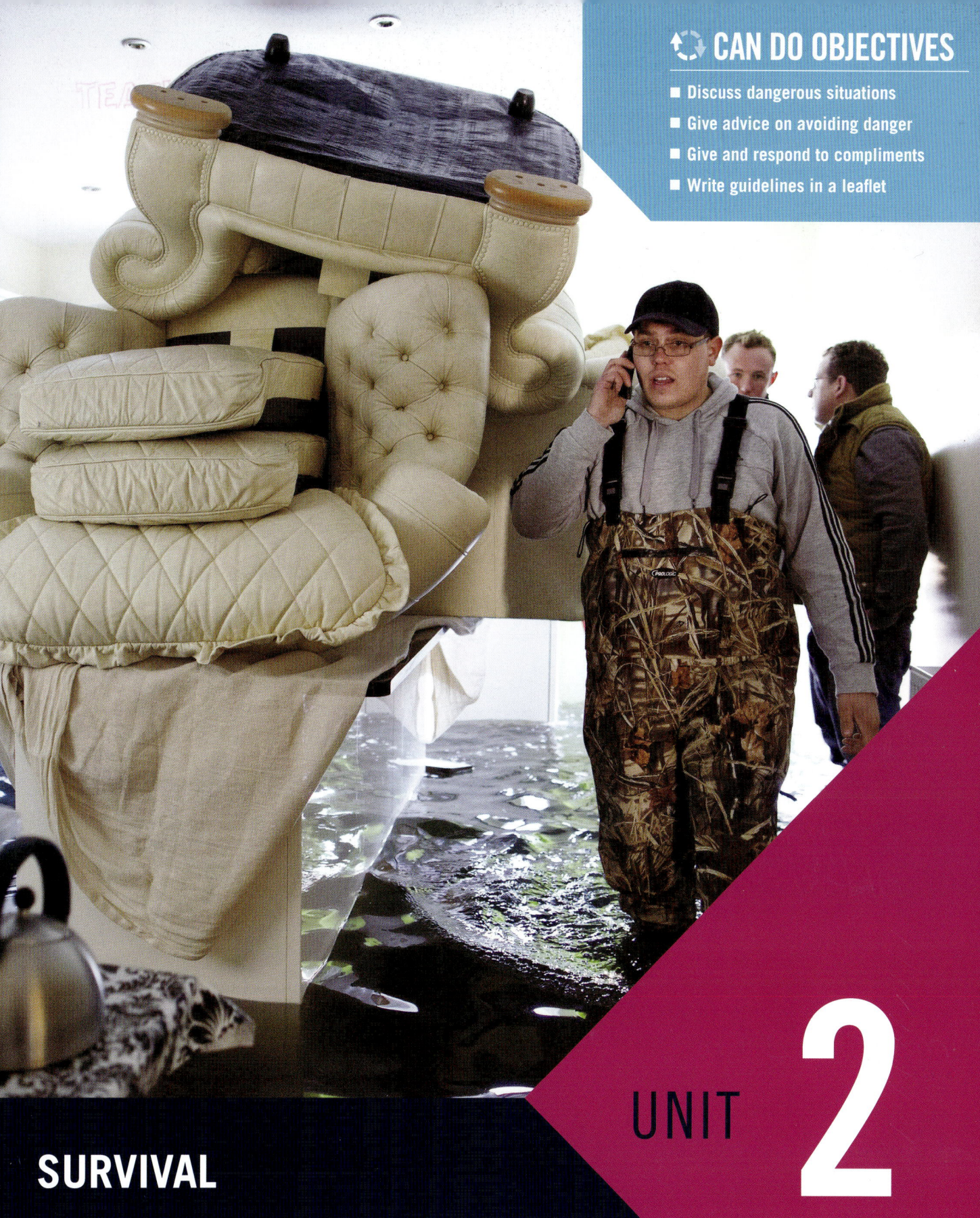

UNIT 2
SURVIVAL

CAN DO OBJECTIVES
- Discuss dangerous situations
- Give advice on avoiding danger
- Give and respond to compliments
- Write guidelines in a leaflet

GETTING STARTED

a 💬 Look at the picture and answer the questions.
1. What do you think has happened here?
2. Who are the people in the picture?
3. What's the man on the phone saying?

b 💬 Discuss the questions.
1. What do you think are the worst kinds of natural disasters? Why?
2. Think of a natural disaster that has happened in your country. How effective was the response of the emergency services? How well did people cope?
3. Why do you think some people cope better with challenging situations than others?

2A IT WAS GETTING LATE AND I WAS LOST

Learn to discuss dangerous situations
- G Narrative tenses
- V Expressions with *get*

1 LISTENING

a Look at pictures a–d. What would you be most afraid of in each situation?

b ▶ 02.01 Listen to someone talking about their holiday. Which of the pictures is being described? Where was the holiday?

c ▶ 02.01 Listen again. Number events a–h in the order that they happened.

a ☐ bought a new surfboard
b ☐ lost the board
c ☐ waved to a lifeguard
d ☐ swam against the current
e ☐ fell off the surfboard
f ☐ learned to surf with instructors
g ☐ went surfing alone
h ☐ was rescued

2 VOCABULARY Expressions with *get*

a Match expressions 1–10 in **bold** with meanings a–j.
1 ☐ I can't wait to **get away**. d
2 ☐ I've always wanted to learn how to surf, and I'll finally **get to** do it. c
3 ☐ I **couldn't get over** just how strong they are. e
4 ☐ Actually, I **got into** a bit of **trouble** once. f
5 ☐ I tried to **get hold of** it. g
6 ☐ It **got swept away** by the wave. b
7 ☐ I soon realised that I **wasn't getting anywhere**. a
8 ☐ I **got the feeling** I was being pulled out to sea. j
9 ☐ So I waved to **get someone's attention**. i
10 ☐ I had a bad experience, but I soon **got over** it. h

a make no progress
b move in a different direction in a powerful way
c have the chance to do something
d go somewhere else
e be very surprised by something
f find myself in difficulty
g take it in my hand
h recover from something negative that happened
i make someone notice
j have the sensation that

b Complete the sentences with the correct form of the phrases in 2a. Write one word in each gap.
1 She ran out on the road to _____ the police officer's _____.
2 They were exhausted and hungry, but after some food and sleep they soon _____ _____ the experience.
3 When he saw the same tree for the third time, he began to _____ _____ _____ that he was lost.
4 He went on a course about surviving in the woods and _____ _____ put into practice his fire-making skills.
5 They decided to ski off the main trail where the snow was fresh, but it was also very dangerous and they soon _____ _____ _____.
6 The boat was sinking, but we all managed to _____ _____ _____ a life jacket.
7 She was crossing the river, but the current was strong and she _____ _____ _____ by the water.
8 They had been walking for hours, but they'd only walked about two kilometres. They felt like they weren't _____ _____.
9 They were in such a rush to _____ _____ to the mountains, they left without taking sensible hiking boots.
10 When they were in the water, they _____ _____ _____ how high the waves were.

c ▶ Now go to Vocabulary Focus 2A on p. 155.

20

3 READING

a Read the article *Lost at sea* and answer the questions.
1 How long was Robert Hewitt in the water?
2 What problems did he have to overcome?

b Can you remember what these numbers refer to? Write sentences about each number. Then read the text again and check your answers.
1 200-metre
2 seven kilometres
3 fourth day
4 three hours
5 half a kilometre
6 third day

c Discuss the questions.
1 What do you think most helped Robert to survive?
2 Do you think that Robert made the right decision on day one not to try to swim for shore? Give reasons.
3 What was the biggest challenge Robert had to overcome?
4 What would you have done in Robert's situation?

REAL DIVING

Stories   Locations   Learn to Dive   Shop

LOST AT SEA

How long could you survive at sea? One day? Two? And when would you start to lose hope?

When Robert Hewitt came to the surface, he [1]**realised** straight away that something was wrong. He [2]**'d been diving** for sea urchins and crayfish off the coast of New Zealand with a friend, and [3]**had decided** to make the 200-metre swim back to shore alone. But instead, strong underwater currents had taken him more than half a kilometre out to sea.

Lying on his back in the middle of the ocean, Robert told himself not to panic. He was a strong swimmer and he [4]**was wearing** his thick wetsuit. 'I'm not going to die. Someone will come,' he told himself. But three hours passed and still no one had come for him. Robert would soon have to make a tough decision.

He was now a long way from the coast, and the tide was taking him further out, but he decided not to try to swim for shore. He felt it was better to save his energy and hold on to his brightly coloured equipment. But the decision was not an easy one. 'I just closed my eyes and said, "You've made the right decision. You've made the right decision" until that's all I heard,' he remembers.

As night approached, Robert established a pattern to help him survive in the water. To stay warm, he kept himself moving and took short naps of less than a minute at a time. Every few hours, he called out to his loved ones. 'Just yelling out their names would pick me up, and then I would keep going for the next hour and the next hour and the next.'

When he woke up the next morning, he couldn't believe he was still alive. Using his bright equipment, he tried to signal to planes that flew overhead. But as each plane turned away, his spirits dropped. He managed to drink rainwater that he collected in his mask to keep himself alive, but as day turned to night again, he started to imagine things.

Robert woke up on the third day to a beautiful blue sky. Now seven kilometres off the coast, Robert decided he had to swim for it. But the sun was so strong and Robert quickly ran out of strength. Hope turned to disappointment yet again. 'I felt disappointed in myself. I thought I was a lot fitter. I thought I would be able to do it.' Robert then started to think he might not survive.

On the fourth day, the lack of food and water was really starting to affect him. Half unconscious, and with strange visions going through his head, he thought he saw a boat coming towards him with two of his friends on board. Another vision, surely.

But no – 'They put me in the boat and I said something like, "Oh, how's it going, what are you guys doing here?"' Then he asked them the question that he'd asked in all his visions, 'Can I have some water?' As they handed him the water and he felt it touch his lips, he knew. This was not a vision. He'd been found! After four days and three nights alone at sea, Robert had been found! Sunburnt, hungry and exhausted, but alive …

GLOSSARY

sea urchin

crayfish

UNIT 2

4 GRAMMAR Narrative tenses

a Look at the verbs in **bold** in *Lost at sea* and match them with the uses a–d.
  a a completed action that takes place before the main events in the story
  b a background activity in progress at the same time as the main events in the story happened
  c a continuous activity that happens before the main events in the story and explains why the main events happen
  d a completed action that tells you what happens at a specific time in the story

b Match the tense names to the meanings in 4a.
  1 ☐ past simple
  2 ☐ past perfect
  3 ☐ past continuous
  4 ☐ past perfect continuous

c ≫ Now go to Grammar Focus 2A on p. 136.

d Work in pairs. Student A: Read *Trapped in the Tham Luang cave*. Student B: Read *Lost in the Sahara*. Answer the questions about your text.
  1 Where does the event take place and who is it about?
  2 How do they survive?

e Underline the correct verbs in your text.

f You are going to tell your partner about your story. Make notes.

g 💬 Tell your partner your survival story. Use correct verb forms.

5 SPEAKING

a Think of a dangerous situation that you or someone you know was in, or it could be something you know about from a book or film. Make notes about the questions.
  • Where and when did it take place?
  • Who was involved?
  • What was the scene or background to the story?
  • What were the main events?
  • How did you / the person feel?
  • What was the outcome?

b 💬 Tell each other your stories. Use different narrative tenses and expressions with *get*. Ask questions.

Student A: TRAPPED IN THE THAM LUANG CAVE

In June 2018, twelve members of a Thai boys' football team and their coach were trapped for 17 days in the Tham Luang cave, the longest cave in Thailand. They ¹*played / had been playing* football nearby and ²*had decided / had been deciding* to explore the cave. They ³*walked / were walking* through the shallow stream which ran through the cave when suddenly there was a flood and the water level ⁴*rose / had been rising* rapidly. To escape the water, they went further into the cave and found a flat rock above the water level, but they were trapped. While they were waiting for help, the coach taught them meditation techniques to help them keep calm. A team of divers found them and raised the alarm, but only after they ⁵*were / had been* there for nine days without food. It wasn't easy to find a way to rescue the boys safely and they had to wait there for eight more days. Finally, pairs of divers rescued the boys, but they had to swim together under water through narrow tunnels. Fortunately, they all survived.

Student B: LOST IN THE SAHARA

When the sun came up, Mauro Prosperi couldn't believe his eyes. He saw desert stretching in every direction. He ¹*took / had been taking* part in a marathon race through the Sahara when a sandstorm ²*had appeared / had been appearing* from nowhere. He spent the night sheltering under a bush, and when morning came, he had expected to see the running trail and carry on. But there was nothing, only sand. He had some dried food and a little water, so he ³*set off / had set off* in what he thought was the right direction – but in fact he was walking deeper into the desert. On the second day while he ⁴*had rested / was resting*, he saw a helicopter, so he fired a signal flare, but the helicopter flew past. In total, Mauro walked for ten days. He ate insects and desert plants in order to survive before he finally reached a nomads' camp and was taken to hospital. There, he learned that he ⁵*walked / had walked* 291 kilometres in the wrong direction and he had lost 16 kilograms.

2B IF IT RUNS TOWARDS YOU, DON'T RUN AWAY

Learn to give advice on avoiding danger
- **G** Future time clauses and conditionals
- **V** Animals and the environment

1 READING

a 💬 Think of three wild places.
- Would you be scared to go for a walk there?
- What dangers could you face?
- What would you do to get out of danger?

b 💬 Look at pictures a–e and answer the questions.
1 Which of the animals do you think are the most and least dangerous? Why?
2 How good do you think your chances are of surviving an attack by these animals?

c Read the text and check your answers.

d Read the text again. Tick (✓) the correct sentences.
1 ✓ Some animals are less dangerous than people think.
2 ✗ If you go walking, you can't avoid meeting dangerous animals.
3 ✓ Not many animals attack without reason.
4 ✓ Having a weapon may help you survive an attack.
5 ✓ Most animals have a part of their body that is vulnerable.
6 ✗ It's better to run away than to try to fight.

e Do you think the text is … ?
a a serious survival guide for travellers
b part of a scientific book about animals
c an article written mainly for interest and amusement

How to survive...
an animal attack

YOU'RE WALKING IN A FOREST WHEN SUDDENLY A WILD ANIMAL APPEARS FROM NOWHERE AND IT DOESN'T LOOK FRIENDLY. WHAT DO YOU DO?

The first important point is that there's not usually much you can do, except hope it goes away again. With luck, you may never have to defend yourself against a wild animal, but it doesn't hurt to know what to do if an escaped leopard attacks you in your back garden, or if you're out on a country walk and you suddenly meet a pack of wolves.

BE AWARE
The first thing is to know which animals are really dangerous. Many people are scared of animals that are in fact harmless, and not scared enough of animals that could kill you. Most animals won't attack people unless you do something to make them angry. Bears, for example, will usually move away as soon as they hear you, and they'll only fight if they think you're attacking them or their young. Wolves won't normally attack unless they are very hungry, and then only if they're in a group. Tarantulas are big, hairy spiders, but they aren't actually dangerous at all – you can even keep them as pets. On the other hand, tigers and crocodiles are serious killers who will be happy to eat you for breakfast.

BE PREPARED
It's a good idea to take a stick, knife or pepper spray when you go for a walk in the wild in case you meet a dangerous animal. Have it in a place where you can easily find it. It may mean the difference between life and death.

KNOW YOUR ENEMY
If you ever find yourself face-to-face with a large and dangerous animal, you'll want to know their strong and weak points. Common weak points are:
- the nose
- the eyes
- the neck.

People have sometimes survived by punching sharks, large cats and crocodiles on the nose, and pushing your thumbs into their eyes will also work well, as long as you press hard enough. Otherwise, you might just make them angry!
You can also try to get a psychological advantage. Provided you seem bigger and more dangerous than the animal, it will probably leave you alone, so make a lot of noise and try to make yourself look bigger.

WHAT NEXT?
If scaring them doesn't work, then you have two options: running or fighting. Remember that most animals are better at running and fighting than humans, so don't expect things to end well. But if you decide to fight, fight back with everything you have. Often during animal attacks, people give up before the fight has even started. If you have any sharp objects or weapons, then use them. Hit the animal's weak points, keep shouting and make sudden movements. Good luck out there!

UNIT 2

f Look at the ideas below for surviving attacks by three different animals. For each animal, decide which ideas are the best. More than one answer is possible.

g ⟫ **Communication 2B** Now go to p. 127 to check your answers.

1 A wolf
a hit it on the nose with a stick
b look it straight in the eyes
c run away immediately

2 A shark
a swim away quickly
b swim towards it
c hit it in the eye if it bites you

3 A bear
a run straight uphill as fast as you can
b lie down and 'play dead'
c hit the trees with sticks if you think bears are nearby

2 GRAMMAR Future time clauses and conditionals

a Look at the words and phrases in **bold** in sentences 1–5 and answer questions a–e.

1 They'll only fight **if** they think you're attacking them.
2 They won't attack people **unless** they're trapped or provoked.
3 Bears, for example, will usually move away **as soon as** they hear you.
4 **Provided** you stay absolutely still, the bear will lose interest and go away.
5 **As long as** you don't panic, it will probably swim away.

a Which two words or phrases have a similar meaning to *if*? 4,5
b What does sentence 2 mean?
  (1) A bear will only attack you if it's trapped or provoked.
  2 A bear will attack you anyway, even if it isn't trapped.
c What does sentence 3 mean?
  1 When bears hear you they will wait, then move away slowly.
  (2) When bears hear you they will move away immediately.
d Look at these examples:
  If you stay still, the bear will go away *as long as*
  (= something good will happen).
  If you move, the bear will attack you *provided*
  (= something bad will happen).
  In which example could we use *as long as* or *provided* instead of *if*?
e What tense is used after the words and phrases in **bold**? *Presente* What tense is used in the other part of the sentence? *Future*

b Find one more example in *How to survive … an animal attack* of each of these words and phrases:
1 as long as
2 unless
3 provided.

c ⟫ Now go to Grammar Focus 2B on p. 136.

d Complete the sentences. There is more than one possible answer. Compare with other students.
1 Sharks won't attack you unless …
2 Wolves will only attack if …
3 A stick may help you provided …
4 If you hit a crocodile on the nose, …

UNIT 2

3 LISTENING AND VOCABULARY
Animals and the environment

a 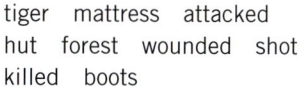 *The Tiger* by John Vaillant tells the true story of a hunter and a Siberian tiger. Use the words in the box to guess what the story is about.

tiger	mattress	attacked
hut	forest	wounded	shot
killed	boots

b ▶ 02.09 Listen to an interview about the book. Was the story similar to yours?

c ▶ 02.09 Which of these questions *doesn't* Miles answer? Listen again and check.
1 Is a Siberian tiger bigger than other tigers? ✓
2 How far can it jump? ✓
3 Have many people been killed by Siberian tigers?
4 Can tigers plan ahead?

d ▶ 02.10 Listen to the second part of the interview. Tick (✓) the things Miles talks about.
1 ☐ his own feelings about the tiger
2 ☐ life in Siberia
3 ✓ the relationship between humans and tigers
4 ✓ tigers as an endangered species
5 ☐ how to survive a tiger attack

e Do you think Miles would agree with statements 1–5? Write *Yes* or *No*. Then explain why.
1 It's a good thing they killed the tiger. _____
2 The tiger was just behaving naturally. _____
3 Tigers have always caused problems for people in Siberia. _____
4 In some ways, humans are more dangerous than tigers. _____
5 We should hunt more tigers to keep them under control. _____

f Which of the words in the box can we use to describe … ?
1 animals   2 places

| at risk | creature | endangered | environment | extinct |
| habitats | hunt | natural | protected | rare | species |

g ▶ 02.11 Complete the sentences with the words in 3f. Then listen and check your answers.
1 … in eastern Siberia, one of the wildest and most _____ _____ on Earth …
2 Imagine a/an _____ that is as active as a cat and has the weight of an industrial refrigerator.
3 Humans and tigers _____ the same animals and share the same _____.
4 Tigers are _____ because of humans.
5 Tigers have become extremely _____.
6 There are 40 million humans but only 500 tigers, so they really are an _____ _____, and although they're _____, they could easily become _____ in a few decades.

4 SPEAKING

a A visitor is coming to stay in your country. Make notes about: forests
• endangered species and where you can see them   Jaguar
• dangerous animals or other creatures (e.g., birds,   deforestation
fish, insects)   and hunting
• other possible risks or dangers (e.g., diseases, dangerous places, travel, weather).

b Imagine what you could tell the visitor and what advice you could give. How could you use the words in the box?

| if | as soon as | in case | unless | as long as | provided |

c Work in pairs. Student A, talk about your country. Student B, you are the visitor. Ask Student A questions. Then change roles.

> Take malaria tablets in case you get bitten by a mosquito.

> Be careful of dogs if you go jogging.

25

2C EVERYDAY ENGLISH
What a great shot!

Learn to give and respond to compliments
- S Giving compliments and responding
- P Intonation in question tags

1 LISTENING

a Discuss the questions.
1 Do you like taking photos? Why / Why not?
2 In your opinion, what makes a good photo?
3 Do you think you are good at taking photos? Why / Why not?

b Look at photo a and answer the questions.
1 What is Becky doing?
2 Why do you think she needs Tessa to help?

c 02.12 Watch or listen to Part 1. Check your answers.

d 02.12 Are the sentences true or false? Watch or listen again to check.
1 Becky asks Tessa to help her check the height of the tripod.
2 Becky is happy with the shots she takes.
3 Tessa wonders if it's necessary to use a lot of equipment.
4 Tessa wants to take a photo of a small animal.

2 CONVERSATION SKILLS Agreeing using question tags

a 02.12 Watch or listen again. How does Tessa respond to Becky's comment 'It's quite difficult'?

b Choose the correct word.
1 We can use statements with question tags to *agree / disagree* with someone.
2 Using a different adjective in the answer is more *interesting / friendly*.

c Complete B's answers with the correct verb forms.
1 A I think she's a lovely person.
   B Yes, she's very charming, _____ she?
2 A Their instructions weren't very clear.
   B No, they weren't helpful, _____ they?

d Complete the rule.

> If the sentence is positive, we use a _____ tag. If the sentence is negative, we use a _____ tag.

e Complete B's replies. Use an adjective from the box in the first gap and the correct verb form in the second gap.

welcoming   soaking   breathtaking   worried

1 A Your clothes are all wet.
   B Yes, they're _____, _____ they?
2 A The scenery there is exceptional.
   B Yes, it's _____, _____ it?
3 A They weren't a very friendly group of people.
   B No, they weren't _____ at all, _____ they?
4 A He looks a bit anxious.
   B Yes, he does look _____, _____ he?

3 PRONUNCIATION Intonation in question tags

a 02.13 Listen to the examples. Does the intonation go up (↗) or down (↘) on the question tag? What's the difference in meaning?
1 No, it isn't very quick, is it?
2 No, they weren't helpful, were they?
3 Yes, you need to make things easy, don't you?

b Practise saying the exchanges in 2e. Try to use the correct intonation in the reply.

c Discuss people and things you and other students know – for example, a person, a café, a film or a car. Use the adjectives below and question tags to agree.
- amusing – funny
- cheerful – happy
- interesting – fascinating
- frightening – terrifying
- exhausting – tiring

> That photo is really amazing.

> Yes, it's impressive, isn't it?

26

UNIT 2

4 LISTENING

a Look at photo b of Becky and Tessa. Which approach to taking photographs would you prefer? Why?

b

b Look at the two photos of flowers. Which do you like more? Why?

Becky's photo

Tessa's photo

c ▶ 02.14 Watch or listen to Part 2. What are Becky and Tessa's opinions of their own photos?

d ▶ 02.14 Watch or listen to Part 2 again. Answer the questions.
1 How did Tessa start taking photos?
2 What do Becky and Tessa have trouble deciding?
3 What does Becky think about her photo of a squirrel? What does Tessa think?
4 Where do they go for coffee?

5 USEFUL LANGUAGE
Giving compliments and responding

a ▶ 02.15 Listen and complete the conversation.
BECKY _____ a _____ shot!
TESSA It's all _____.
BECKY You _____ just _____ to get a really good shot. The light is amazing.
TESSA Thanks. Guess it's _____ bad.

b Answer the questions about the conversation.
1 Do Becky's compliments sound excited?
2 Is Tessa's response grateful or neutral?

c Look at the **bold** words in compliments 1–4. Match them to the words and phrases in a–d.

1 ☐ That's a **lovely** picture!   a talented / skilled
2 ☐ You're so **good** at taking photos.   b excellent / amazing / beautiful / striking
3 ☐ I **love** the way you caught the light. c were able to / succeeded in
4 ☐ You really **managed to** get it just right. d really like / am impressed by

d Which of these responses are grateful and which are neutral?

Do you think so?   It's OK, I guess.

Thanks, I'm glad you like it.   I'm really pleased you like it.

e 💬 Work in pairs. Imagine you have both finished writing an essay and have read each other's essays. Use the ideas below to have a short conversation. Take turns to be A and B.

A
- Tell your partner how easy/difficult it was to write the essay.
- Say you've read your partner's essay and compliment him/her.

B
- Agree with A using a question tag.
- Respond gratefully.

6 SPEAKING

a Work alone. What compliments can you give to your classmates? Think about:
- things they do or make as hobbies
- their jobs
- things they have done in your English classes
- the clothes they are wearing.

b 💬 Talk to different students in your class. Give compliments and respond.

That's a really nice jumper you're wearing.   Thanks, It's not bad, is it?

✓ **UNIT PROGRESS TEST**

→ **CHECK YOUR PROGRESS**

You can now do the Unit Progress Test.

27

2D SKILLS FOR WRITING
Make sure you know where you're going

Learn to write guidelines in a leaflet

G Organising guidelines in a leaflet

1 SPEAKING AND LISTENING

a 💬 Discuss the questions.
1 When was the last time you went to some kind of natural environment?
2 What did you do there?
3 How did you prepare for your trip?

b ▶ 02.16 Listen to Luiza talk about an experience she had in Canada. Answer the questions.
1 Which natural environment does she talk about?
2 Near the beginning, she says, 'I got in trouble'. What was the trouble?

c ▶ 02.16 Listen again and answer the questions.
1 Why did Luiza get lost?
2 How did she decide which way to go?
3 What helped her find the clearing?

d 💬 At the end, Luiza says, 'I suddenly had the strange feeling I was not alone'. What do you think happened next? Discuss your ideas.

e ▶ 02.17 Listen to the rest of Luiza's story. Were your ideas correct?

f ▶ 02.17 Listen again. Are the sentences true or false?
1 Luiza knew what to do.
2 She felt calm and wasn't afraid.
3 The helicopter saw Luiza the first time it flew over.
4 Luiza was surprised to find out she was close to the main track.

g 💬 What would you have done in Luiza's situation?

2 READING

a 💬 Think about Luiza's experience. Imagine you are going hiking in a forest. What do you need to remember in order to be safe?

b Read the leaflet *Be wise and survive!* Were your ideas similar? Put headings in spaces A–C in the leaflet. There is one extra heading.
1 In the forest
2 If you get lost
3 Identifying useful plants
4 Preparation

c Read the leaflet again. What should you … ?
1 take with you when you go hiking
2 not do when you are hiking
3 do about food and drink if you are lost
4 do if you are lost: move around or stay in one place

desert

beach

forest

mountains

28

BE WISE AND SURVIVE!

We all enjoy being in the great outdoors. There are lots of amazing environments, but some of them can be quite challenging, even dangerous, and it's important that you think about safety. Here are some simple guidelines to help you stay safe.

A _____

1. Get a map of the area and make sure you know where you are going.
2. Check the weather forecast.
3. Wear clothes and shoes that are suitable for the conditions. If you think the weather may change suddenly, take extra clothing.
4. If you are going on a longer walk, take some emergency food with you.

B _____

5. Provided you follow the signs, you shouldn't get into trouble.
6. Never take shortcuts unless you're absolutely sure where they go.
7. Allow plenty of time to get to your destination or get back before it gets dark.

C _____

8. As soon as you realise you're lost, stop, keep calm and plan what you will do next.
9. Don't eat all your food at once. Have a little at a time.
10. Try to find a source of water you can drink from, like a river or a stream. Being able to drink is more important than being able to eat.
11. Don't keep moving around. Find somewhere that is dry and get plenty of rest. It's easier for rescuers to find you if you stay in one place.
12. Always try to stay warm. You can cover yourself with dry plants.
13. If you need to keep moving, make sure you use rocks or pieces of wood as signs that show rescuers where you are going.
14. As long as you tell yourself you'll survive, you probably will!

UNIT 2

3 WRITING SKILLS
Organising guidelines in a leaflet

a Notice these verb forms used in the leaflet.
1. **Check** the weather forecast. (positive imperative)
2. **Don't eat** all your food at once. (negative imperative)
3. **Never take** shortcuts … (frequency adverb + imperative)
4. **If** you **think** the weather may change suddenly, **take** extra clothing. (*if* + present tense + imperative)

Find one more example of each verb form in the leaflet.

b Choose the correct answers.
1. What's the function of the verb forms in 3a?
   a to give advice
   b to make indirect suggestions
2. Why are those forms used?
   a to make the information clear and direct
   b to show hikers they have a strong obligation

c Correct the incorrect sentences.
1. Not eat any plants you don't recognise.
2. Never leave the group of people you are hiking with.
3. If you will hear a rescue team, make a lot of noise.
4. Always carries a pocket knife.
5. As soon as it starts getting dark, stop and think about what to do next.
6. If you have a map, take it with you.

4 WRITING

a Choose one of the situations in the box and take notes on advice you could include in a leaflet.

camping in a forest   backpacking in a foreign country
swimming in the sea   hiking in the mountains

b Write a leaflet for the situation you chose above. Remember to:
- use headings
- include the different imperative forms in 3a
- make the information clear and direct.

c Swap leaflets with another student. Does the leaflet include headings and different imperative forms? Is the information clear and direct? What improvements could be made?

d 💬 Give your leaflet to other students. Read other leaflets and decide which leaflet you think is the clearest and the most useful.

UNIT 2
Review and extension

1 GRAMMAR

handwritten notes: 4- had been travelling 12- could see 7- had told 11- was diving

a Complete the text with the verbs in brackets. Use the past simple, past continuous, past perfect or past perfect continuous forms.

The first time I ¹_tried_ (try) scuba diving ²_was_ (be) when I ³_lived_ (live) in Thailand. I ⁴_____ (travel) around Southeast Asia and I ⁵_decided_ (decide) to stop and work for a few months. I ⁶_was_ (be) on a gap year between finishing university and beginning my career. Years before, someone ⁷_told_ (tell) me the best way to see coral reefs ⁸_was_ (be) by scuba diving. The diving I ⁹_did_ (do) in Thailand ¹⁰_was_ (be) fantastic. As I ¹¹_____ (dive), I ¹²_____ (see) spectacular marine life.

b Make sentences by matching the halves. Put the linking expression in brackets in the correct place.

1 ☐ you won't find it difficult to learn to ski
2 ☐ you won't make much progress
3 ☐ you'll make steady progress
4 ☐ you won't be able to control your skis
5 ☐ you'll stay warm
6 ☐ you'll start making progress after a week

a you can move your toes in your boots (unless)
b you're generally fit and healthy (if)
c you keep moving (provided)
d you choose an easy ski slope (as long as)
e you're patient with yourself (provided)
f you're prepared to fall down a lot at first (unless)

2 VOCABULARY

a Correct the errors in the sentences.
1 I dropped my hat in the sea and it got swept by a wave away.
2 She couldn't get it over how hot it was.
3 He got trouble for being late.
4 I got feeling they didn't like guests.
5 She's now getting over it the shock of losing her job last week.
6 They're planning to get to the countryside this weekend.

b Complete the words.
1 In North America, red wolves are considered an e _ _ _ _ _ _ _ _ _ _ s _ _ _ _ _ _ _.
2 In the UK, Large Blue butterflies are a _ r _ _ _ and are p _ _ _ _ _ _ _ _ _.
3 The South American Spix's Macaw, featured in the film *Rio*, is now e _ _ _ _ _ _ in the wild.
4 It's possible to find many Chinese alligators in zoos and research centres, but there are fewer living in their n _ _ _ _ _ _ h _ _ _ _ _ _ _.
5 In Australia, just over 20 percent of the native plants are considered r _ _ _ and need to be conserved.

3 WORDPOWER *face*

a Match examples 1–8 with definitions a–h.
1 ☐ Although he said he enjoys the taste of raw fish, he still **made a face**.
2 ☐ She **faced a difficult choice** between the two jobs she was offered.
3 ☐ Her **face fell** when I told her the painting was worthless.
4 ☐ I've been studying all day, and I **can't face** doing my homework now.
5 ☐ It's not good news, but I feel I need to **say it to his face**.
6 ☐ We just have to **face the fact** that we haven't got enough money to buy a house.
7 ☐ I tripped on a loose brick and **fell flat on my face**.
8 ☐ I could tell my boss wasn't happy about the outcome. Now I have to talk to her and **face the music**.

a to be disappointed
b to accept another person's criticism or displeasure
c to accept an unpleasant situation
d to show from your expression that you don't like something
e to fall over badly and feel embarrassed
f to make a difficult decision
g to say something directly to someone
h to not want to do something unpleasant

b In which of the expressions in 1–8 is *face* used as a noun and in which as a verb?

c Which one of the following nouns doesn't collocate with *face*?

1 a problem   2 the truth   3 a difficult decision
4 the facts   5 a success   6 reality

d Add words to the gaps.
1 When did you last fall _____ on your face?
2 What was the last _____ choice you had to face?
3 What happened the last time you saw someone's face _____?
4 What's something difficult you've had to say _____ someone's face?
5 What food causes you to _____ a face when you eat it?
6 When was the last time you had to face _____ music?

e 💬 Ask and answer the questions in 3d.

🔄 REVIEW YOUR PROGRESS

How well did you do in this unit? Write 3, 2 or 1 for each objective.
3 = very well   2 = well   1 = not so well

I CAN ...	
discuss dangerous situations	☐
give advice on avoiding danger	☐
give and respond to compliments	☐
write guidelines in a leaflet.	☐

CAN DO OBJECTIVES

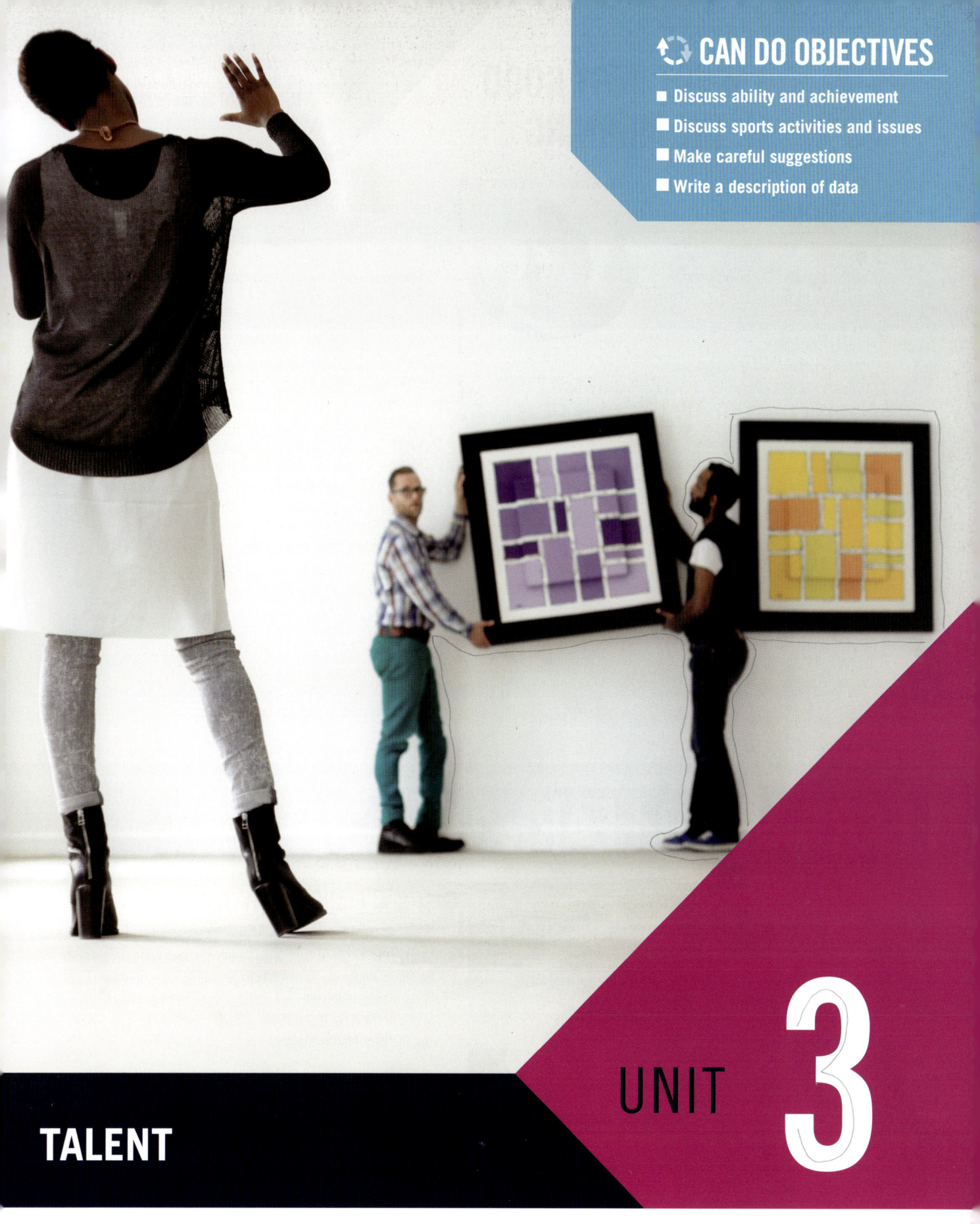

- Discuss ability and achievement
- Discuss sports activities and issues
- Make careful suggestions
- Write a description of data

UNIT 3

TALENT

GETTING STARTED

a Look at the picture and answer the questions.
1. What are the people doing?
2. Why do you think three people are needed for the job?
3. What could the woman be thinking?

b Discuss the questions.
1. What makes something a work of art?
2. Do famous artists have natural talent? Or is their success due to luck, hard work or something else? Why do you think so?

3A I'M NOT VERY GOOD IN THE MORNING

Learn to discuss ability and achievement
- **G** Multi-word verbs
- **V** Ability and achievement

1 LISTENING

a Think about how to learn something new. Do you agree or disagree with sentences 1–5? Why?
1 My teacher will get angry if I make mistakes.
2 Children learn faster than adults.
3 I must practise every day in order to make progress.
4 If something seems very easy, I must be doing it wrong.
5 Long practice sessions are best.

b 03.01 Listen to an experienced teacher talk about the same sentences. Are his ideas similar to yours? Do you agree with his ideas?

2 READING

a Discuss the questions.
1 How long does it take to learn something well?
2 What's the best time of day to learn something new?
3 What techniques do people use to help remember things?

b Read *Learning to learn*. Match texts a–c with the questions in 2a.

c Read questions 1–6 from people who have to learn something. Use information in the texts to answer the questions.
1 I have to learn a lot of historical dates for an exam. What's a good way to do this?
2 I want to join a beginners' kickboxing class. Is it better to join the morning or afternoon class?
3 I know I have a natural talent for tennis. Do I need to practise hard to do well?
4 If I study first thing in the morning after my brain has rested, I'm sure I'll learn more. Do you agree?
5 I have to find out about the way car engines work, but the book I'm reading is really boring. Should I just stick with it?
6 I don't just want to be a good computer programmer – I want to be a brilliant one. What can I do to achieve that?

d Discuss the questions.
1 What information in the texts surprised you?
2 What information made sense to you?
3 Have you had any experience of the ideas discussed in the text?
4 Do you think you'll change your learning practice as a result of the information?

LEARNING TO LEARN

a IT'S ALL ABOUT RHYTHM

Bodies and brains need time to warm up.
'Early bird' or 'night owl', we all have different body clocks and rhythms. However, research is beginning to show that we're all quite similar in the way our minds and bodies behave at different times of the day. Understanding these rhythms helps us figure out the best time to learn.

If learning means having to use your brain, then morning is the best time.
But not first thing. Our bodies and brains need time to warm up, and our body temperature rises slowly from the moment we wake up. Between ten in the morning and midday, most people are at their best in terms of their ability to concentrate and learn.

If we want to learn something physical, then it pays to wait until the afternoon.
Between 2 pm and 6 pm, our muscle strength is at its peak and our hand-eye coordination is very efficient. This means the afternoon is probably better for learning a new sport or maybe a new dance style.

UNIT 3

3 VOCABULARY
Ability and achievement

a Look at the adjectives in **bold** and answer questions 1–4.

And when you look at all the people who are **outstanding** at what they do …
… they seem so much more **talented** …
… that's what it takes to become really **skilled**.
Those who became **exceptional** practised about 2,000 hours more …
… in order to learn something and become very **successful** at doing it, all you'll need is about 10,000 hours!
Without a doubt, there are people who are **brilliant** at certain things …
All the musicians in the study had the **potential** to become world famous …

1 Which two adjectives describe a good level of ability?
2 Which adjective describes a good level of achievement?
3 Which three adjectives describe a very high level of ability or achievement?
4 Look at the noun in **bold** in the last sentence. Are the musicians world famous now or are they likely to be in the future?

b Write the noun forms of the adjectives.
1 skilled _____
2 talented _____
3 brilliant _____
4 able _____

c Complete the sentences with the words in the box.

| at   for   to (x2) |

1 He's very talented _____ playing the guitar.
2 He has a lot of potential _____ succeed in his career.
3 She's got a real talent _____ drawing.
4 She has the ability _____ become an exceptional actor.

d Think of an example of someone who:
1 is skilled at some kind of sport or art
2 has a talent for some kind of musical instrument
3 is famous and you think is brilliant
4 is exceptional in their field
5 is the most successful person you know

e 💬 Tell each other about your answers in 3d. Give reasons for your opinions.

b GIVE ME STRENGTH
A new word suggests a picture.

Isn't it strange how we can remember the words of a much-loved poem that we learned at primary school more than twenty years ago, but we can't remember where we left our keys about ten minutes ago? More than 130 years ago, this problem caught the attention of the German psychologist Hermann Ebbinghaus, and he came up with a theory: the strength of memory.

Ebbinghaus believed that if we find new information interesting, then it'll probably be more meaningful to us. This makes the information easier to learn and also helps the strength of memory. It also helps if we associate the new information with something else. For example, a new word we learn might make us think of a picture. This association can also build memory strength.

Using associations to help us remember what we learn is known as 'mnemonics'. For example, some people are able to remember a long sequence of numbers because the shape of all those numbers reminds them of a specific physical shape, such as a guitar. Mnemonic techniques are often used by competitors in the World Memory Championships held every year.

Popular spelling mnemonics:
BECAUSE
  Big **E**lephants **C**an't **A**lways **U**se **S**mall **E**xits.
HERE or **HEAR?**
  We h**ear** with our **ear**.

c A QUESTION OF TALENT?
'All you'll need is about 10,000 hours!'

We've all had the experience of trying to learn something new only to find out that we're not very good at it. We look around at other people we're learning with who seem more talented and are doing so much better. It seems to come naturally to them. And when you look at all the people who are outstanding at what they do – the really famous people who are superstars – all you see is natural ability. The conclusion seems obvious: talented people must be born that way.

Without a doubt, there are people who are brilliant at certain things – they have a talent for kicking a ball around a field, or they pick up a violin and immediately make music. However, there's also a lot to be said for practice. Psychologist K. Anders Ericsson studied students at Berlin's Academy of Music. He found that even though all the musicians in the study had the potential to become world famous, only some of them actually did. What made the difference? The answer is simple: time. Those who became exceptional were more competitive and practised about 2,000 hours more than those who only did well. So, according to Ericsson, that's what it takes to become really skilled. It turns out that practice really does make perfect, and in order to learn something and become very successful at doing it, all you'll need is about 10,000 hours!

33

UNIT 3

Seamus, comic book creator

Fiona, chemist

Henry, saxophonist

4 LISTENING

a ▶ 03.02 Listen to Seamus, Fiona and Henry talk about their learning experiences. Answer the questions.
1 Who talks about … ?
   a the best time to learn
   b learning hours
   c the strength of memory
2 Do the speakers think the learning ideas they talk about work for them?

b ▶ 03.02 Listen again and make notes about the things they talk about.
1 Seamus
   a copying comics
   b friends
   c graphic design
2 Fiona
   a chemistry
   b system for remembering symbols
   c colleagues' attitudes
3 Henry
   a tour preparation
   b daily learning routine
   c results

c 💬 Whose ideas do you think make most sense? Why?

5 GRAMMAR Multi-word verbs

a What is the meaning of the multi-word verbs in **bold**? Which multi-word verb is most similar to the verb on its own?
1 ☐ … none of them tried to **come up with** their own stories.
2 ☐ I think my career in comics is beginning to **take off**.
3 ☐ I want to **look into** these techniques in more depth.
4 ☐ I also started **making up** my own stories.

b Match the examples in **a** with the patterns below:
1 two-word verb: intransitive verb + particle (no noun following)
2 two-word verb: verb + particle, followed by a noun
3 three-word verb: verb + two particles, followed by a noun

c Look at the two examples which have pattern 2. In which one could you move the particle to the end of the sentence?

d ≫ Now go to Grammar Focus 3A on p. 138.

6 SPEAKING

a Think of something you've done that you have put a lot of effort into. For example:
- your job
- a free-time activity
- study of some kind
- playing a musical instrument
- learning a language.

Take notes about these questions:
1 What special skills or talent do you need?
2 What level of ability do you think you have achieved?
3 How have you learned new information necessary for this activity?
4 Do you need to remember a lot of things to do this well?
5 How much time have you put into it?

b 💬 Work in small groups. Tell each other about your activity. Ask questions.

c 💬 Who in your group do you think has put in the most effort? Who has been successful?

3B THERE ARE A LOT OF GOOD RUNNERS IN KENYA

Learn to discuss sports activities and issues
- **G** Present perfect and present perfect continuous
- **V** Words connected with sport

1 READING

a Look at the photos. What sports do they show?

b What do you think makes a successful athlete or sportsperson? Choose the five things in the box you think are the most important. Are there any you think are unimportant?

> attitude   general level of fitness   luck
> desire for money   genetic make-up
> support from the community   technique
> parents   training and practice

c Compare your ideas with other students.

d Read the text *Born to be the best* about professionals in four sports. In what way are they all similar?

e Read the text again and answer the questions about each sport.
1. What sport is it?
2. Who is given as an example?
3. What unusual features are mentioned?
4. What is the result?

f Which of the things in 1b are mentioned in the text? Do you think this is important for all sports activities or only for top professional players?

Born to be THE BEST

CHAMPION SKIER
Champion cross-country skier Eero Mäntyranta had an unusual gene which made him produce too many red blood cells. Cross-country skiers cover long distances and their red blood cells have to send oxygen to their muscles. Mäntyranta had about 65% more red blood cells than the normal adult male and that's why he performed so well. In the 1960, 1964 and 1968 Winter Olympic Games, he won a total of seven medals. In 1964, he beat his closest competitor in the 15-kilometre race by 40 seconds.

CENTRE OF GRAVITY
When American-Croatian football star Christian Pulisic dribbles the ball past the opposing team to score a goal, people often comment that the ball seems 'glued to his feet'. How does he achieve this? Partly through training and technique, of course, but it also helps that he is shorter than many footballers and as a result has a lower centre of gravity. This accounts for his ability to stay on his feet in spite of being pushed and tackled by the opposing team.

THE WORLD'S BEST RUNNERS
Why do so many of the world's best distance runners come from Kenya and Ethiopia? Because a runner needs not just to be thin, but also to have thin legs and ankles. Runners from the Kalenjin tribe in Kenya – where most of the country's best athletes come from – are thin in exactly this way. Compared to Europeans, Kalenjins are shorter but have longer legs, and their lower legs are over half a kilogram lighter.

BEST AT BASKETBALL
The average height of players in the National Basketball Association is just over two metres (compared with the national average for men of 1.76 m). But some top players are not that tall – the NBA's first three-time slam-dunk champion player Nate Robinson, for example, is only 1.75 m. So how does he play so well? Well, it turns out that although he's short, he has an arm span of 1.85m, so he's taller than he looks! And he's no exception – nearly all top professional basketball players have an arm span far longer than the average, which makes it easier for them to catch the ball and score points.

UNIT 3

2 VOCABULARY
Words connected with sport

a Find words in the text that have a similar meaning to the words in *italics*.
1 Eero Mäntyranta was a cross-country skier *who often won competitions*.
2 He *did so well* because he had more red blood cells than most skiers.
3 He easily beat the closest *person competing with him*.
4 Christian Pulisic is successful because of *regular practice* and also because of *the special way he plays*.
5 The team *playing against him* find it hard to keep him from scoring goals.
6 Most of Kenya's best *sportspeople* are from the Kalenjin tribe.
7 Basketball players *who play for a living* often have a long arm span.

b ≫ Now go to Vocabulary Focus 3B on p. 156.

3 LISTENING

a ▶03.06 The text in 1d is from a book called *The Sports Gene*. Listen to the first part of a programme in which people discuss the book. Answer the questions.
1 What do we know about Barbara McCallum?
2 What does she think of the ideas in the book?

b ▶03.06 Answer the questions. Then listen again and check.
1 What is the main message of the book?
   a The best athletes are often genetically different from most other people.
   b There is a particular gene which makes you a good athlete.
   c Being a good athlete is mainly a question of luck.
2 Which of the following factors does Barbara say are important in Kenyans' success in running?
   a They start running at an early age.
   b Many people have long legs.
   c Children learn to run in bare feet.
   d They train for hours every day.

c ▶03.07 Listen to the second part of the programme and answer the questions.
1 What do we know about Marta Fedorova?
2 What does she think of the ideas in the book?

d ▶03.07 💬 Listen again and discuss the questions.
1 What does Marta notice about the people she has played against?
2 What conclusion does she reach from that?
3 In what way does she say sporting events like the Olympics are 'unfair'?
4 Do you agree with her conclusion? Why / Why not?

UNIT 3

4 GRAMMAR Present perfect and present perfect continuous

a Match sentences 1–4 with the uses of the present perfect and present perfect continuous (a–d).
1. ☐ You**'ve been playing** tennis since you were a child.
2. ☐ I**'ve** also **read** the book.
3. ☐ I**'ve been thinking** a lot about this recently.
4. ☐ I**'ve lived** in Kenya myself.

  a to talk about a past action with no time reference, e.g., *I've lost my glasses.*
  b to talk about an activity that started in the past and is still continuing, e.g., *We've been waiting since this morning.*
  c to talk about an experience at some unspecified time in your life, e.g., *He's climbed Mount Everest.*
  d to talk about a recent activity which continued for a while (and will likely continue into the future), e.g., *I've been reading a lot of good books lately.*

b ≫ Now go to Grammar Focus 3B on p. 138.

c Add a sentence using the present perfect or present perfect continuous.
1. I don't think I could play squash any more. I …
   I haven't played it for years.
2. She's really fit. She …
3. Of course I can play chess. I …
4. Why don't you buy a new pair of skis? You …

d Think about a sport (or another free time activity) that you have been doing for a while. Make notes about questions 1–4.
1. How long have you been doing this sport or activity? Why did you start?
2. How good are you at it?
3. What are the main reasons you have/haven't become good at it? Does it have to do with … ?
   - your genetic make-up and natural ability
   - developing technique and practising
   - support from other people
4. Do you think any of the things you have read or heard in this lesson are relevant to the activity you've been doing?

e 💬 Tell other students about your activity.

5 READING AND SPEAKING

a Read about three famous athletes and answer the questions.
1. How are they similar?
2. How are they different?

b Think about the questions.
If 'sport isn't as fair as we like to think', should players be allowed to find ways to improve their performance? Which of the following do you think are acceptable? Why?
- training hard
- having an operation (e.g., replacing arm muscles, improving eyesight)
- taking legal substances to enhance their performance (e.g., energy drinks)
- taking illegal substances to enhance their performance (e.g., drugs)

c 💬 Compare your ideas. Do you agree?

CHRIS FROOME

World class British racing cyclist Chris Froome is well known for his outstanding performance in international races, including the Tour de France, which he has won four times, and the 2016 Olympics, where he was awarded a bronze medal. Froome suffers from asthma, which is a common problem among racing cyclists. He takes medication to control his asthma, but this caused problems when he was given a blood test after a win in 2017. The test revealed that he had twice the permitted amount of salbutamol, a drug used to treat asthma that also builds muscle and improves performance. Froome claimed he took the medication on the advice of his doctor to control a severe asthma attack and after an investigation, the case against him was dropped.

MIKE WEIR

Mike Weir is one of Canada's best-known champion golfers and he is the only Canadian player ever to win a major world championship. When he found that his eyesight was deteriorating, he decided to have laser surgery on his eyes. This restored his vision, not just to the normal 20/20 vision, but to 20/15, which is better than normal eyesight. After the operation, he went on to win a series of top golfing championships. Laser surgery is commonly used by professional golfers and tennis players and often results in 'super-vision', which gives them a huge competitive advantage over players with normal eyesight.

MARIA SHARAPOVA

Because of her spectacular sporting career, Russian tennis star Maria Sharapova has become a household name, known even to people who don't follow tennis. She was ranked the world's number one player five times and she has won 35 singles titles in her career, including five major international tournaments. However, her professional career has not been free of controversy. In 2016, Sharapova was banned from playing for two years after a drug test found meldonium, which can be used to improve performance, in her blood. She claimed that she took the medication for health reasons and had not realised it was banned in most countries. The ruling caused a widespread public outcry and after her appeal, the ban was reduced to 15 months. She retired from professional tennis in 2020.

3C EVERYDAY ENGLISH
Who should we invite?

Learn to make careful suggestions
- S Keeping to the topic of the conversation
- P Consonant sounds

1 LISTENING

a Discuss the questions.
1. What kind of events do people usually celebrate?
2. Do you prefer small or big celebrations? Why?

b Look at photo a and discuss the questions.
1. Where do you think Becky and Tom have been?
2. What do you think has happened?

c 03.09 Watch or listen to Part 1 and check your ideas in 1b.

d 03.09 Watch or listen again. Tick (✓) the topics that Becky and Tom talk about.

photographs Becky has taken		Tom's colleagues
dinner	Becky's café job	Tom's promotion
Becky's classmate, Tessa		

e 03.09 Watch or listen again. What do they say about the topics?

f 03.10 Watch or listen to Part 2. What wedding plans do Becky and Tom talk about?

g 03.10 Watch or listen to Part 2 again and answer the questions.
1. What's the first decision they have to make?
2. Who seems more focused on wedding plans? Why do you think so?

2 CONVERSATION SKILLS Keeping to the topic of the conversation

a Read this conversation from Part 1. How does Becky return to the original topic of the conversation? Underline the expression she uses.

BECKY So when are you going to tell your parents about your promotion?
TOM This weekend, I think. We're seeing them on Saturday, remember?
BECKY Oh yes. Anyway, as I was saying – about Tessa …
TOM Tessa, yes, your classmate …

b Join words from A and B to make expressions.

A	B
as I	were saying …
to go/get	back to …
just	was saying …
as we	getting/going back to …

c We can put two of these words before the expressions in 2b. Which words are they?

so   actually   oh   anyway

d Work in pairs. Have short conversations. You need to agree on an English language study plan and organise what to study, how much to study, when, etc.

Student A: Explain your ideas for your study plans. Make sure you keep to the topic of the conversation.

Student B: Answer your partner's questions about the study plans, but keep trying to change the topic of conversation to something else.
Swap roles.

I think we should start with vocabulary.

As I was saying, we should start with …

Why don't we go to the café first?

UNIT 3

3 PRONUNCIATION
Sound and spelling: Consonant sounds

a Look at the examples from Parts 1 and 2. Underline words that begin with the sounds in the box.

/b/ /f/ /g/ /k/ /p/ /v/

1 I've gradually got better …
2 … guests, a venue for the reception, the cake.
3 But don't you agree that she'd be perfect …
4 We'll need a photographer.

b ▶03.11 Listen to these two words. Which begins with a voiced sound? Which begins with an unvoiced sound?

better   people

Do you use your lips differently in the /b/ and /p/ sounds?

c ▶03.12 Listen to six words. Which word do you hear in each pair?

1	bill	3	van	5	lap
---	pill		fan		lab
2	goat	4	leave	6	bag
	coat		leaf		back

d 💬 Work in pairs. Take turns saying one word from each pair. Which word does your partner say?

4 LISTENING

a 🎥▶03.13 Watch or listen to Part 3. What is the main topic of Becky and Tom's conversation?
1 food for the wedding
2 their wedding clothes
3 the guests they'll invite

b 🎥▶03.13 Watch or listen again. What do they say about the topics below? Make notes.
1 Aunt Clare
2 Uncle Fred
3 Tom's colleagues
4 Regent's Lodge
5 after they get married

5 USEFUL LANGUAGE
Making careful suggestions

a ▶03.14 Becky and Tom make careful suggestions to each other. Can you remember the missing words?

BECKY   We _____ _____ invite them to the evening reception.
TOM   But don't you agree that it'd _____ _____ not to invite them?

Listen and check.

b Why do Becky and Tom make careful suggestions? Choose the best answer.
1 They feel the subject matter is a bit sensitive and they don't want to offend each other.
2 The wedding won't happen for a few months, so it doesn't feel real to them.

c Look at these examples of careful suggestions. Match the examples to the correct uses below.
a Don't you think it's a good idea to … ?
b How does it sound if we/I … ?
c Another idea might be to …
d I think maybe we should …
e I thought maybe we could …

1 Putting forward an idea carefully
2 Asking the other person to give their point of view

d Correct the careful suggestions.
1 Another idea might to be booking a DJ for the reception.
2 Don't you think a good idea to invite more people?
3 Maybe I thought we could get married at home.
4 How does it sound we only have a small cake?

e ≫ **Communication 3C** Student A: Go to p. 128. Student B: Go to p. 129.

6 SPEAKING

a You are going to have a class party. Work alone and think of ideas for the party. Think about:
- when
- where
- party theme and music
- food and drinks

b 💬 Discuss your ideas and make careful suggestions. Make sure everyone keeps to the topic of the conversation.

> We could always do it at college.

> Another idea might be to hire a hall.

✓ UNIT PROGRESS TEST

→ **CHECK YOUR PROGRESS**

You can now do the Unit Progress Test.

3D SKILLS FOR WRITING
It doesn't matter what sport people choose

Learn to write a description of data
W Describing data

1 SPEAKING AND LISTENING

a Discuss the questions.
1 What's the most unusual sport you've seen or heard of? Have you ever tried it?
2 What do you think are the most popular sports in your country to participate in? Why do you think they are popular?
3 How do you think new sports become popular?

b Look at photos 1–3. What are the names of the sports? Which of these sports have you tried? Which would you like to try?

c 03.15 Marco talks to three people at a sports centre: Lizzie, Barry and Patricia. Listen and match the speakers to the sports in the photos.

d 03.15 Listen again and make notes about each speaker:
1 reasons for choosing their sport
2 experience of the sport
3 future plans.

e Are any of these sports popular in your country? Why / Why not?

2 READING

a Look at the bar chart. Are the sentences true or false?
1 The data only shows information about the different kinds of programmes members do.
2 The data doesn't give information about age or gender of members.
3 The data shows changes that happen every second year.
4 The most growth in participation is in gym training.

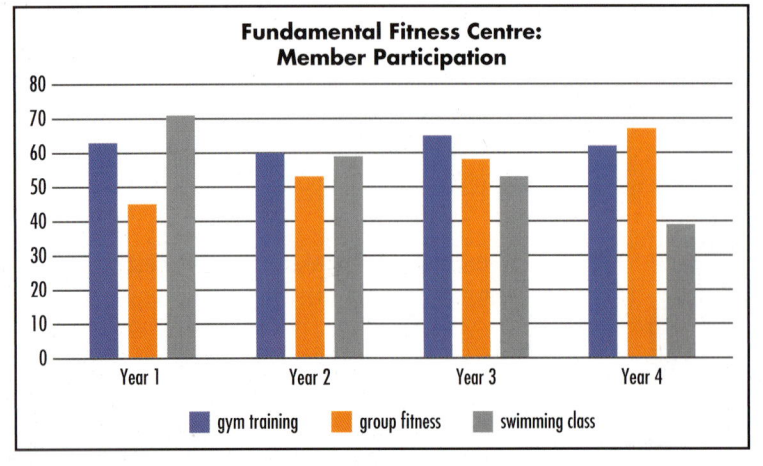

b Read the article *Fitness: Seattle snapshot*. Does it give the same information as the bar chart?

c Read the article again and answer the questions.
1 Why are the sports that people like doing different from the ones that they like watching?
2 What was a big attraction for members when the gym first opened?
3 Why were fewer people swimming by the fourth year?
4 In which programme has participation not changed a lot? Why?
5 Why was participation in group fitness classes low to begin with?
6 Why have they been so successful?

3 WRITING SKILLS
Describing data

a Look at paragraphs c, d and e. They are all organised in the same way. In each one, what is the order of these points? Number them 1 to 3.
☐ a reason for the change in percentages
☐ a description of the activity
☐ a report on important increases/decreases.

b Look at paragraphs c, d and e again and complete the table.

	Adjective	Noun
there is a/an	¹____ / dramatic	increase
	obvious / significant	²____
	³____ / ⁴____	decrease
	Verb	**Adverb**
the number(s) / size	has/have / hasn't/ haven't increased	⁵____ / ⁶____ / slightly
	has/have ⁷____	dramatically

c Which adjectives and adverbs describe … ?
1. a big change
2. a small change
3. a sudden change
4. a slow change
5. an important change
6. a change you can see clearly

d Answer the questions.
1. What verb phrase in paragraph d shows that there has been no change to member participation?
2. Does the underlined *this* in paragraphs c and d refer back or forward to other information in the paragraphs?

e Use the data about use of equipment when people work out in the gym to write sentences. Use language from 3b.
1. Members who use free weights: year 1 = 43%; year 4 = 46%
2. Members who use cardio machines: year 1 = 64%; year 4 = 41%
3. Members who use weight machines: year 1 = 48%; year 4 = 57%

4 WRITING

a Look at the bar chart and read the notes below. What does the information show?

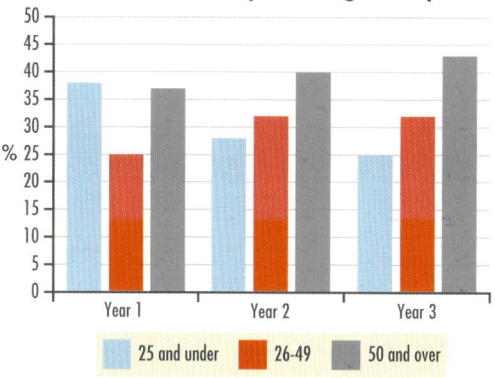

Fundamental Fitness Centre Member Participation: Age Groups

[Bar chart showing percentages for age groups 25 and under, 26-49, and 50 and over across Year 1, Year 2, and Year 3]

Notes
Ages 25 and under: change gyms often – like to try something new
Ages 26-49: many have families and less time for fitness
Ages 50 and over: getting older, free of responsibility – more time for fitness

b Work in pairs. Plan an article about the data and notes in 4a. Then write your article.

c Swap your article with another pair. Does the article use language from 3b correctly? Does it include verbs and nouns? Does it have the same organisation as 3a? Was it easy to understand?

FITNESS: SEATTLE SNAPSHOT

ᵃSurveys show that people in Seattle love watching team sports like basketball, baseball and football, but if they want to get moving, they need to do activities that don't involve watching other people chasing a ball around a pitch or court. Activities can include workouts at a gym, swimming and group fitness classes. Below is an example of participation in different fitness programmes at a gym in Seattle.

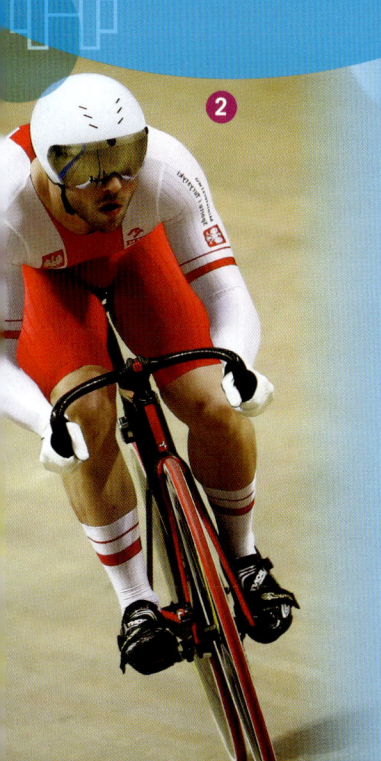

ᵇThe Fundamental Fitness Centre (FFC) opened four years ago. We have group fitness classes and our aquatic centre offers a range of swimming lessons.

ᶜA lot of our members do more than one activity each week, so overall, our participation rates are very high. To begin with, our swimming programme had the highest participation of all our programmes. After the first two years, there was a gradual decrease in the number of members using the pool because it was crowded at peak times. Last year, participation decreased dramatically. This was because a new gym opened nearby with an Olympic-sized pool, so a lot of members moved there.

ᵈFFC also has an excellent range of machines for cardio and building strength. Participation in members' individual gym programmes has remained steady over the four-year period. There was a slight decrease after the first year and then a noticeable increase in our third year. However, participation hasn't increased or dropped below 60%. This is the result of a stable group of members who enjoy their workouts on a regular basis.

ᵉThe real success story of FFC has been our group classes, which offer a lot of variety. To begin with, a lot of members thought group workouts were just dance classes. But there has been an obvious boost in participation in group fitness over the four-year period, and last year was the most popular year for our members. Word is getting out that this is a great way to get fit – and have fun. Just recently, we've added yoga to the schedule, and numbers in those classes have increased noticeably. The reason for all of this is that we're lucky to have some really creative and motivating instructors who have helped establish these classes for our members.

ᶠFFC offers a range of activities, so there is something for everyone. Also, many activities don't require as high a level of expertise as team sports do. However, it is interesting that the group classes have become increasingly popular. While people may not always like joining teams, they seem to benefit from working out in a group.

UNIT 3
Review and extension

1 GRAMMAR

a Put the words in *italics* in the correct order.
1 I didn't know Spanish before I went to Mexico, but I managed to *up / pick / it* very quickly.
2 I'm just as good as you. There's no need to *me / down / look / on* just because I didn't go to university.
3 It's still raining. This weather is starting to *get / down / me*.
4 I don't believe she was ever married to a film star. I think she *it / up / making / is*.
5 She's very creative. She keeps *up / with / coming* new ideas.
6 I don't know how to do this task. I just can't *out / figure / it*.

b Choose the correct verb tenses in the conversations.
1 **A** Come in. Sorry the flat is such a mess.
   B What have you ¹*done / been doing*? There are things all over the floor.
   A I've ²*sorted / been sorting* things out, but I haven't quite ³*finished / been finishing* yet.
2 **A** How are things? I haven't ⁴*seen / been seeing* you for ages. What have you ⁵*done / been doing*?
   B Oh, nothing much. I've got exams coming up next month, so I've ⁶*studied / been studying* most of the time.

c Think of things you could say to answer these questions using the present perfect or present perfect continuous.
- What have you been doing these days?
- How's your family?
- You're looking fit. Have you been doing a lot of sport?
- So what's new?

d 💬 Have conversations, starting with the questions in 1c.

2 VOCABULARY

a Rewrite the sentences, using the words in brackets, so that they keep the same meaning. More than one answer is sometimes possible.
1 We're looking for someone who can lead a team of researchers. (ability)
2 She can design things very well. (skilled)
3 The members of the band all play music extremely well. (outstanding)
4 He could become a very good politician. (potential)
5 He's better than most goalkeepers. (exceptional)
6 My sister can cook very well. (extraordinary)

b Give a different form of the words in *italics* to complete the definitions.
1 Someone who *trains* athletes is a __trainer__ .
2 A person who *competes* in a sport is a _____ .
3 *Athletes* are usually very fit and _____ .
4 Someone who does sport as a *profession* is a _____ sportsperson.
5 If you *perform* well, you give a good _____ .
6 A team that wins a *victory* is _____ .

3 WORDPOWER *up*

a Match the comments with the pictures.

1 ☐ '**Drink up**. We need to go.'
2 ☐ 'Could you **speak up**? We can't hear you.'
3 ☐ 'I've **used up** the shampoo. Is there any more?'
4 ☐ 'Let me see the bill. I think they've **added** it **up** incorrectly.'

b Adding *up* often gives an extra meaning to a verb. In which examples in 3a does *up* mean … ?
a to the end   b together   c louder

c What does *it* mean in each example below?

a suggestion   a language   a glass   a word

1 You dropped it, so I think you should **clear** it **up**.
2 I don't know. I'll have to **look** it **up**.
3 It was easy. I **picked** it **up** in about six months.
4 Why don't you **bring** it **up** at the meeting?

d ▶ 03.16 Listen and check your answers. What was the problem in each case?

e Here are some more multi-word verbs with *up*. Match the two parts of the sentences.
1 Walk more slowly! I can't   **look up to** him.
2 He's a good father. His children really   **turned up**.
3 We invited 50 people, but only a few   **put up with** him.
4 He's so rude. I don't know why people   **keep up with** you.

f Match the multi-word verbs in 3e with these meanings.
a tolerate   c appear or arrive
b go at the same speed   d admire or respect

g 💬 Work in pairs. Choose two of the multi-word verbs in 3a, c or e. Think of a situation and write a short conversation which includes both verbs.

h 💬 Act out your conversation. Can other students guess your situation?

♻ REVIEW YOUR PROGRESS

How well did you do in this unit? Write 3, 2 or 1 for each objective.
3 = very well   2 = well   1 = not so well

I CAN …	
discuss ability and achievement	☐
discuss sports activities and issues	☐
make careful suggestions	☐
write a description of data.	☐

CAN DO OBJECTIVES

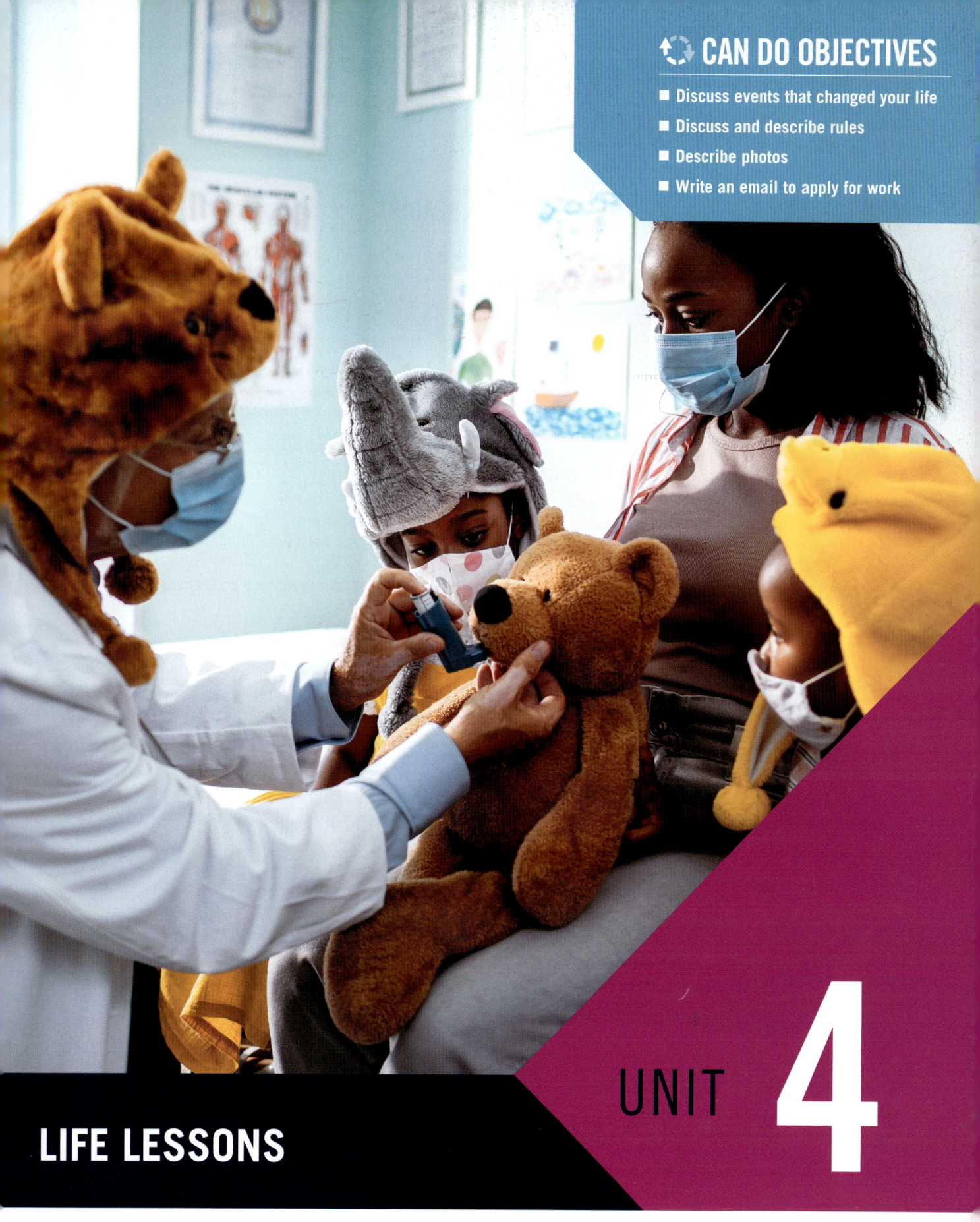

■ Discuss events that changed your life
■ Discuss and describe rules
■ Describe photos
■ Write an email to apply for work

UNIT 4

LIFE LESSONS

GETTING STARTED

a Look at the picture and answer the questions.
1. Where are these people? What are they doing?
2. What is the doctor showing the children? Why?
3. What do you think the children are thinking?

b Discuss the questions.
1. Is it important to help children prepare for what might happen to them later in life? Why?
2. Which of your childhood experiences have had an impact on your adult life?
3. In general, how much do you think experiences in childhood influence the choices you make in your life?

43

4A I'M MORE CAUTIOUS THAN I USED TO BE

Learn to discuss events that changed your life

G *used to* and *would*
V Cause and result

1 SPEAKING

a What people do you know of in your country or the world who ...?
- are extremely rich
- went from being poor to being very rich

Do you think these people ... ?
- are happy
- spend their money wisely

Say why you think so.

b Imagine you are a millionaire. What would you do with your money? Think about:
- ways to spend it
- ways to invest it
- using it to help people.

THE DECISION THAT CHANGED MY LIFE

How a boy from Southern India went from having just £600 to being a London millionaire

Rupesh Thomas runs a company worth over £2 million and lives with his wife and son in a £1 million home in the southwest of London. The secret of his success is chai tea, a traditional Indian drink which his company sells in Britain and all round the world. But how did he come to be so successful? It all started with a single life-changing decision.

2 READING

a Read the first part of two texts about people who went from being very poor to being very rich. In each text, what do you think happened that changed the person's life?

b The words in the boxes are keywords from each story.

Rupesh Thomas
low-income university engineering dream
motorbike single ticket London McDonalds
wife chai company award

Mark Pearson
mother Liverpool trouble catering college
competition restaurants idea fridge discount
vouchers online website £55 million

Read the definitions and complete the gaps using some of the words from the boxes.

1 If you go to _____, you study food and cooking.
2 You can collect _____ from the newspaper or online and use them to buy products more cheaply.
3 If a product is very good or high quality, it may get an _____.
4 People in _____ families don't earn much money.
5 If you keep arriving late to school, you may get into _____ with the head teacher.

c What do you think happened to the two people? Use the keywords in 2b to help you guess.

d **Communication 4A** Work in pairs – you are either Pair A or Pair B. Pair A: Read the story of Rupesh Thomas on p. 127 and answer the questions. Pair B: Read the story of Mark Pearson on p. 128 and answer the questions. Then practise telling your story.

e Work in new pairs, with one A and one B.
1 Take turns to tell your stories using the keywords in 2b. Ask questions about your partner's story to check anything you don't understand.
2 What similarities and differences are there between the two stories?

TWO THINGS HAPPENED THAT CHANGED EVERYTHING

The events that set Mark Pearson on the path to becoming a multi-millionaire

Mark Pearson is a multi-millionaire and runs an investment company which supports young entrepreneurs. But when he left school at the age of 16 to go to catering college, it didn't look as if he was headed for success. So, what happened that helped him to become so successful?

herdeiro – heir

UNIT 4

f 💬 Discuss the questions.
1 How much was Rupesh's and Mark's success a result of … ?
 • luck
 • following their dream
 • hard work
2 What 'message' comes out of these stories for you? Write it down and compare your idea with other students.

3 GRAMMAR *used to* and *would*

a Look at sentences a–c and complete the rules with the words in the box.
 a His father **used to** travel for his work, and he once gave him a picture of London.
 b When he was young, he **used to** be afraid that he would never find a good job.
 c She **used to** make it herself and she **would** often drink ten cups of it a day.

 now   past   used to (x2)   would (x2)

> We use *used to* and *would* to talk about things in the ¹_____ that are no longer true ²_____.
> To talk about states, thoughts and feelings in the past, we can only use ³_____, not ⁴_____.
> To talk about habits and repeated actions, we can use either ⁵_____ or ⁶_____.

b Look again at the text about Rupesh Thomas on p. 127. Find and underline other examples of *used to* and *would*.

c Look at the sentences and answer the questions.
 a And of course, his mother and sister **don't** live in a small flat **any more**.
 b Although he **no longer** needed to work, he decided to set up an investment company.
1 What do the words in **bold** mean?
 (a) things are the same as before
 (b) things are different now
2 Rewrite sentence a with *no longer* and sentence b with *not any more*. How does the word order change?

d ≫ Now go to Grammar Focus 4A on p. 140.

e Express these ideas in a different way, using expressions from 2a–c. Try to think of two ways to say the same idea.
1 Money isn't important to me, but it was before.
 Money used to be very important to me.
 Money isn't important to me any more.
2 When I was younger, I went shopping for clothes every Saturday, but not now.
3 I eat healthier food now.
4 I don't go out much these days. I usually stay at home.

4 LISTENING

a You are going to listen to an interview with Monica Sharpe, a researcher in the psychology of money. How do you think she will answer these questions?
1 Does having lots of money make you happy? *No ya, generally*
2 Does suddenly having lots of money make you behave badly? *Isolated cases, people like to think that*
3 Does buying things make you happy? *Experiences type & long term happiness*

b ▶ 04.04 Listen and check your answers.

c ▶ 04.04 Tick (✓) the points Monica makes. Listen again and check.
1 ☐ The happiest people are those who have between $1 million and $2 million.
2 ✓ Most people who get a lot of money spend (it sensibly).
3 ✓ We enjoy hearing stories about people who won a lot of money and then lost it all.
4 ☐ Suddenly having lots of money usually has a negative effect on you.
5 ✓ Very few people who win money go back to being poor again.
6 ✓ In the long term, being rich doesn't always make you happier.
7 ☐ It's better to spend money on things you can see, like houses and cars.

d 💬 Which of the points in 4c do you agree with? Can you think of examples from people you know or have heard about?

45

UNIT 4

5 VOCABULARY Cause and result

a ▶ 04.05 Underline the correct words in **bold**. Then listen and check your answers.
1. Of course, people like to believe that winning money leads **into** / **to** disaster.
2. The idea that winning a lot of money **causes** / **is caused by** misery is actually a myth.
3. Suddenly having a lot of money is just as likely to have a positive effect **on** / **to** you as a negative effect.
4. They measured how happy people are as a result **from** / **of** winning the lottery.
5. Getting richer doesn't actually **effect** / **affect** how happy you are.
6. But spending money on experiences usually results **in** / **on** longer-term happiness.

b Answer the questions about the expressions in 5a.
1. Which expressions have a similar meaning to 'causes'?
2. Which expression has a similar meaning to 'caused by'?
3. What is the difference between *affect* and *effect*?
4. Look at sentences 4 and 6. In which sentence is *result* a verb and in which is it a noun?

c Complete the sentences with the words in the box.

affect   effect   cause   lead   result (x2)

1. He's much friendlier than he used to be. Getting married has had a positive _____ on him.
2. Having no money at all can often _____ to problems in a relationship.
3. I hear John and Barbara have split up. I hope it won't _____ our friendship with them.
4. It's well known that smoking can _____ cancer.
5. Hundreds of villagers' lives were saved as a _____ of the government's help.
6. Be careful! Borrowing large amounts of money can _____ in serious financial problems.

d Think about an important event in your own life and another event that happened as a result. Write three sentences about it using expressions in 5a.

e 💬 Read your sentences to each other and ask questions.

6 LISTENING

a Look at the information about Alfonso and Dragana. How do you think their lives have changed? Think about:

lifestyle   attitude to life   daily routine   work   money   leisure

LIFE-CHANGING EVENTS

Sometimes a single big event can change your life. Two people tell us their stories.

Dragana studied abroad for a year.

Alfonso and Carmen have just had their first baby.

b ▶ 04.06 Listen to Alfonso and Dragana. Which of the topics in 6a do they talk about?

c ▶ 04.06 Are the sentences true or false? Correct the false sentences. Listen again and check.

Alfonso
1. They both used to work.
2. They didn't have much money.
3. The baby hasn't changed his attitude to life much.

Dragana
4. She's from a big city in Croatia.
5. She didn't enjoy being in Berlin.
6. The experience has changed her attitude to other cultures.

7 SPEAKING

a Think about yourself now and how you have changed in the last ten years. Make notes on some of these topics:
- work
- free time
- attitude to life
- daily routine
- family and relationships
- money.

b 💬 Tell each other how you think you have changed using *used to* / *would*.

4B WE WEREN'T ALLOWED TO TALK IN CLASS

Learn to discuss and describe rules
- **G** Obligation and permission
- **V** Talking about difficulty

Have, must, can, need

1 SPEAKING

a 💬 Look at photos a–d. Which of the jobs would you most like to do? Why?

b Read what these people say about training. Do you agree with their opinions?

2 GRAMMAR Obligation and permission

a <u>Underline</u> all the modal verbs or phrases (e.g., *can*, *have to*) in the quotes.

b Complete the rules with the correct modal verb or phrase in 2a.

1. We use __must__, __need to__ and __have to__ when we talk about something that's necessary.
2. We use __don't have to__ to talk about something that isn't necessary.
3. We use __can__ when we talk about something that's possible.
4. We use __can't__ to talk about something that's not possible.

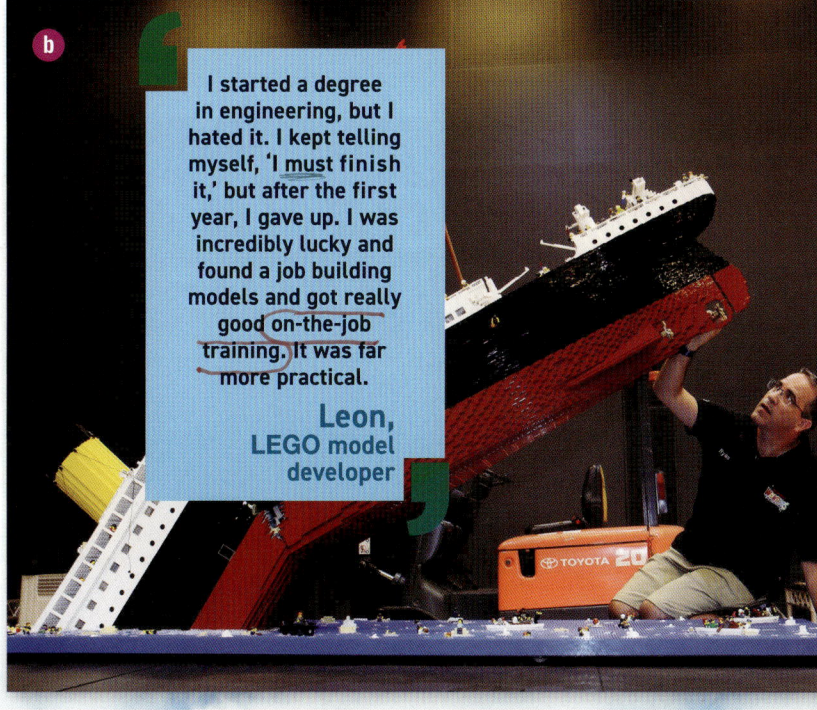

> You <u>can</u> do all the studying you like, but until you've done the actual job, you don't know what it really involves.
> **Sheela,** pilot

> I started a degree in engineering, but I hated it. I kept telling myself, 'I <u>must</u> finish it,' but after the first year, I gave up. I was incredibly lucky and found a job building models and got really good on-the-job training. It was far more practical.
> **Leon,** LEGO model developer

> These days you <u>need to</u> have a degree no matter what you do; you simply <u>can't</u> get a job without one. It's getting a bit silly, really. Most of the time, all you require is common sense and practical skills.
> **Amelia,** forest ranger

monitor protect wildlife

> You <u>don't have to</u> have a university degree to get a good job these days – it's as much about training and practice.
> **Tony,** stuntman

47

UNIT 4

3 READING

a Look at photos a–d and answer the questions.
1 What jobs are shown in the photos?
2 What kind of training do you need for this work?

b Read the texts. Were your ideas correct?

c Read the texts again. Who do you think would say this: Joe (J), Amelia (A) or both (B)?
1 [B] There are some situations I can never really prepare for.
2 [J] I couldn't rush things with the training course.
3 [J] I really needed the strength I developed doing workouts at the gym.
4 [A] It's necessary to have a degree, but you also need to keep up to date with new practices and procedures.
5 [B] Sometimes when I get home, I just feel exhausted.
6 [J] I need to take care not only of myself but also the other members of the team.
7 [A] I try not to let my feelings show.
8 [B] I never stop training and learning.

d Which of the two kinds of training seems harder to you? Which one would you choose to do? Why?

4 VOCABULARY Talking about difficulty

a Match these definitions to the **bold** adjectives in the text. Notice the differences in meaning. Which word in **bold** is not as strong as the others?
1 1 very difficult because the training is thorough and detailed
6 2 difficult because you need a lot of effort and energy
2 3 hard because you need to give it a lot of time and attention
3 4 difficult and extremely tiring
5 5 involves hard physical work that makes your body sore
4 6 extremely tiring and difficult – you need a lot of effort and determination
7 7 difficult to deal with and needs careful attention or skill
8 8 difficult to deal with or do – you need to be physically and emotionally strong
9 9 difficult because there are rules that must be obeyed
10 10 so difficult you have to push yourself almost to the point of hurting yourself

Training for the EMERGENCY FRONT LINE

Training to Rescue

You go for an easy hike in the mountains. Suddenly the weather changes and you lose sight of the trail. What should you do? Call for help and wait for Joe Conte to appear.

Joe is a Mountain Search and Rescue volunteer who risks his life to save people who get into trouble in the wilderness. Based in Colorado, Joe is a computer programmer by day. But his real passion is anything to do with mountains. Joe is one of the most experienced volunteers and often undertakes extremely dangerous rescue missions.

Can anyone become a volunteer? 'Well, we welcome anyone who wants to get involved,' says Joe, 'but if you want to do serious rescues, you must undergo a ¹**rigorous** training course.'

To begin with, you have to be an experienced mountaineer and you have to be fit. 'On rescue missions, you often face ²**arduous** conditions, so you need strength and ability,' Joe points out.

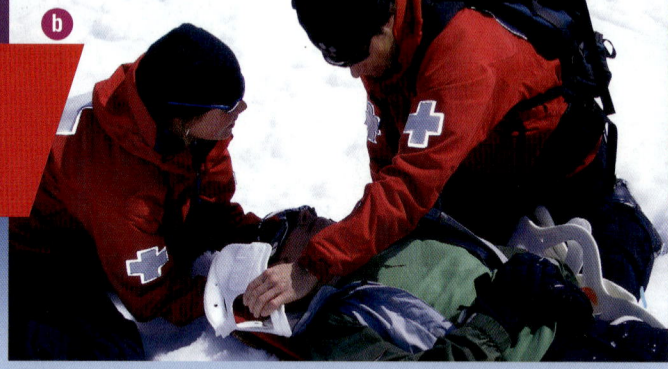

The training takes two years and is ³**demanding** and ⁴**exhausting**. 'In one training scenario, you have to rescue someone from a gap between rocks. You have to pull them up by a rope, so you need to be really strong. In another scenario, you dig someone out of an avalanche. It's ⁵**backbreaking** work, and you have to be fast because victims can only survive for about 40 minutes buried in snow.'

Apart from the ⁶**gruelling** physical training, volunteers need expert risk assessment skills. They often find themselves in ⁷**tricky** situations where not only the lives of the victims are in danger but also those of volunteers. 'You have to make smart decisions and you have to make them quickly.'

And the training never stops. Fully-trained volunteers still do about 300 hours of ongoing training every year.

'Yes, it's a big commitment, but the reward of bringing someone to safety makes it worth it.'

Training to Save Lives

Being a nurse is demanding, but some nurses want an even bigger challenge and move into Accident and Emergency (A&E) nursing. The A&E department is fast-paced and often chaotic, so A&E nurses not only need to be patient and understanding, but they must also know how to multitask and stay calm under pressure.

Amelia Davis has been an A&E nurse for the past six years at one of the busiest hospitals in Manchester. She is the first point of contact for patients who arrive at A&E. Many have life-threatening medical conditions, such as heart attacks. Amelia has to know exactly what to do before a doctor can see the patient.

How do you train for such a ⁸**tough**, high-stress job? 'In some ways, you don't!' was Amelia's surprising answer. 'Obviously, you have to have a nursing degree, but you also continue to learn by further training. It's our duty to be aware of changes relevant to our role in order to ensure we deliver the very best care we can to our patients,' Amelia explains.

UNIT 4

b Answer the questions about the differences in meaning.
1 You can describe training as *arduous* or *gruelling*. Which has a stronger meaning?
2 Environmental conditions can be *tough* or *arduous*. Which has a stronger meaning?
3 Work can be *demanding*, *exhausting* or *backbreaking*. Which adjective means it makes you tired? Which means it challenges you physically? Which means it can be both a physical and an emotional challenge?
4 A situation can be *tough* or *tricky*. Which adjective suggests the situation is difficult and complicated?
5 Pace can be *demanding* or *punishing*. Which has a stronger meaning?
6 Discipline can be *tough* or *strict*. Which adjective gives a stronger idea of being careful about following rules?

c Ask and answer the questions. Give extra details.
1 What is something tough you have done?
2 Can you remember a teacher you had at school who was very strict?
3 What's a job that requires rigorous training?
4 Have you ever been in a tricky situation? What happened?

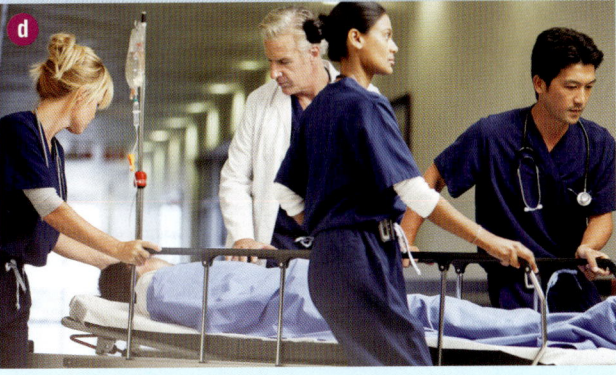

'When I first started, much of my training was on the job, and the discipline was ⁹**strict**. The head nurse was hard on the inexperienced nurses, but she knew what she was doing. I really respected her, and she prepared us for dealing with all kinds of situations.'

A&E nurses never know who's going to show up, so they must be ready for anything. Also, they never know when patients are going to arrive, and there are times when A&E gets unbelievably busy.

'At the beginning, I found the pace ¹⁰**punishing**. In my first week, there was a bus crash with a lot of injured people. One of the passengers was pregnant and in pain. I had the feeling she was in labour and not injured, so I called a doctor quickly. Sure enough, the baby was about to arrive. It was a complicated birth, and the doctor told me it was good I called him as soon as I did. Despite all the training, you also have to trust your instincts.'

A key part of Amelia's on-the-job training was not letting her emotions get in the way. An A&E nurse needs to keep a clear head at all times.

'Even after six years, some days are really hard and stressful. But it's never boring and you do save lives. That's why I'm a nurse.'

d Now go to Vocabulary Focus 4B on p. 157.

5 LISTENING

a ▶ 04.09 Listen to Miranda, who trained at a drama school, and Fred, who trained at a football academy. Which sentence describes their experience best?
1 They both enjoyed the training but felt they missed a part of growing up.
2 They weren't sure about the training, but they know they'll do well anyway.
3 They weren't sure about the selection process, but they feel they did well during the training.

b ▶ 04.09 Listen again. Are the sentences true or false?
Miranda
1 During the audition process, she had to perform scenes from plays twice.
2 She was confident she would get into drama school.
3 All her tutors were tough.
4 The school was flexible when she wasn't sure if she wanted to continue training.
Fred
5 His parents were unsure whether he should join the academy.
6 They knew they would have to sacrifice a lot of time to help Fred.
7 He was surprised to find that he enjoyed analysing football matches.
8 He felt disappointed for his friend, Jack.

c Do you think the kind of sacrifice that Miranda and Fred made was worth it? Why / Why not?

6 GRAMMAR
Obligation and permission

a Look at the words and phrases in **bold** in sentences 1–6. Which show obligation (*O*) and which show permission (*P*)?
O 1 ☐ I **was supposed to** prepare a song as well, but they forgot to let me know.
O 2 ☐ … there was a workshop for a day where they **made** us work on new scenes from plays …
P 3 ☐ … in her class we **weren't allowed to** talk or use our voices in any way.
P 4 ☐ … they could see this was a pretty unique opportunity, so they **let** me do it.
P 5 ☐ … we **were allowed to** see the games for free.
O 6 ☐ … there were some boys who **were forced to** give it all up …

b Now go to Grammar Focus 4B on p. 140.

7 SPEAKING

a Think of a time (at school or work or in sports or music) when you had to do some training and follow rules. Make notes about the questions.

What was the situation?
Who made the rules?
Were some of the rules very strict?
Were there some rules you didn't follow?
How did you feel about the experience?

b Discuss your experiences. What similarities and differences were there?

49

4C EVERYDAY ENGLISH
Thank you, you've saved my life

Learn to describe photos
- P Contrastive stress
- S Expressing careful disagreement

1 LISTENING

a Discuss the questions.
1 How do you feel about showing your work to other people? Do you … ?
   a always show other people what you've done
   b only show your work if you think it's good
   c never show your work unless you really have to
2 How do you feel about people commenting on it or criticising it?
   ↳ negative

b Look at photo a from Part 1. Where do you think Becky and Tessa are? Who are they talking to?

c 📹 ▶ 04.12 Watch or listen to Part 1 and check your ideas.
close-up shots, sharp details and light colours

d 📹 ▶ 04.12 Answer the questions. Watch or listen again and check.
1 Whose photos are they?
2 What does the tutor especially like?
3 What's the topic for the next assignment?

2 USEFUL LANGUAGE
Describing photos

a Which of the expressions below could describe the photos? Write 1, 2, neither (N) or both (B).

1 [2] And here's a <u>close-up</u> of some leaves.
2 [2] We tried to get a <u>closer shot</u> with this photo.
3 [1] Here's <u>a more distant shot</u> of the tree.
4 [1] And this is the same tree, but <u>from further away</u>.
5 [B] Here's another shot of the tree, but <u>from a different angle</u>.
6 [1] As you can see, there are mountains <u>in the background</u>.
7 [N] That's my car <u>in the foreground</u>.
8 [N] This one's a bit <u>out of focus</u>!

b 📹 ▶ 04.12 Which <u>underlined</u> expressions in 2a did Becky use? Watch or listen again and check.

c ≫ **Communication 4C** Student A: Go to p. 128. Student B: Go to p. 130.

d Work in pairs (one student from A and B in each pair). Take turns to show your photos to your partner and discuss them. Ask questions about your partner's photos.

e Discuss the photos. In what ways are the photos similar? In what ways are they different?

3 LISTENING

a 📹 ▶ 04.13 Watch or listen to Part 2. Answer the questions.
1 What are Becky and Tessa talking about?
2 Where is Becky going next?

b Who thinks these things, Becky (B) or Tessa (T)?
1 ☐ Bridges are an interesting topic.
2 ☐ The theoretical part of the course is boring.
3 ☐ She is missing information for the essay.

UNIT 4

4 CONVERSATION SKILLS
Expressing careful disagreement

a ▶ 04.14 Look at the exchange between Tessa and Becky. Then listen to what they actually say. What is the difference?
TESSA Yes, bridges. So boring.
BECKY I don't agree. They're not at all boring.

b Why does Becky use careful ways to disagree?

c The sentences below are replies to what another person said. What do you think each speaker is talking about? Match the replies with the topics in the box.

| 1 a football match 2 a film 3 bank managers |
| 4 a restaurant meal 5 a party |

1 <u>Really, did you think so? I thought</u> he played quite well. 1
2 <u>I'm not sure about that.</u> It doesn't seem that expensive. 4
3 <u>I know what you mean, but on the other hand</u> it's a very responsible job. 3
4 <u>Oh, I don't know.</u> I think it could be quite good fun. 5
5 <u>Maybe you're right</u>, but I enjoyed some bits of it. 2

d ▶ 04.15 Listen to the conversations and check your answers.

e 💬 How could you disagree with the comments below? Prepare replies using <u>underlined</u> expressions from 4c. Then take turns to reply.
1 I love Café Roma. It's a great atmosphere.
2 I'd never want to have a cat. All they do is sit around and sleep.
3 I don't know why people play golf. It's such a boring sport.

5 PRONUNCIATION Contrastive stress

a ▶ 04.14 Listen again to Becky's reply and answer the questions below.
TESSA Yes, bridges. So boring.
BECKY Oh, I don't know. *It's not that boring.*

1 Underline the word which has the strongest stress in the sentence in *italics*.
2 Does the sentence mean … ?
   a They're not all boring.
   b They're not as boring as you think they are.
   c They're not as boring as other kinds of architecture.

b 💬 Reply to the comments below, using *not that*.
1 I thought that was a really interesting lecture.

> Oh, I don't know. …

2 I find photography a very difficult subject.
3 Look at that bridge. It's so unusual.
4 I thought the questions in the exam were incredibly easy.

c ▶ 04.16 Listen and check. Were your replies similar?

6 LISTENING

a 🎥 ▶ 04.17 Watch or listen to Part 3. Which of these is the best summary of what happens?
1 Becky gives Tessa a coffee and some books she found in the library. Then they talk about the wedding. Then Tessa notices Phil and asks who he is.
2 Becky gives Tessa her lecture notes, then they talk about the wedding. Then Tessa meets Phil and they talk about his book.

b 💬 Are the sentences true or false? Discuss the false sentences – what actually happens?
1 Becky gives Tessa her lecture notes.
2 Tessa is grateful to Becky for her help.
3 Becky wants Tessa to be their wedding photographer.
4 Tessa refuses because she thinks she's not good enough.
5 Phil finishes typing and saves what he's written.
6 Phil asks who Tessa is.
7 Tessa wants to read Phil's novel.

7 SPEAKING

a ≫ **Communication 4C** Student A: Go to p. 127. Student B: Go to p. 129.

b Present an opinion on one of the topics to the rest of the class. Do they agree with you?

✓ UNIT PROGRESS TEST

➡ **CHECK YOUR PROGRESS**

You can now do the Unit Progress Test.

4D SKILLS FOR WRITING
I'm good at communicating with people

Learn to write an email to apply for work
W Giving a positive impression

1 SPEAKING AND LISTENING

a 💬 If you go to live in a different country, do you think it's important to … ?
- learn the local language
- make friends with local people
- go somewhere beautiful with a good climate

Why do you think these things are important or not important?

b ▶04.18 Listen to three people talking about living in the places in the photos. Which topics do they mention?

meeting people   the climate   food and drink
the culture of the country   speaking the language

c ▶04.18 Listen again. Answer these questions about each speaker.
1 What did he/she like?
2 What did he/she find difficult?
3 How was it different from his/her own country?

d Which speakers make these points? How did their own experience support these opinions?
1 It's important to learn the local language.
2 Beautiful cities aren't always the best places to live.
3 The weather influences the way people live.
4 Foreigners often don't make an effort to get to know the local culture.
5 Living abroad can be worthwhile even if you don't always have a good time.

e 💬 The speakers say that meeting local people is important when you live in a different country. Think of three ways you could meet local people. Which is your most interesting idea? Why?

2 READING

a Read the advert about becoming an international student 'buddy' in London. Answer the questions.
1 What is a 'buddy' and what does he/she do?
2 What are the advantages of becoming a buddy?
3 What kind of person are they looking for?

Nick from England
Katowice, Poland
Jean from France
Muscat, Oman
Eva from Colombia
Toronto, Canada

Be a buddy for
THE INTERNATIONAL STUDENTS' CLUB

Are you curious about other cultures? Are you eager to get to know and meet new people from all over the world?
Volunteer to offer assistance and friendship to international students as a 'buddy' at your university or college.

RESPONSIBILITIES
After an international student has been assigned to you, you will show them around during the first weeks of their stay. You'll give them an insight into the student life in your area and generally help them out.

WHAT WE OFFER YOU
- free membership and benefits of belonging to the International Students' Club
- free training courses, which will look great on your CV (a certificate of participation will also be awarded)
- the opportunity to get a wide range of cross-cultural experiences

b Maurizio wrote an email applying to be a buddy and saying why he is suitable. Which of the reasons below do you think he should use?

he understands the needs of foreign students
he loves living in London
he's outgoing and sociable
he's interested in other cultures
he speaks several languages
he has plenty of free time
he knows London well

Read the email and compare your answers.

3 WRITING SKILLS
Giving a positive impression

a Maurizio uses phrases in his email which give a positive impression. Underline the phrases which have these meanings.

1 *I speak* English *well*.
2 *I like being with other people*.
3 *I have no problem talking to people*.
4 *I am able to* understand the needs of students.
5 *I know* the city *well*.
6 *I have always been interested in* learning about other countries.
7 *I would be willing to* give up some of my free time.
8 *I could help* your programme.

b Maurizio writes *I am sure* … instead of *I think* … in order to sound more confident. Find four more expressions like this in the email.

c What is the advantage of using the expressions in 3a and 3b when applying for a job? Which answer is not correct?

1 They make the writer sound positive and enthusiastic.
2 They make the email more interesting to read.
3 They give the impression that the writer could do the job well.

QUALIFICATIONS
- You're open-minded and interested in other cultures.
- You have a knowledge of English as well as other languages.

Dear International Students' Club,

[1] I saw the information about international student buddies on your website, and I am writing to apply for the role.

[2] I am an Italian student at Birkbeck, University of London, where I am studying international law. I am fluent in English, Spanish, French and Italian, which would help me to communicate with students from different countries. I am also very sociable and good at communicating with people, which I am sure would help me to establish a good relationship with new students.

[3] As a foreign student in London myself, I am in an excellent position to understand the needs of students coming from other countries. I have a thorough knowledge of the city and the student life here. I am confident that I would be able to help students to feel at home and find their way around.

[4] I have always been very keen on learning about other cultures and my own circle of friends in London is completely international. I strongly believe we should encourage people from different cultures to come together to help promote intercultural understanding.

[5] I would be more than happy to give up some of my free time to work as an international student buddy, and I'm certain I could make a valuable contribution to your programme.

I look forward to hearing from you.

Best regards,
Maurizio Cavaliere

4 WRITING

a Plan an email applying to do volunteer work. Choose one of these situations. Make a list of reasons why you would be suitable.

- A website is advertising for volunteers to work in an international summer camp and organise activities for teenagers.
- A volunteer organisation wants helpers to make contact with English-speaking families living in your country and help them to adapt to your culture.
- A large secondary school in your area wants volunteers to give talks to students about different jobs and to help them decide on a future career.

b Write the email. Include:
- an opening sentence, explaining why you are writing
- two or three paragraphs, explaining why you are suitable
- phrases from 3a and 3b
- a final sentence to conclude the email.

c Work in pairs. Look at your partner's email. Does it … ?
- make it clear why he/she is suitable
- have a clear structure
- use expressions from 3a and 3b to give a positive impression

d Swap your email with other students. Would they choose you to be a volunteer?

UNIT 4
Review and extension

1 GRAMMAR

a Use the words in brackets to rewrite the sentences. Make sure the meaning doesn't change.

1 I was a nurse, but now I work for a pharmaceutical company. (used to)
2 I don't do shift work now. (no longer)
3 When I was a nurse I sometimes slept in, but now I always get up early. (would)
4 I no longer take my lunch to work because there's a cafeteria at the pharmaceutical company. (any more)
5 I wore a uniform in my old job, but now I wear my own clothes. (used to)
6 I don't have to deal with difficult patients now. (no longer)
7 I'm much happier than I was before. (used to)

b Correct five obligation and permission expressions in the text.

I went to a very strict primary school when I was a child. I wasn't allowed to do about two hours of homework every night, which meant there was little time to play with my friends. But often my parents told me just to study for an hour and wrote a note for the teacher excusing me from homework. In class we weren't let to talk to each other when we were working on a task because teachers didn't like noisy classrooms. However, we allowed to put up our hand and ask our teacher a question as she felt it was good to help students. We weren't allowed to do some kind of physical exercise every day after lunch, but that made us very tired in the afternoon. One good thing is that they supposed us learn a musical instrument and I learned to play the clarinet, which I still enjoy doing.

2 VOCABULARY

a Complete the sentences with a preposition followed by your own idea.

1 Tiredness is usually caused ___ …
2 A sunny day always has a positive effect ___ …
3 Too much exercise can result ___ …
4 Visiting a foreign country can lead ___ …
5 As a result ___ learning English, I …

b Work in pairs. Compare your ideas. Ask your partner why they completed the sentences in that way.

c Which words in the box collocate best with the nouns?

| rigorous | tough | punishing | strict | arduous | tricky |

1 _____ training programme / schedule
2 _____ laws / parents
3 _____ plastic / teachers
4 _____ journey / task
5 _____ testing / training
6 _____ situation / question

d Talk about three examples in 2c that you have experienced.

3 WORDPOWER as

a Replace the underlined words with as expressions in the box.

as a whole   as far as restaurants are concerned
as for   as a matter of fact   as far as I'm concerned
as far as I know   as if   as follows

1 I'm glad you're happy. But speaking of Alan, it's impossible to please him.
2 Everyone in the class is improving their speaking.
3 I'm not English. To tell you the truth, I'm from Denmark.
4 My list of complaints is below: 1) There was no hot water …
5 It felt like we had always lived there.
6 In my opinion, the cost of food here is very high.
7 Talking about restaurants, there are some excellent ones in our neighbourhood.
8 From what I've seen and from what people tell me, she's usually on time.

b Add a word to the gaps in 1–8 and then match to a–h.

1 [c] As far as I ____ 'm / ____ am
2 [ ] The key reasons for our success are as ____
3 [ ] I'm fit and well. As ____
4 [ ] As far as I ____
5 [ ] The team as ____
6 [ ] She's not boring. As ____
7 [ ] It looks as ____
8 [ ] As far as sport is ____

a … whole played very well.
b … they make the best coffee in town.
c … concerned, I go running twice a week.
d … matter of fact, she's a really interesting person.
e … my husband, he has the flu.
f … football is more about the money than the sport.
g … 1) We trained very hard …
h … it's going to be a sunny day.

c Complete the sentences with your own ideas.

1 As far as I'm concerned, …
2 As far as I know, …
3 It looks as if …
4 Our class as a whole …
5 As far as English is concerned, …

d Tell another student your sentences and ask questions.

REVIEW YOUR PROGRESS

How well did you do in this unit? Write 3, 2 or 1 for each objective.
3 = very well   2 = well   1 = not so well

I CAN …

discuss events that changed my life	☐
discuss and describe rules	☐
describe photos	☐
write an email to apply for work.	☐

CAN DO OBJECTIVES

- Discuss possible future events
- Prepare for a job interview
- Discuss advantages and disadvantages
- Write an argument for and against an idea

UNIT 5

CHANCE

GETTING STARTED

a Look at the picture and answer the questions.
1. What is the woman doing?
2. Would you like to try something like that? Why / Why not?
3. What could the woman be thinking?
4. Imagine you're on the beach in the picture. What would you be thinking?

b Discuss the questions.
1. Why do you think some people like doing extreme and dangerous things?
2. Do you think they do these things in spite of the risk or because of the risk?

55

5A YOU COULD LIVE TO BE A HUNDRED

Learn to discuss possible future events
- G Future probability
- V Adjectives describing attitude

Are you an OPTIMIST or a PESSIMIST?

1 If you take a test at the end of this course, how well will you do?

I'll get a perfect score. ⟷ I'll probably fail.

2 Do you expect the coming week to be … ?

exciting/great ⟷ boring/terrible

3 Imagine you left your bag on the bus. Do you expect to get it back?

Yes. ⟷ No.

4 You start a new workout routine and you're really tired the next day. Do you expect it to be easier the next time?

Yes. ⟷ No.

1 SPEAKING

a Are you an optimist or a pessimist? Mark your place on this scale, then compare with others in your group.

Optimist ⟷ Pessimist

b Decide what you think about the questions in the quiz above, then compare your answers.

c ≫ Communication 5A Now go to p. 129.

d Based on your answers in 1b, decide who in your group … ?
- is the most optimistic
- is the most pessimistic
- is the most realistic

e Write a question to find out if other students are optimistic or pessimistic. Add a) and b) answer choices.
Example:
You want to buy a shirt you like, but the shop has sold out. What do you think?
a I'm sure I can find it somewhere else.
b Why am I always so unlucky?

WHY WE THINK WE'RE GOING TO HAVE A LONG AND HAPPY LIFE

Researchers have found that people all over the world share an important characteristic: optimism. Sue Reynolds explains what it's all about.

WE'RE ALL ABOVE AVERAGE!
Try asking a 20-year-old these questions:
- What kind of career will you have?
- How long do you think you'll live?

Most people think they'll be able to earn above-average salaries, but only some of the population can make that much. Most young men in Europe will say they expect to live well into their 80s, but the average life expectancy for European men is 75. Most people will give an answer that is unrealistic because nearly everyone believes they will be better than the average. Obviously, they can't all be right.

Most people are also optimistic about their own strengths and abilities. Ask people, 'How well do you get on with other people?' or 'How intelligent are the people in your family?' and they'll usually say they're above average. Again, they can't all be right. We can't all be better than everyone else, but that's what we think.

LOOKING ON THE BRIGHT SIDE
There is a reason for this. Research has shown that, on the whole, we are optimistic by nature and have a positive view of ourselves. In fact, we are much more optimistic than realistic and frequently imagine things will turn out better than they actually do. Most people don't expect their marriages to end in divorce, they don't expect to lose their jobs or to be diagnosed with a life-threatening disease. Furthermore, when things do go wrong, they are often quick to find something positive in all the gloom. Many people who fail exams, for example, are convinced they were just unlucky with the questions and they'll do better next time. Or people who have had a serious illness often say that it was really positive because it made them appreciate life more. We really are very good at 'looking on the bright side'.

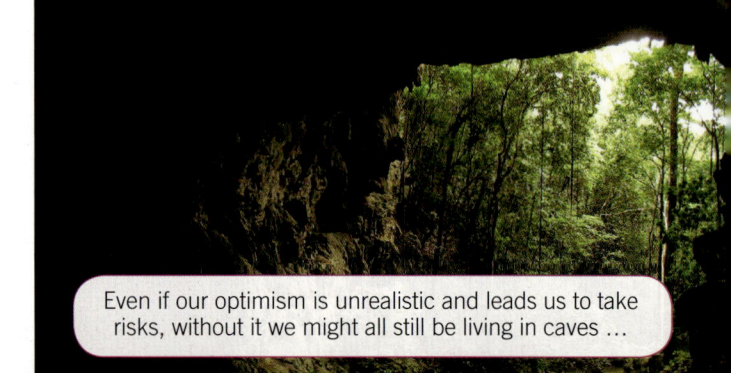

Even if our optimism is unrealistic and leads us to take risks, without it we might all still be living in caves …

... we carry on polluting the planet because we're sure that we'll find a way to clean it up some day ...

THE OPTIMISM BIAS
This certainty that our future is bound to be better than our past and present is known as the 'Optimism Bias', and researchers have found that it is common to people all over the world and of all ages. Of course, the Optimism Bias can lead us to make some very bad decisions. Often, people don't take out travel insurance because they're sure everything will be all right, they don't worry about saving up for old age because the future looks fine, or they smoke cigarettes in spite of the health warnings on the pack because they believe 'It won't happen to me'. Or on a global scale, we carry on polluting the planet because we're sure that we'll find a way to clean it up some day in the future.

OPTIMISM IS GOOD FOR YOU
But researchers believe that the Optimism Bias is actually good for us. People who expect the best are generally likely to be ambitious and adventurous, whereas people who expect the worst are likely to be more cautious, so optimism actually helps to make us successful. Optimists are also healthier because they feel less stress – they can relax because they think that everything is going to be just fine. Not only that, but the Optimism Bias may also have played an important part in our evolution as human beings. Because we hoped for the best, we were prepared to take risks such as hunting down dangerous animals and travelling overseas to find new places to live, and this is why we became so successful as a species. Even if our optimism is unrealistic and leads us to take risks, without it we might all still be living in caves, too afraid to go outside and explore the world in case we get eaten by wild animals.

Many people who fail exams are convinced they were just unlucky with the questions ...

UNIT 5

2 READING

a Read the article *Why we think we're going to have a long and happy life* quickly. Choose the correct words to complete the summary.

Most people are naturally *optimistic / pessimistic*, and this is generally *an advantage / a disadvantage* for the human race because it helps us to be *realistic about the future / more successful*.

b Read the article again. Tick (✓) the five points made in the article.
1 ☐ Pessimists usually have fewer friends than optimists.
2 ☐ Humans are naturally positive about their future.
3 ☐ Reality is often worse than we imagine it to be.
4 ☐ People who live in warmer countries are usually more optimistic.
5 ☐ We often act (or don't act) because we're confident everything will work out.
6 ☐ If we imagine a better future, we will take more risks.
7 ☐ Optimists spend a lot of time daydreaming.
8 ☐ Optimism about the future makes us feel better in the present.

c Discuss the questions.
- Look again at your answers in 1b. Do you think you have the 'Optimism Bias'?
- Do you agree that it's better to be optimistic than realistic? Why / Why not?
- How do you see yourself 20 years from now?

3 VOCABULARY
Adjectives describing attitude

a Find adjectives in *Why we think we're going to have a long and happy life* that mean:
1 expecting the future to be good
2 seeing things as they are
3 not seeing things as they are
4 prepared to take risks
5 not prepared to take risks
6 wanting to be successful.

b Which of these adjectives best describe you?

c ⟫ Now go to Vocabulary Focus 5A on p. 158.

UNIT 5

4 LISTENING

a Read the statistics and guess which numbers complete the sentences.

| 8,000 | 6 | 18 million | 1 million | 4 |

WHAT ARE YOUR CHANCES?

Chance of living to be 100 (man):
1 in _____

Chance of living to be 100 (woman):
1 in _____

Chance of having a road accident:
1 in _____

Chance of winning the lottery:
1 in _____

Chance of being in a plane crash:
1 in _____

b ▶05.04 Listen and check your answers. Do you think any of the statistics would be different where you live?

c ▶05.04 According to the speaker, how can you increase your chances of doing these things? Listen again and check.
1 surviving a plane crash
2 getting to the airport safely
3 living to be 100

5 GRAMMAR Future probability

a ▶05.05 Complete the sentences with the words in the box. Then listen and check.

likely   unlikely   could   may   probably (x2)
certainly (x2)   chance

1 It's very _____ that your plane will crash.
2 Even if it does, you'll _____ be fine because 95% of people in plane crashes survive.
3 So, if you're worried about getting on that plane, don't be, because you'll almost _____ survive the journey.
4 You're more _____ to have an accident in the car going to the airport.
5 You have quite a good _____ of living to be 100.
6 Modern medicine _____ well make the chances higher still during your lifetime.
7 You _____ won't die in a plane crash and you _____ live to be 100.
8 But the bad news is, you almost _____ won't win the lottery.

b Which phrases in 5a mean … ?
1 it's certain / nearly certain   3 it's possible
2 it's probable   4 it's not probable

c Which words in the box in 5a are used in these patterns?
1 will _____ (+ verb)
2 _____ won't (+ verb)
3 is/are _____ to (+ verb)
4 It's _____ that …
5 There's a _____ that …

d 💬 Change these predictions, using words from 5a.
1 I'll meet someone famous in my life: 70%.
2 I'll have children: 50–60%.
3 I'll fall in love at least once in my life: 90%.
4 I'll become a millionaire: 0.05%.
5 Someone will steal from me: 80%.
6 I'll live in the same place all my life: 20%.

e ≫ Now go to Grammar Focus 5A on p. 142.

6 SPEAKING

a Do you think these things will happen in your lifetime? Decide if each event is certain, probable, possible, unlikely to happen or if it will certainly not happen. Then add a question of your own.
1 Will we find a cure for all forms of cancer?
2 Will people go to live on Mars?
3 Will sea levels continue to rise?
4 Will there be another world war?
5 Will people stop using cars?
6 Will Spanish become the world's most used language?

b 💬 Ask other students their opinion.

c 💬 Tell the class what you found out.
- How many people agreed with your opinion?
- What were the most interesting comments?
- Are people in your class generally optimistic, pessimistic or realistic?

5B I'LL BE SETTLING INTO MY ACCOMMODATION

Learn to prepare for a job interview

G Future perfect and future continuous
V The natural world

1 READING

a Look at the pictures of Antarctica and answer the questions.
1 What can you see in the pictures?
2 What do you know about Antarctica?
3 Would you like to go there? Why / Why not?

b Do the quiz. Then compare your answers with a partner.

THE UNKNOWN CONTINENT

1 HOW BIG IS ANTARCTICA?
(a) the size of Russia
(b) the size of the USA and Mexico
(c) the size of Australia

2 HOW MUCH OF ANTARCTICA IS COVERED BY ICE?
(a) 98%   (b) 86%   (c) 77%

3 WHICH OF THE FOLLOWING CAN'T YOU FIND IN ANTARCTICA?
(a) rivers   (c) trees
(b) deserts

4 WHICH OF THESE ANIMALS CAN YOU FIND THERE?
(a) polar bears
(b) seals
(c) wolves

5 WHO WAS THE FIRST PERSON TO REACH THE SOUTH POLE IN 1911?
(a) Richard Byrd (American)
(b) Robert Scott (British)
(c) Roald Amundsen (Norwegian)

c Communication 5B Now go to p. 129.

d Read the first part of an article about working in Antarctica. What would your reaction be to a job advertisement like this?

MY LIFE ON ICE

Imagine you saw a job advertised with the following conditions:
- no leaving your place of work for six months – you must stay inside
- work six days a week, but always be available
- socialise only with your colleagues – no contact with other friends and family

You'd be mad to apply, wouldn't you? Probably. But if you want to work in Antarctica during the winter, this is what you'll have to put up with.

UNIT 5

e 💬 Discuss the questions.
- Why do you think people want to work in Antarctica?
- What kinds of jobs can people do there?
- What kinds of leisure activities do they do during the winter months when it's difficult to go outside?

f Read *Cooking in Antarctica*. Does it include any of your ideas from 1e?

g Read the article again. Make notes about:
- Fleur's background
- her role at the base
- her free time
- her thoughts about Antarctica
- her colleagues at the base.

h 💬 What do you think are … ?
- the advantages of a job like Fleur's
- possible frustrations in this kind of job

Would you ever consider doing a job like this?

2 VOCABULARY The natural world

a Don't look at the article. Match words from A with words from B to make collocations.

A	B
rough	environment
environmentally	energy
solar	atmosphere
fragile	footprint
ecological	weather
global	change
carbon	warming
climate	impact
the Earth's	friendly

b Check your answers in the article.

c Complete the sentences with the collocations in 2a.
1. We're going to change our energy supply to _____ _____ to reduce our _____ _____.
2. When the steam engine was invented, not many would have thought about the _____ _____ of burning so much coal.
3. Our boat trip was cancelled due to _____ _____.
4. The factories on the outskirts of town burn their waste and release toxic gases into _____. I think they should be shut down.
5. If there is an oil spill from a ship, it will damage the _____ marine _____ in this bay.
6. Most scientists agree that irregular weather patterns are evidence of _____ _____ and _____ _____.
7. Travelling by train is slower but it's far more _____ _____ than going by plane.

Cooking in ANTARCTICA

When she saw an online advertisement for a Chef Manager at the British Antarctic Survey (BAS) base in Rothera, chef Fleur Wilson was certainly given food for thought. Fleur, in her mid-thirties, felt it was time for an adventure and a life experience that really was different.

Fleur is part of a group of key support staff at Rothera. The main focus of BAS is scientific research into the climate, the oceans and ecosystems of Antarctica. In order to carry out this research successfully, scientists need the help of people like Fleur to make their lives as comfortable as possible.

A key responsibility for Fleur is keeping everyone happy, and one of the best ways of doing this is by making sure they are well fed. This doesn't mean preparing high-end restaurant food, but it does mean organising lots of social events to boost the mood. However, everyone has to play their part, and Fleur makes sure no one escapes doing the dishes.

One thing that all staff at BAS share is their love of the continent. 'I don't mind the harsh weather,' Fleur says, 'and I've always found landscapes with ice and snow amazingly beautiful. Sure, I don't get to see much for six months of the year, but for the other six months there's plenty of light and the scenery is stunning.' But, quite apart from admiring the natural beauty of Antarctica, the staff all have a clear understanding of the fact that it's a fragile environment because, compared to the rest of the world, it is largely untouched. They're aware that the presence of human beings can have a significant ecological impact on the continent and therefore they treat it with care. BAS research stations use solar energy to heat air and hot water. 'We try to be as environmentally friendly as possible,' says Fleur; 'we don't want to leave a carbon footprint down here.'

As Fleur notes, 'Antarctica can tell us a lot about what's happening in the world. It can tell us a lot about global warming and climate change. In an extreme climate like this, you can really notice if things are changing.'

During the winter months, all Rothera staff try to keep themselves entertained either by making mid-winter gifts for each other or creating Murder Mystery parties. Fleur has also taught herself Spanish to intermediate level. However, during the summer months she does cross-country skiing and enjoys penguin and whale-watching trips.

Fleur realises that living and working in Antarctica isn't for everyone. 'If you're the kind of person that likes shopping, going out for dinner and clubbing, then forget it.' She's now in her fourth year here and still finds it a unique and rewarding experience.

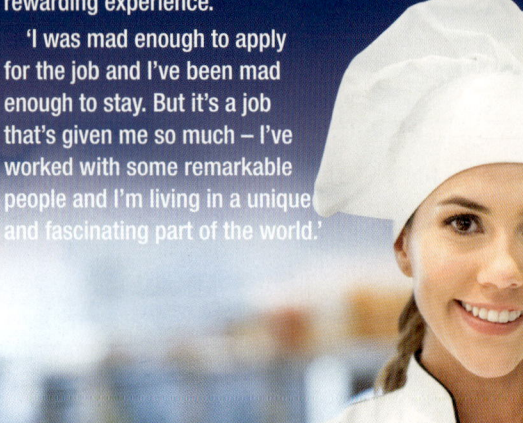

'I was mad enough to apply for the job and I've been mad enough to stay. But it's a job that's given me so much – I've worked with some remarkable people and I'm living in a unique and fascinating part of the world.'

d Work on your own. Answer the questions and make notes.
- Are there any environments near you that are considered fragile? What kind of environments are they?
- What different human inventions have a negative ecological impact?
- What kinds of things could you do to reduce your carbon footprint?

e 💬 Discuss your answers.

3 LISTENING

a ▶ 05.08 Martha's going to Antarctica to do research on penguins. She talks to her friend Joe about her work. Listen and answer the questions.
1 How well does Joe understand Martha's research?
2 Are his questions serious or light-hearted?
3 What do we learn about the personality of the penguins?
4 Why is the research important?

b ▶ 05.08 Listen again. Number the actions in the correct order from 1 to 5.
- [ ] The eggs are laid.
- [ ] Tags are put on the penguins.
- [ ] Penguins find mates.
- [ ] Martha arrives in Antarctica.
- [ ] Penguin chicks are born.

4 GRAMMAR
Future perfect and future continuous

a Look at these future verb forms from the conversation in 3a and match them to the uses a–c below.
1 … this time next week **I'll be settling** into my accommodation.
2 … I think **I'll be doing** similar things every day.
3 … by the time I arrive **the penguins will already have got** into pairs.

> a talk about an action that will be in progress at a specific time in the future
> b talk about an action that will be completed before a specific time in the future
> c talk about routine actions in the future

b ≫ Now go to Grammar Focus 5B on p. 142.

c Work on your own. Make notes about the questions.
- What will you be doing for the rest of the week or over the weekend? Think about your routine for the next few days.
- Where do you think you'll be living this time next year?
- What do you think you'll have achieved five years from now?

d 💬 Tell each other your answers to 4c and ask follow-up questions.

5 SPEAKING

a Read the job advert. Would you like this job?

Communications Officer in Antarctica

Responsibilities:
❄ interview researchers and collect information about their projects
❄ update our blog regularly
❄ assist all staff with IT requests

You need a friendly personality and excellent people skills.
This job is from October to March.

b Prepare a job interview role play for the job in 5a.
Student A: You want to apply for the job. Imagine you have the skills and experience that make you a suitable job applicant. Think of questions you can ask the interviewer.
Student B: You are the interviewer. Think of questions you can ask the applicant. Think of any useful information you can tell the applicant.

c 💬 Work in pairs. Do the role play.
Student A: Do you still want the job?
Student B: Do you think Student A is suitable for the job? Why / Why not?

61

5C EVERYDAY ENGLISH
We're not making enough money

Learn to discuss advantages and disadvantages
- **P** Intonation groups
- **S** Responding to an idea

1 SPEAKING and LISTENING

a Discuss the questions below.
- What kind of cafés are there near where you live? e.g., traditional, modern, part of a chain
- What kind of cafés do you like? Why?
- What do you usually do in a café?

b 05.11 Watch or listen to Part 1. Put four of these events in the correct order. One event doesn't appear in the scene. Which is it?
- ☐ Sam talks about money.
- ☐ Becky offers to help.
- ☐ Phil finishes his chapter.
- ☐ Phil asks about Tessa.
- ☐ Phil suggests staying open longer.

c 05.11 Answer the questions. Watch or listen again and check.
1. Why is Sam worried?
2. What are the problems with serving meals?
3. Why does Phil think serving meals is a good idea?
4. What does Phil want to know about Tessa?

2 LISTENING

a 05.12 Look at photo b of Sam and Emma. Which of these topics do you think they're talking about? Watch or listen to Part 2 and check.

money problems   staying open later   Sam's birthday
hiring a cook   investing money in the café

b 05.12 Watch or listen again. Make notes about the ideas Sam and Emma discuss. What are the positive and negative points for each idea?

3 USEFUL LANGUAGE Discussing advantages and disadvantages

a Sam and Emma discuss the advantages and disadvantages of making changes to the café. What do you think they say? Complete the sentences.
1. Of course, the _____ is we'd have to invest even more money.
2. Yes, but the _____ is it might be a way to get more business.

b 05.13 Listen and check.

c Which of these words/phrases could you use in the sentences in 3a?

problem   advantage   disadvantage
best thing   drawback

d 05.14 Add prepositions from the box to the expressions. Then listen and check.

of (x2)   with (x2)   about

one good thing _____
the advantage/disadvantage _____
the only drawback _____
another problem _____
the trouble _____

e Look at some people's ideas for the future. Use an expression from 3d in each second sentence.
1. 'I might sell my car and go everywhere by bike. I'd get fit.'
2. 'I'd love to live in London. It would be very expensive.'
3. 'I could work in China for a year. I don't speak the language.'

UNIT 5

4 PRONUNCIATION Intonation groups

a ▶ 05.15 Listen to these sentences. Answer the questions.

The good thing about it is it might be a way to get more business.
The trouble is we'd have to invest even more money.
1 Where do you hear a slight pause?
2 Which words are stressed in the bold phrase?
3 Does Sam's voice go up (↗) or down (↘) on the word *is*?

b ▶ 05.16 Listen to these sentences. Practise saying them, pausing after *is*.
1 The trouble is we don't have enough money.
2 The point is we still owe money to the bank.
3 The problem is we'd need to employ more staff.
4 The advantage is we'd attract more customers.

5 LISTENING

a ▶ 05.17 Watch or listen to Part 3. Who suggests doing these things (Sam or Emma) and what do they say about it?
1 have live music
2 get students to play music
3 have photo exhibitions
4 ask people to read poems and stories

b Which of these adjectives and phrases describe Emma? Which describe Sam?

full of ideas   cautious in making decisions
enthusiastic   worried about the future
careful with money   fair to other people

6 CONVERSATION SKILLS Responding to an idea

a Read what the speakers say. Complete the replies with the words in the box.

bad   possibility   lovely   worth

1 **A** I don't know, it's a big risk.
  B I think it's a _____ idea.
2 **B** Well, how about entertainment? We could have live music, get locals to play at the weekend.
  A That might be _____ a try.
3 **B** Or display paintings or photos.
  A That's not a _____ idea.
4 **B** Or readings. Have poetry readings.
  A Yeah, that's a _____.

b ▶ 05.18 Listen and check. Which of the replies is … ?
1 more enthusiastic   2 more cautious

c Look at these ways to respond to an idea. Order them from 1–6 (1 = very cautious, 6 = very enthusiastic).
☐ It's an idea, I suppose.
☐ Yes, that makes sense.
☐ That's a great idea.
☐ What a brilliant idea!
☐ 1 Mm, I don't know about that.
☐ Yes, good idea.

d You want to do something with the whole class at the end of the course. Write down three ideas.

We could go on a day trip.

e 💬 Work in groups. Take turns to suggest your ideas. Respond to other students' ideas, using expressions in 6a and 6c. Which idea is the best?

7 SPEAKING

a ≫ **Communication 5C** Now go to p. 128.

b Take a class vote. Whose café sounds the best?

✓ UNIT PROGRESS TEST

➔ **CHECK YOUR PROGRESS**

You can now do the Unit Progress Test.

5D SKILLS FOR WRITING
We need to change the way we live

Learn to write an argument for and against an idea

W Arguing for and against an idea

1 SPEAKING AND LISTENING

a Discuss the questions.
1 What environmental problems are suggested by photos a–d?
2 What environmental problems exist in your country or region? Which do you think are the most serious?
3 What action can people take to help solve them?

b ▶ 05.19 Listen to the news reports and match them with photos a–d. What key words helped you decide?

c ▶ 05.19 What did the news reports say about these topics?
1 beekeepers – bees – pesticides – farmers – fruit trees
2 air pollution – smog – masks – coal – exhaust fumes
3 plastic – birds, sea animals and fish – the sea – 2050
4 fires – rainforest – wildfires – clearing forest for land – football pitches

Retell the reports. Listen again if necessary.

d Discuss the questions.
1 Have you ever heard a news report like those in 1b about your own country or a country you know? What happened?
2 Which of these statements do you agree with the most and why?
   - We are responsible as individuals for protecting the environment. We can solve most environmental problems by behaving in a more responsible way.
   - The main responsibility for protecting the environment should lie with governments and large companies. There isn't much that individuals can do to change things.
3 What actions do you think (a) governments, (b) large companies and (c) individuals can take to protect the environment?

How can we help protect the environment?

Leon

[1] Modern technology has many benefits – we can produce food more cheaply and in greater quantities, we can manufacture the things we need more efficiently and we can travel and communicate more easily. On the other hand, our activities often have negative impacts on the environment. It is well known that we are polluting our oceans with plastic and chemicals, many species are dying out and natural areas are disappearing as cities spread. Scientists agree that we need to take urgent action to protect the world we live in before it's too late. But how can we do this?

[2] Most people accept that in order to protect the environment, we need to change the way we live. As individuals, we can help the environment by living simpler: we can buy fewer things and keep things we buy longer. We can also use public transport and only use cars and planes when necessary; we can eat locally-produced food to cut down on transport costs; and we can recycle more. People with their own houses and gardens can compost their food, grow organic vegetables and invest in solar panels to provide energy.

[3] However, not everyone agrees that the responsibility for protecting the environment lies with individuals. They point out that most environmental destruction is caused by companies, not individual people. For example, many people are worried that widespread use of fertilisers and pesticides threatens wildlife and pollutes soil and water, and that cutting down forests destroys the habitats of birds and animals. Also, pollution of the sea is often caused by waste from factories or by spills from oil tankers, and scientists warn that overfishing by large commercial fishing fleets could lead to fish disappearing from our oceans. Some people believe these things can only be changed by introducing new laws, not by asking individuals to change their lifestyle.

[4] My own view is that both of these opinions are correct. We can do a lot as individuals to help the environment by behaving in a more responsible way, but that is not enough. We also need governments to take action to reduce pollution and improve the environment, and rich countries should lead the way in doing that.

UNIT 5

2 READING

a Leon wrote an essay discussing the topic of protecting the environment. Read the essay and answer the questions.
  1 Which of these sentences best summarises the essay?
     a Leon considers whether individuals or governments can do the most to protect the environment.
     b Leon describes different ways in which we are damaging the environment.
  2 What is Leon's conclusion?
     a It's not clear how we can best protect the environment.
     b Both individuals and governments should act to protect the environment.

b Read the essay again and make brief notes on the main points Leon makes.

3 WRITING SKILLS
Arguing for and against an idea

a Match four of the descriptions below to paragraphs 1–4 in the essay.
  • Introduction – stating the problem
  • Introduction – giving Leon's point of view
  • How individuals can help protect the environment
  • How large companies damage the environment
  • How large companies can help the environment
  • Conclusion – restating the problem
  • Conclusion – Leon's point of view

b Answer the questions.
  1 Why does Leon ask a question in the first paragraph?
  2 How does Leon make his arguments seem more objective (i.e., not just his own opinion)?

c Notice how Leon uses expressions like these to report people's opinions.

> It is well known that …
> Scientists agree that …

Find more expressions in the essay that:
  1 report what other people say or think (x3)
  2 report how people feel
  3 report what scientists say
  4 report what Leon thinks himself.

d Write sentences in response to these questions, using expressions from 3c.
  • Does recycling plastic really make much difference to the environment?
  • Would eating less meat help protect the environment?
  • Are pesticides causing bees to die out?

4 WRITING

a Work in pairs. Choose one of the essay topics.
  Are extreme weather events a sign of a climate crisis?
  Is building nuclear power stations the best way to provide 'clean' energy?
  Should airfares be increased to discourage people from travelling by plane?

b 💬 Discuss the topic you chose and make notes on possible arguments for and against. Then decide on your conclusion.

c Work on your own. Plan your essay using the structure in 3a.

d 💬 Compare your notes with your partner and explain roughly what you plan to write.

e Write the essay in about 150–200 words, using expressions in 3c.

f Swap essays with another student. Does the essay … ?
  1 have a clear structure
  2 set out the arguments in a clear way
  3 use suitable expressions for reporting opinions

Do you agree with the conclusion? Why / Why not?

UNIT 5
Review and extension

1 GRAMMAR

a Change these sentences using the words in brackets so that the meaning stays the same.
1 Cities will probably become more dangerous over the next 50 years. (likely)
2 Scientists will probably find a way to delay the ageing process soon. (chance)
3 It's quite possible that the Alliance Party will win the election. (could well)
4 There are bears in this forest, but you probably won't see one. (unlikely)

b Complete the gaps with the verbs in brackets. Use either future continuous (*will be + -ing*) or future perfect (*will have* + past participle).

I'm in my 20s, but I sometimes imagine my life at 70. When I'm 70, I'll [1]_____ (retire), so I won't [2]_____ (work) and I'll have plenty of free time. But I will [3]_____ (have) a successful career, and I will [4]_____ (save) a lot of money, so I'll be rich. I will [5]_____ (get) married in my 30s, and we will [6]_____ (have) two or three children. By the time we're 70, we'll have a nice house by the sea, and our children will [7]_____ (live) nearby.
Of course, my life could turn out differently, but it's always good to have positive dreams!

c 💬 Imagine yourself 30 years from now. What will you be doing? What will you have done by then?

2 VOCABULARY

a What adjective could describe these people? Use words from the box.

well-organised   critical   adventurous
reliable   sympathetic   realistic

1 Dana has started a pop group, but she knows she probably won't ever become famous.
2 Mia always keeps her desk tidy and she knows where to find everything.
3 Tom listens to people's problems and knows how to make them feel better.
4 Pedro gave up work for six months to travel through Central America on a motorbike.
5 Christine's very hard to please. If you get something wrong, she'll notice it and she'll tell you.
6 If you ask Hamid to do a job, he'll always do it well and on time.

b What is the opposite of these words?
1 reliable   3 responsible   5 well-organised
2 sensitive   4 thoughtful   6 realistic

c 💬 Work in pairs. Which words in 2b (or their opposites) are true of people you know? Tell your partner and give a few examples of things the people do or don't do.

3 WORDPOWER *side*

a Look at these examples and match the word *side* with the meanings in the box.

group or team   point of view   part of a person's character

1 She's friendly but she also has a rather unpleasant **side**.
2 He usually plays for Fenerbahçe, but tonight he's playing for the national **side**.
3 We need to look at both **sides** of the argument.

b Here are some common expressions with *side*. Use them instead of the underlined parts of the sentences.

on your side   look on the bright side
to one side   from side to side   on the side
side by side   see the funny side

1 They sat on the bench <u>next to each other</u> without talking.
2 We think he was wrong. We're all <u>supporting you</u>.
3 Well, let's <u>see things positively</u> – we're both still alive.
4 I didn't earn much as a taxi driver, but I made quite a bit of money <u>doing other work</u>.
5 I was very embarrassed at the time, but now I can <u>laugh about what happened</u>.
6 She took me <u>away from the other people</u> and said quietly, 'I'll call you this evening.'
7 As the sea got rougher, the lamp in my cabin started swinging <u>from left to right</u>.

c Read these extracts from stories. Which sentences in 3b do you think go in the gaps?

❶ The first few days of the voyage were calm, but then the weather changed. _____
I lay in my bed watching it, feeling sick.

❷ She saw a man approaching. It was Tom. 'OK if I sit here?' he asked. She nodded. _____
Then he turned to her and said, 'Do you still have the letter?'

d Work in pairs. Choose another sentence from 3b. Imagine it's from a story and write a sentence before and after it.

e 💬 Read out your sentences. Which were the most interesting?

🔄 REVIEW YOUR PROGRESS

How well did you do in this unit? Write 3, 2 or 1 for each objective.
3 = very well   2 = well   1 = not so well

I CAN ...	
discuss possible future events	☐
prepare for a job interview	☐
discuss advantages and disadvantages	☐
write an argument for and against an idea.	☐

66

CAN DO OBJECTIVES

- Discuss choices
- Discuss changes
- Introduce requests and say you are grateful
- Write a travel blog

UNIT 6

AROUND THE GLOBE

GETTING STARTED

a Look at the picture and answer the questions.
1. Where are the man and the boy?
2. Why aren't they talking to each other?
3. What's on the man's phone? What's on the boy's phone?

b Discuss the questions.
1. Do you prefer travelling alone or with other people? Why?
2. What do you usually do while you're waiting in an airport or a train/bus station?
3. What are the positives and negatives of going on long trips?

6A I'M NOT GOING TO TRY TO SEE EVERYTHING

Learn to discuss choices
G Infinitives and *-ing* forms
V Travel and tourism

1 READING AND LISTENING

a Look at photos a–d and read about the four tourist attractions. Have you visited any of these places? Which one would you most like to visit?

b Read the tourist comments. Which are positive and which are negative?

1. ❝ To see all these amazing things in gold and silver with precious stones like diamonds, and to know they've been used by kings and queens – it was wonderful! ❞

2. ❝ It was too modern for me. I mean, it was interesting to see an amazing building and setting, but I like buildings with more historical objects. ❞

3. ❝ All these incredible, old religious objects – they were in glass cases and too far away. I wanted to get much closer than that. ❞

4. ❝ I've never seen so many beautiful, old paintings in one place – it was extraordinary. ❞

5. ❝ We spent hours enjoying the amazing shapes and materials of the building – I could have stayed longer. ❞

6. ❝ We had to keep walking and couldn't stop and look at the crown. It felt like high-pressure tourism. ❞

7. ❝ Absolutely fascinating – I learned so much about the Ottoman Empire. ❞

8. ❝ Overcrowded – and everyone rushing to take a photo of just one famous painting – not a pleasant experience. ❞

c Match comments 1–8 with the tourist attractions in 1a.

d ▶ 06.01 Listen to two tourists, Di and Bernie. Which places in 1a do they mention? Do they have the same idea about sightseeing tours?

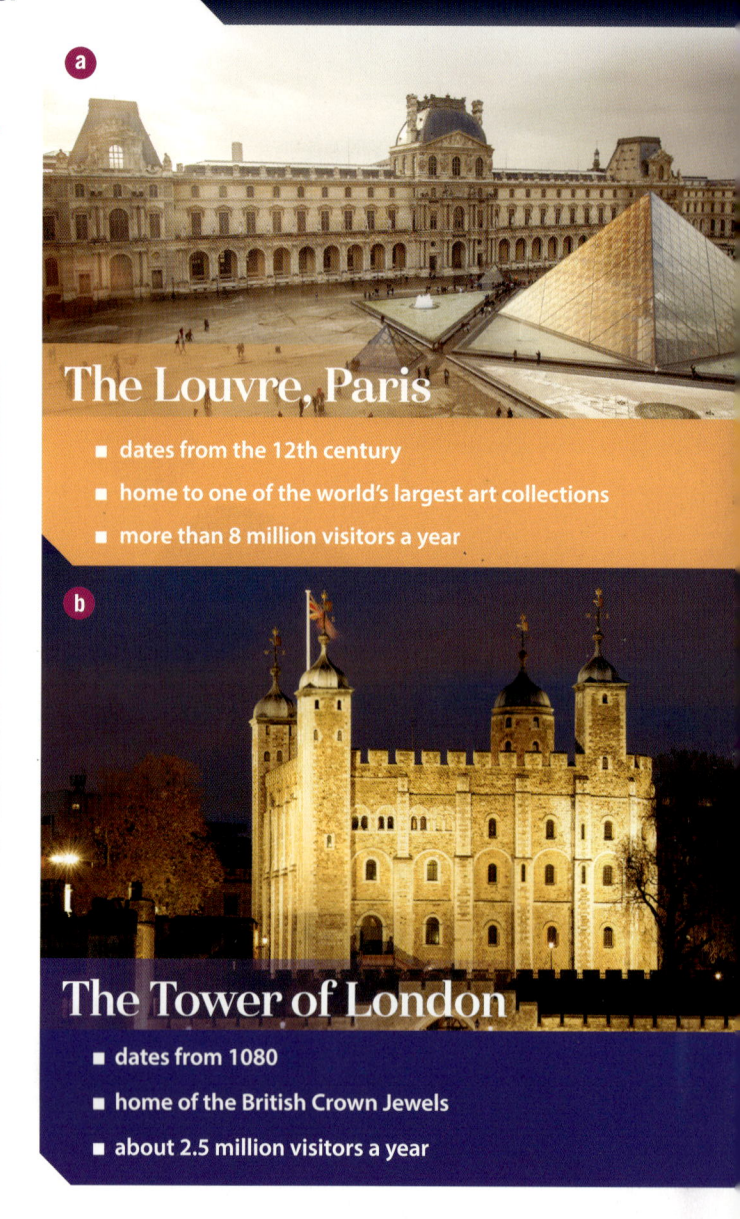

The Louvre, Paris
- dates from the 12th century
- home to one of the world's largest art collections
- more than 8 million visitors a year

The Tower of London
- dates from 1080
- home of the British Crown Jewels
- about 2.5 million visitors a year

e ▶ 06.01 Listen again and answer the questions.

Di
1. Why did Di join a tour?
2. What was her impression of the organisation of the tour?
3. Where did she want to spend more time?
4. What did she and her friend do?

Bernie
1. How many people did Bernie travel with?
2. What was the problem with guidebooks and maps?
3. Why did they almost have an accident in Paris?
4. What was disappointing about the *Mona Lisa*?

f 💬 Discuss the questions.
1. Have you had experiences similar to Di and Bernie?
2. How do you prefer to go sightseeing?
3. Di and Bernie and some of the tourists in 1b mention some negative aspects of tourism. What others can you think of?
4. Do these negative aspects stop you from wanting to see traditional tourist sights? Why / Why not?

68

Guggenheim Bilbao, Spain

- designed by Canadian architect Frank Gehry and built in 1997
- modern museum made of titanium, glass and limestone
- over 1 million visitors a year

Topkapi Palace, Istanbul

- main residence of Ottoman Sultans from 1465 to 1856
- contains holy relics from Islamic world
- about 3 million visitors a year

2 GRAMMAR Infinitives and -ing forms

a ▶ 06.02 Underline the correct verbs. Listen and check.

1 … it would be easy *to meet / meeting* people …
2 *Drive / Driving* in Paris was really hard work …
3 … we took off together *travel / to travel* around Europe.
4 This felt like *to be / being* in the army.
5 Before *going / to go* to the next place, I decided to leave the tour.
6 I decided *booking / to book* a place on a coach tour.
7 I might try *going / to go* on a tour of some kind.

b Match the rules a–f to sentences 1–6 in 2a.

- a ☐ We use verb + -ing after prepositions.
- b ☐ We use verb + -ing when it is the subject of the sentence.
- c ☐ We use verb + -ing in time phrases (with *before*, *after*, *while* …).
- d ☐ We use verb + -ing after some verbs.
- e ☐ We use *to* + infinitive after adjectives.
- f ☐ We use *to* + infinitive after some verbs.
- g ☐ We use *to* + infinitive to talk about the purpose or reason for something.

c Match the verbs in **bold** with meaning a or b in each pair of sentences.

1 … the people organising these tours **try** to fill every hour in the schedule.
2 I might **try** going on a tour of some kind.
  a do something to see what effect it has
  b attempt to do something (often unsuccessfully)

3 I **remember** visiting the incredible Guggenheim Museum …
4 … **remember** to be back at 10:30.
  a have a memory of doing something
  b not forget to do something

d Where do the objects (in brackets) go in these sentences?

I could hear shouting behind me. (the tour guide)
I noticed waving their arms at us. (all these people)

We can also use this pattern with *see*, *watch*, *observe*, *listen to*, *feel*, *smell*. What kinds of verbs are they?

e ⟫ Now go to Grammar Focus 6A on p. 144.

f Complete the sentences with the correct form of the verbs in brackets.

1 After _____ (arrive) in Venice, we went to St Mark's Square.
2 You can't leave London without _____ (visit) the British Museum.
3 It's not possible _____ (go) to the museum in the evening. It closes at 5:00 pm.
4 When you visit the Hermitage, remember _____ (look for) the two paintings by Leonardo da Vinci.
5 The guide was _____ (have) an argument with another tourist.
6 _____ (discover) Topkapi Palace in Istanbul was the highlight of my trip.
7 We went to Rome _____ (visit) the Colosseum, but we found the baroque architecture just as interesting.
8 I remember _____ (see) the Sagrada Família for the first time – it was so original.

g 💬 Discuss the questions.

1 Why do you think we all like visiting the same tourist attractions?
2 Do you think it's important to see all the famous sights and landmarks if you visit a new place? Why / Why not?
3 How do you think tourism will change in the future?

69

UNIT 6

3 READING

a Read the comments from a tourism website about three destinations. Answer the questions.
1. What countries are the tourist destinations in?
2. Are the places well known?
3. Is the main tourist attraction in each place part of nature or is it man-made?

b Read the texts again. Are the sentences true or false?
1. Uruapan is an ancient city.
2. The Parícutin volcano is still active.
3. Colin and his girlfriend left Hanoi because of bad food.
4. The people of Ha Long Bay don't live on the islands.
5. The wooden constructions on Kizhi Island were built in the 1950s.
6. Emmy and her friends felt that visiting Kizhi Island was a special experience.

c Which place do you think sounds the most interesting? Which place sounds the least interesting? Why?

4 VOCABULARY
Travel and tourism

a Look at the adjectives in **bold** in the text. Do they have a positive or negative meaning?

b Answer the questions about the adjectives.
1. If something is *remarkable*, is there something special about it or is it quite normal?
2. If you see something *memorable*, is it something that stays in your mind for a long time or do you forget it easily?
3. If you think something's *exotic*, does it seem foreign and unpleasant or foreign and interesting to you?
4. If a landmark is *breathtaking*, is it exciting and surprising or really high up?
5. If you feel that something's *impressive*, is it something you admire or just something that's very big?
6. If something's *unique*, how many are there of them in the world?
7. If you think something's *superb*, do you believe it's very spicy or of very high quality?
8. If you see something *astonishing*, are you very bored or very surprised?
9. If something's *stunning*, does it feel almost as though you've been hit by its beauty or does it mean you think it's quite old-fashioned?
10. If you think scenery is *dramatic*, is it pleasant and interesting or beautiful and exciting?

WHERE TO GO?

Have you planned your next holiday? Tell us about your favourite places and send us a photo.

URUAPAN
People always seem to go to the same places. I live in Mexico and tourists always visit places like Mexico City and Cancún. Not many tourists come to my home town, Uruapan. It's one of the oldest cities in Mexico. A beautiful river – it's called 'The river that sings' – runs through it, and there are spectacular waterfalls on the outskirts of the city. However, the most amazing feature you can see here is the nearby volcano, Parícutin. It really is quite **impressive**. You can go trekking up the volcano (it's about 420 metres high). The volcano is extinct, so it's perfectly safe. So for some history and some really **remarkable** scenery, Uruapan is a good choice. *Teresa*

HA LONG BAY
Last year, my girlfriend and I went to Vietnam for the first time. We loved it – the people were great and the food was **superb**. Hanoi is a busy city, but there are more **exotic** places you can escape to in Vietnam. The place we loved the most was Ha Long Bay where everyone lives in a floating house! On top of that, all around the bay there are **astonishing** islands made of limestone. Some of them look like beautiful towers – they're really **breathtaking**. And there are lakes and caves on some of the islands, as well as some very cheeky monkeys. Ha Long Bay is **dramatic** and beautiful. Many tourists have already discovered it – but it's still worth a visit. *Colin*

KIZHI ISLAND
If you want to see something original and **unique**, you should go to Kizhi Island in Russia. The whole island is like a museum of **stunning** wooden structures that look like they are straight out of a fairy tale. The island's in the middle of Lake Onega in the Russian part of Karelia. In the 1950s, a lot of historic wooden buildings were moved from different parts of Karelia to the island in order to preserve them. A couple of years ago, a group of us went to St Petersburg first, then on to Kizhi Island. It's the most **memorable** holiday I've ever had, and I felt like I'd been transported to another world. Although it's a UNESCO site, not too many people know about it, so you won't meet loads of tourists. *Emmy*

c 06.07 **Pronunciation** Look at these adjectives from the text and mark the stress. Then listen and check.

impressive	stunning	breathtaking
remarkable	dramatic	memorable
superb	exotic	
astonishing	unique	

d Think of some interesting and beautiful things you've seen as a tourist. Choose adjectives from 4c to describe them. Then tell each other about the things you've seen.

e Now go to Vocabulary Focus 6A on p. 159.

5 READING AND SPEAKING

a **Communication 6A** Student A: Go to p. 133. Student B: Go to p. 132.

b Tell the class what you decided.

6B ABOUT HALF THE WORLD'S LANGUAGES WILL DISAPPEAR

Learn to discuss changes
- G The passive
- V Describing changes

1 READING AND LISTENING

a Work in small groups. Do the quiz together.

b ▶ 06.11 Listen to the first part of an interview with a language expert and check your answers. Then answer these questions.
1 What languages are most in danger of disappearing?
2 What is a 'language hotspot'?

How much do you know about … ?

LANGUAGES of the WORLD

Can you answer these questions?

1 How many independent countries are there in the world?
   a) 120   b) nearly 200   c) nearly 500

2 How many spoken languages are there in the world?
   a) around 500   b) around 3,000   c) around 7,000

3 Which one of these languages has over 400 million native speakers?
   a) Portuguese   b) French   c) Spanish

4 What percentage of the world's population speaks Mandarin Chinese?
   a) 4%   b) 14%   c) 24%

5 On average, how many languages die out every year?
   a) 5   b) 25   c) 120

2 VOCABULARY Describing changes

a Match the verbs in the box with the meanings.

be lost   decline (x2)   decrease   deteriorate   die out
disappear   increase   preserve   revive

1 keep as it is
2 stop existing (x3)
3 become more
4 become less or go down (x2)
5 bring back into existence
6 get worse (x2)

b Complete the sentences with the correct forms of the verbs in 2a and the information in 1b. More than one answer is possible.
1 The number of people who speak English is _____.
2 The number of minority languages is _____.
3 Many languages are in danger of _____.
4 Educating children may help to _____ a language.

c ▶ 06.12 **Pronunciation** Listen to the verb and noun forms of these words. Are they pronounced differently?
verb: increase   decrease   decline
noun: increase   decrease   decline

d ▶ 06.13 Say the words in **bold** in sentences 1–4. Then listen and check.
1 There has been a steady **increase** in world literacy.
2 The number of different English dialects is slowly **decreasing**.
3 There has been a gradual **decline** in student numbers.
4 The number of bilingual children has **increased** over the last 50 years.

e What is the noun form of these verbs? Choose the correct ending in the box. What changes do you need to make?

-al   -ance   -tion

1 disappear   2 deteriorate   3 revive   4 preserve

f Think of three things which have increased or decreased in your country recently. Then compare with a partner.

71

UNIT 6

3 READING

a Read about three languages. In what ways are they similar? In what ways are they different?

DANGER!
DYING LANGUAGES

About half the world's languages are in danger of dying out, and many have already been lost, sometimes without any written record to show what they were like. We look at three languages: one dead, one dying and one that is being brought back to life thanks to one woman's dream.

BO In 2010, the last speaker of Bo, an ancient tribal language, died in the Andaman Islands, off the coast of India, breaking a 65,000-year link to one of the world's oldest cultures. Boa Sr was the last native who was fluent in Bo, which had been spoken since pre-Neolithic times.

Though the language was being studied and recorded by researchers, Boa Sr spent the last years of her life as the only speaker of the language, so she was unable to converse with anyone in her mother tongue. The Bo songs and stories which the old woman told couldn't be understood even by members of related tribes.

Andaman Islands

N|U

Hannah Koper is one of the few remaining speakers of a southern African language called N|u (the vertical line represents a clicking sound made with the tongue). Now most young people have no interest in learning N|u, which they see as an 'ugly language, just for old people'. Although efforts are being made to save the language from dying out by recording stories and by giving language classes for children, it seems unlikely to survive as a spoken language for more than a few years.

Hannah remembers: 'We all used to get together and speak the language. We gathered together, we discussed issues, we laughed together in N|u'.

WAMPANOAG

When the first European settlers landed in North America in 1620, they were helped by a Native American tribe called the Wampanoag, who showed them how to plant corn. The language died out in the early 19th century, and there were no fluent speakers of Wampanoag for more than 150 years.

However, one night a young woman named Jessie Little Doe Baird dreamed that her ancestors spoke to her in the Wampanoag language. Inspired by this, she first studied the language herself and then started a programme to revive the language, using old written records and books written in the language. She and her husband are raising their daughter entirely in Wampanoag, and every summer they organise a 'language camp', which is attended by a group of about 50 young people and where only Wampanoag is spoken. This is the first time a language with no living speakers for many generations has been revived in a Native American community, and there's a good chance that it will be spoken more widely by future generations of Wampanoag.

UNIT 6

b Read the text again and make notes about each language:
  1 number of speakers
  2 increasing or decreasing
  3 other important facts.

c 💬 Imagine you could ask each of the three people mentioned in the text a question. What would you ask? What answer do you think they would give?

4 GRAMMAR The passive

a Complete sentences 1–8 with the passive forms of the verbs in a–h.
  1 Many languages _____ lost.
  2 Bo was a local language which _____ since pre-Neolithic times.
  3 The language _____ by researchers.
  4 Her songs and stories couldn't _____ even by members of related tribes.
  5 N|u _____ now only _____ by a few people.
  6 Efforts _____ to save the language from dying out.
  7 They _____ by a Native American tribe called the Wampanoag.
  8 There's a good chance that it _____ more widely by future generations.

  a is spoken
  b were helped
  c have already been
  d will be spoken
  e are being made
  f was being studied
  g had been spoken
  h be understood

b How do we form the passive?
  a *be* + past participle
  b *have* + past participle
  c *be* + infinitive

c Find and underline other examples of the passive in the text. What tense are they?

d ≫ Now go to Grammar Focus 6B on p. 144.

e Rewrite the paragraph using the passive so that the subject remains 'the N|u language'.

> The N|u language is in serious danger because people only speak it in a few small villages. In the past, people spoke it in a large region of South Africa and Namibia. Linguists have now recorded it and they've written it down, and teachers who have learned the language themselves are teaching it to children in schools.

f 💬 Think about languages in your country and discuss the questions.
  1 What languages are spoken? What about dialects? Is there one 'official' language or more than one?
  2 Which languages or dialects do you think are spoken more and which are spoken less? Why?
  3 Do you think people should be encouraged to use their own language, dialect or accent? Why / Why not?

5 LISTENING AND SPEAKING

a You are going to listen to the rest of the interview with Professor Barnett, who tries to preserve endangered languages. How do you think he will answer these questions?
  1 Does it matter if small languages die out … ?
    • to the people who speak that language
    • to the wider world
  2 Isn't it a good idea for everyone to learn a global language?
  3 Is it possible to stop languages from dying out?

b ▶ 06.16 Listen and check your ideas.

c ▶ 06.16 Listen again. Tick (✓) the points he makes.
  1 ☐ No one feels happy about their language dying out.
  2 ☐ Languages are just as important as buildings.
  3 ☐ You can translate everything from one language to another.
  4 ☐ You can learn a 'big' language and still keep your own language.
  5 ☐ It's not good for children to be bilingual.
  6 ☐ Children are the key to keeping languages alive.
  7 ☐ Technology can help keep languages from dying out.

d Which points in 5c do you agree with? Are there any you disagree with? Why?

e ≫ Communication 6B Work in two pairs. Pair A: Go to p. 130. Pair B: Go to p. 133.

f 💬 Work with a partner from the other pair. Have a discussion, using the arguments you prepared. Report back to the class which points you agree on.

73

6C EVERYDAY ENGLISH
It's time you two had a break together

Learn to introduce requests and say you are grateful
- S Introducing requests
- P Consonant sounds

1 LISTENING

a Discuss the questions.
1 When was the last time you had to ask a friend or a family member for a favour?
2 What kind of favour was it?
3 How do you feel about asking someone a favour?

b Look at photo a. Who do you think is asking for a favour? What do you think they're saying?

c ▶ 06.17 Watch or listen to Part 1. Were your ideas in 1b correct? What is the favour?

d ▶ 06.17 Watch or listen to Part 1 again. Answer the questions.
1 What do Sam and Emma want to do?
2 How does Sam feel about asking Becky?
3 How do Sam and Emma feel afterwards?

2 CONVERSATION SKILLS Introducing requests

a ▶ 06.18 Read the conversation below and then listen to an excerpt from Part 1. What is the difference?

SAM Becky?
BECKY Yes, Sam.
SAM Could you look after the café this weekend?
BECKY Yes, that's fine.

b ▶ 06.18 Sam and Emma go through four steps to introduce the request. Put the steps in the correct order. Listen again and check.
1 They make the request.
2 They show that they realise they're asking a big favour.
3 They say they want to make a request.
4 They give a reason for needing to make the request.

c Why do Sam and Emma introduce their request carefully? Choose the correct answer.
1 They don't know Becky very well.
2 Sam and Becky had an argument recently.
3 They realise they're asking Becky a big favour.
4 They're worried about paying her overtime.

d Complete the beginnings in A with a word in the box. Then match A and B to make expressions that introduce requests.

like   if   mind   to   if

A
1 Do you mind _____ …
2 I'm really sorry _____ …
3 There's an idea I'd _____ …
4 I was wondering _____ …
5 I hope you don't _____ …

B
a … ask you this, but …
b … you wouldn't mind … ?
c … I ask you something?
d … my asking, but …
e … to run past you

e Answer the questions about the requests in 2d and the replies below.
1 What do you say to the requests to encourage the speaker?
2 Which two replies can be used with requests 1–2 and 4–5?
3 Which reply matches request 3?

What is it?   No, that's fine.   No, not at all.   Go right ahead.

74

3 USEFUL LANGUAGE
Showing you are grateful

a Sam thanks Becky and then shows how grateful he is. Complete Sam's sentence.

Thank you. That's _____ _____ of you.

▶ 06.19 Listen and check.

b Put the words in the correct order to make expressions.
1 really it appreciate we
2 really grateful we're
3 it's of kind you so
4 don't to I thank know you how

c Look at these replies to the expressions in 3b. Which one is not suitable? Why?
1 Oh, don't worry about it.
2 I'm happy to help.
3 It's no trouble at all.
4 I'm glad you're grateful.
5 It's not a problem.
6 My pleasure.

4 LISTENING

a 💬 Look at photos b and c and discuss the questions. Why do you think … ?
1 Tessa has come to visit Becky at the café
2 Phil is saying 'great'
3 Becky is saying 'sorry'

b 🎬 ▶ 06.20 Watch or listen to Part 2 and check your answers.

c 🎬 ▶ 06.20 Watch or listen again. Are the sentences true or false?
1 Tessa is interested in science fiction.
2 She asks Phil if she can read his book.
3 Tessa suggests that she and Becky begin their photography project.
4 Tessa offers to make sandwiches at the café.
5 Becky suggests that Tessa works in the café every Saturday.

5 PRONUNCIATION
Sounds and spelling: Consonant sounds

a Notice the **bold** consonant sounds. Match the underlined sounds in a–h with consonant sounds 1–8.

1 /θ/ **th**irty
2 /ð/ **th**ey
3 /s/ **s**ay
4 /z/ **z**ero
5 /ʃ/ **sh**op
6 /ʒ/ u**s**ually
7 /tʃ/ **ch**oose
8 /dʒ/ **j**eans

a I'm really sorry to ask you …
b My pleasure …
c Do you think it'll be a problem?
d I need to check with Becky …
e I'm quite into science fiction.
f It's time you had a break together.
g … this project photographing bridges.
h I could close up on Friday.

▶ 06.21 Listen and check.

b Find a sound from 5a in the following words:
1 ideas
2 earth
3 television
4 jewel
5 bother
6 sugar
7 science
8 future

▶ 06.22 Listen and check. Then practise saying the words.

6 SPEAKING

a Think of a big favour to ask your partner. Think of a reason why you need to ask this favour.

b 💬 Take turns making your requests. Make sure you introduce your request carefully. If your partner agrees to your request, show that you're grateful.

> I hope you don't mind my asking.
>
> No, not at all.
>
> I know that you're usually really busy at weekends …
>
> Well, this weekend looks OK at the moment.

✓ UNIT PROGRESS TEST
→ CHECK YOUR PROGRESS

You can now do the Unit Progress Test.

6D SKILLS FOR WRITING
The scenery was fantastic

Learn to write a travel blog

W Using descriptive language

1 SPEAKING AND LISTENING

a 💬 Look at the photos of the top five tourist attractions in the USA. What do you know about them? Why do you think people want to see them? Which place would you most like to visit? Why?

TOP 5 USA TOURIST ATTRACTIONS

1. Manhattan, New York City
2. The Grand Canyon, Arizona
3. The White House, Washington, DC
4. Niagara Falls, New York
5. Las Vegas, Nevada

Manhattan

The White House

Las Vegas

The Grand Canyon

Niagara Falls

b ▶06.23 Listen to Kirsten and John telling a friend about a trip to the Grand Canyon. Which of these topics do they NOT talk about?

the people   the views   camping   birds
cars   the desert   cowboys   meals

c ▶06.23 Listen again and answer the questions.
1. How did they travel?
2. What is unusual about the Mojave Desert?
3. Where did they stay: the first night? the second night? What do they say about it?
4. What two events did they watch at the Grand Canyon?
5. Where did they go next?

d Work on your own. What do you think are the top tourist destinations in your country?

e 💬 Compare your destinations with other students' ideas. Why do you think tourists find these places interesting?

This is me in the salt desert.

76

UNIT 6

2 READING

a Read Kirsten's travel blog about their trip. What information does it contain that was not in the recording?

Around the
GRAND CANYON

Driving to the Grand Canyon was an experience in itself. On the historic Route 66, we passed through the heart of the Mojave Desert, which is a huge, flat salt desert – it was the first time we had seen salt plains. We stopped off at a small town called Williams, where we saw cowboys and a re-enactment of an old shootout that had taken place there in the 1800s.

It was late when we finally found a restaurant, where they let us put up our tent behind the building. To our horror, the airbed had a hole in it, so we had another uncomfortable night's sleep. I could feel stones pressing into my back all night! In the morning, we woke and drove the final 20 kilometres to the canyon. It was literally breathtaking ... it's hard to describe in words the grandeur and beauty of this natural phenomenon – it was the experience of a lifetime. We drove around the South Rim, which has superb views down into the canyon itself, until we found a campsite. Luckily, we found a spot even though it was peak season. We ate, then went to the Desert Watchtower to watch the sun going down – just amazing.

At 4:45 am, we woke up and took a walk to watch the sun rise, which was a whole new experience as the light and the shadows made everything look different. After breakfast, we headed up to the village where a bus took us to the other part of the South Rim. We took a short walk and we were very lucky to see a condor, as their numbers have declined and there are now fewer than 300 left in the wild – they are huge and very impressive. We watched it circling right above our heads. Again, the scenery was fantastic and we saw the canyon from a few different viewpoints.

After that we drove to Lake Mead for a few days to relax before the madness of Las Vegas. Vegas – here we come!

John looking down into the canyon.

3 WRITING SKILLS
Using descriptive language

a Kirsten says the sunset was *amazing*. Find five other adjectives in the blog that mean *very beautiful* or *very big*.

b Look at the adjectives and phrases in the box. Which of them have a positive meaning and which have a negative meaning?

disappointing   fabulous   awesome
uninspiring   mind-blowing   ordinary
unbelievable   out of this world   dull
awe-inspiring   unforgettable

c Which adjectives/phrases in 3b can be used to complete these sentences?
1 Without a doubt, the scenery was absolutely _____.
2 I don't know. The scenery was a little _____.

Can you think of adverbs to replace *absolutely* and *a little*?

d Change these sentences to make the meaning stronger. Use adjectives and phrases from 3a and 3b. More than one answer is possible.
1 Manhattan was good, and I thought the buildings were very nice.
2 Niagara Falls was beautiful. We went on a boat below the falls – it was very good.
3 People say that Las Vegas is a nice place to visit, but I thought it was not very good.

e Kirsten also uses three expressions with *experience* to describe the trip. Find the examples in 2a and complete 1–3.
1 It was an experience _____.
2 It was the experience _____.
3 ... which was a whole _____ experience.

f 💬 Think of a place you have visited. Write sentences about your experience using language in 3a–e. Then discuss it.

4 WRITING

a Choose one of the photos, or think of one of your own travel photos. Plan a travel blog around this photo. Take notes on:
- where you went
- what you did
- what you saw
- what it was like.

b Write the travel blog. Include language from 3a–e.

c 💬 Swap travel blogs with other students. Ask and answer questions. Do the descriptions make you want to visit the place? Why / Why not?

UNIT 6
Review and extension

1 GRAMMAR

a Correct the mistakes in these sentences.
1 Do you find it easy relax at the weekend?
2 What kinds of things do you do for help you relax?
3 Do you have a series of household tasks you need to remember doing?
4 In your neighbourhood, do you notice people to do the same kinds of things as you do?
5 Do you remember to do the same kinds of things at the weekend when you were a child?

b Ask each other the corrected questions.

c Put the verbs in brackets in the correct passive or active form.

This small pot [1]_____ (give) to me by my great-grandfather about ten years ago. It's Egyptian. He [2]_____ (buy) it about 60 years ago. Apparently it [3]_____ (discover) in the desert by an Egyptian farmer. Then it [4]_____ (see) by a soldier during the war. He [5]_____ (pass) through a village where the pot [6]_____ (clean). My great-grandfather [7]_____ (say) the pot [8]_____ (sell) to the soldier for the price of a cup of coffee. He [9]_____ (pay) about £50 for it after the war. It [10]_____ (value) recently by an expert, and it's now worth more than £2,000.

2 VOCABULARY

a Write the correct adjectives in the gaps.
1 We had a fantastic meal followed by a brilliant concert. It really was a m_____ evening.
2 They have a really i_____ collection of old film posters – I've never seen so many.
3 I come from Tahiti so for me, somewhere like Ireland is e_____.
4 She paid a lot of money for her new evening dress. But it was worth it – she looks s_____ in it.
5 My favourite act in the circus was the high-wire acrobats. They were so skilled – their performance was b_____.

b Choose the correct word in *italics*.

Grayson's used to be my favourite department store. However, in the past few years, I've noticed there's been a [1]*decreasing / deterioration* in service. Years ago, the owners used to walk around the store and chat with customers, but not any more. I wish they'd [2]*revive / increase* that, and [3]*preservation / preserve* those old traditions with a personal touch. However, the Grayson family ties have all [4]*died out / been lost* now, and the store's owned by some anonymous company. They've [5]*declined / decreased* the number of shop assistants who can help you. Instead there's been an [6]*increased / increase* in self-service check-outs and face-to-face contact has [7]*been lost / revived*. I think it's a shame.

3 WORDPOWER *out*

a ▶ 06.24 Listen to the short conversations. What multi-word verb with *out* is used to replace the underlined words?
1 Yes, if I keep working 14-hour days, I'll <u>become exhausted</u>. _____ out
2 I feel like I'm going to <u>faint</u>. _____ out
3 I just need to <u>calculate</u> the total cost. _____ out
4 I've <u>argued</u> with my brother and we're not speaking. _____ out
5 Yes, but haven't we <u>finished the</u> milk? _____ out
6 But of all the applicants, Maria really <u>is noticeably better</u>. _____ out
7 But he's <u>become</u> a very nice young man. _____ out
8 I'm going to lie by the swimming pool with a cold drink and just <u>relax</u>. _____ out

b Write multi-word verbs with *out* in the gaps. Think carefully about the correct verb form to use.
1 The weather was terrible this morning, but it's _____ to be a beautiful day.
2 His way of _____ is to play video games and forget daily life.
3 She was getting annoyed with the bad behaviour of the class, and her patience was beginning to _____.
4 All the staff are saying that they're going to _____ if they keep working so hard.
5 This model really _____ as being more economical than all other cars of this size.
6 I'm trying to _____ how much tax I have to pay, but it's really hard.
7 The sight of blood makes him _____.
8 He always _____ with his friends – he's very difficult to get on with.

c Make notes about the following questions.
1 Have you ever fallen out with another family member? Why?
2 What do you like to do to chill out?
3 Have you ever passed out? If so, how did it happen?
4 Who's a famous person that you think really stands out? Why do you think so?
5 What kinds of jobs do you think could result in burnout?

d Discuss your answers to the questions.

⟳ REVIEW YOUR PROGRESS

How well did you do in this unit? Write 3, 2 or 1 for each objective.
3 = very well   2 = well   1 = not so well

I CAN ...	
discuss choices	☐
discuss changes	☐
introduce requests and say I am grateful	☐
write a travel blog.	☐

CAN DO OBJECTIVES

- Discuss living in cities
- Discuss changes to a home
- Imagine how things could be
- Write an email to complain

UNIT 7

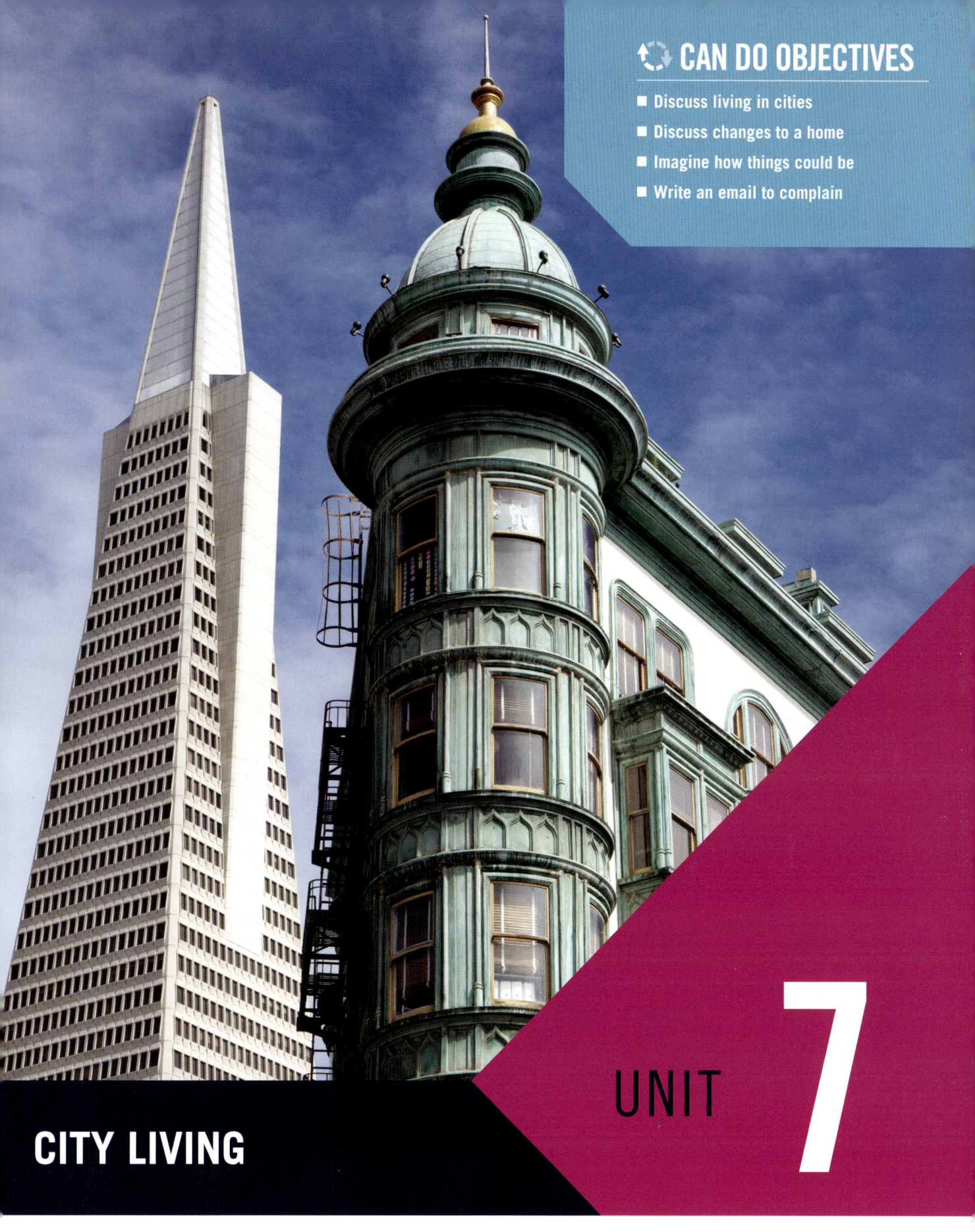

CITY LIVING

GETTING STARTED

a Look at the picture and answer the questions.
1 Look at the buildings. Which one is new or modern? How is it different from the older building beside it? How is it similar?
2 What do you think of the modern building? Do you think it is … ?
  interesting   outrageous   ridiculous   amusing
  ugly   harmonious
3 What do you think the architect of the modern building was aiming to achieve? How successful was he/she?

b Discuss the questions.
1 Think of modern buildings that you know. What do you like / not like about them?
2 Do you think new buildings should fit in with their surroundings or stand out from them? Why?
3 Do you think it's right to develop and alter city neighbourhoods or should they be preserved?

7A THERE'S VERY LITTLE TRAFFIC

Learn to discuss living in cities

G too / enough; so / such
V Describing life in cities

1 SPEAKING

a What kind of stress is caused by crowds? How do you think the people in the two photos feel?

b Imagine a third photo of city life. What might it show? Discuss your ideas.

2 READING

a The article below is from an online group called The Slow Movement. Read the title. What do you think the group believes?
1 Success isn't as important as people think.
2 You shouldn't let work take over your life.
3 Modern life is bad for our health.

Quick – slow down!

Speed worship

We love speed. When it comes to doing business and connecting with people, speed is important. We need to get our work done faster. We worry that we're too slow, that we aren't efficient enough or productive enough to succeed. We need to get there first. How do we do this? We speed up. Why? Because we seem to associate 'slow' with failure, inefficiency and even worse: laziness.

City life

Many people complain that they don't have enough time. They have too much work to do every day, and there are always too many things that they haven't done. There is pressure to be available 24/7 – to colleagues, clients and friends. We spend around 13 hours a week on emails and an average of three hours a day on social networking sites. City living can make things worse – we spend 106 days of our life looking for a parking space and up to three days a year in traffic jams. We have less time to relax, and this makes us more impatient and less polite. Even birds are affected by the pace of urban living – blackbirds in cities get up earlier and go to sleep later than rural blackbirds.

Time poverty and sleep debt

Economist Juliet Schor calculated that people in most jobs now work the equivalent of a full month more each year than they did two decades earlier. In addition to this, scientist Russell Foster says that people get about two hours' less sleep than they did 60 years ago.

This results in 'sleep debt'. In other words, people have so little sleep over such a long period of time that they are permanently tired. Studies done on doctors who didn't get enough sleep showed that they had a much slower reaction speed than average. Being so tired can also seriously affect your health – scientists have discovered a link between sleep debt and cancer, heart disease, diabetes, infections and obesity.

Slow seeing

We are in such a hurry that we are creating big problems for ourselves. The answer to this is simple: slow down! Slowing down gives us the opportunity to see things more clearly and make the right decisions, and in the end it may help us to have better ideas and a healthier life. Einstein, one of the greatest scientific minds of all time, spent a lot of time daydreaming, and psychologists agree that this helps us to be more creative. So sit back and do nothing for a little while – your brain and body will thank you for it.

b Read *Quick – slow down!* quickly and check your ideas from 2a.

c Read the article again. What connection does the writer make between … ?
1 speed and business
2 slowness and laziness
3 time and city life
4 relaxing and our mood
5 work and sleep
6 'sleep debt' and reaction speed
7 tiredness and health

d 💬 How could you live more slowly? Compare your ideas.

e Read *Rules for slowing down*. Are they the same as your ideas in 2d? Which ones are … ?
- things you do already
- things you don't do, but you think are a good idea
- things you think are a bad idea

Rules for slowing down

1 Put your feet up and stare idly out of the window. (Warning: Do not attempt this while driving.)
2 Think about things; take your time. Do not be pushed into answering questions. A response is not the same as an answer.
3 Yawn often. Medical studies have shown that yawning may be good for you.
4 Bright lights and screens before bed will make sleeping difficult. So avoid gaming and social networking late in the evening.
5 Spend more time in bed. When it's time to get out of bed in the morning, don't. Sit there for half an hour and do nothing. Then get up slowly.
6 Read long, slow stories.
7 Spend more time in the bath.
8 Practise doing nothing. (Yes, this is the difficult one.)

3 GRAMMAR *too / enough; so / such*

a Put *too*, *too much*, *too many* or *enough* in the correct place in each sentence. Then check your answers in the article *Quick – slow down!*
1 We worry that we're slow.
2 We aren't efficient or productive to succeed.
3 Many people complain that they don't have time.
4 They have work to do every day.
5 There are always things that they haven't done.

b Look at the sentences in 3a again. Did you put the words before or after … ?
1 an adjective   2 a noun

c Complete the rules with the words in the box.

> an adjective   countable   after
> a noun   before   uncountable

1 We use *too* before _____, but *too much* or *too many* before _____.
2 We use *too much* before _____ nouns and *too many* before _____ nouns.
3 *Enough* always comes _____ an adjective but _____ a noun.

d Complete the sentences with *so* or *such*.
1 People get _____ little sleep over _____ a long period of time that they are permanently tired.
2 Being _____ tired can also seriously affect your health.
3 We are in _____ a hurry that we are creating big problems for ourselves.

e ⟫ Now go to Grammar Focus 7A on p. 146.

f Find and correct the mistake in each sentence.
1 I have such much work to do that I often have to work at weekends.
2 You spend too many time in front of the computer.
3 We don't have money enough to buy a new car.
4 He doesn't like his job, but he's too much lazy to look for a better one.
5 Cheer up! Why are you always in so a bad mood?
6 I'll have to draw the plan again. It isn't enough clear.

g Write four sentences about your everyday life and work/studies. They can be true or false. Include *too*, *enough*, *so* or *such*.

I have so many clothes that I never know what to wear.

h Work in groups. Read your sentences from 3g. Can your group guess which sentences are true and which are false?

UNIT 7

81

UNIT 7

4 READING AND LISTENING

a Look at the cities in photos a–d. What do you think the term 'smart city' means?

b ▶ 07.05 Listen to the interview. What are the two main ideas of a 'smart city'? Choose two of the answers below.
1 People in it have a good quality of life.
2 It responds to people's needs.
3 It encourages people to have new ideas.

c ▶ 07.05 Listen again. What new information do you hear about … ?
1 traffic in London, UK
2 parking in Dublin, Ireland
3 energy use in Masdar, UAE
4 life in Songdo, South Korea

5 VOCABULARY
Describing life in cities

a Match 1–7 and a–g to make collocations.
1 local — a development
2 traffic — b pollution
3 quality — c transport
4 urban — d of life
5 public — e congestion
6 air — f space
7 parking — g residents

b Find collocations in a that mean:
1 the level of enjoyment and health in someone's life
2 the people in a particular area
3 the problem of too many vehicles in the streets
4 a place to leave your car
5 the process in which a city grows or changes
6 buses, trains, trams, etc.
7 damage caused to the air by harmful substances.

c Use two or three of the collocations in sentences about the place where you are now.

d 💬 Read your sentences aloud. Do other students agree?

SMART CITIES: Are these the cities of the future?

a In London, UK, cars pay to enter the city centre, and you only need a single card for the whole public transport system.

b In Dublin, Ireland, they have a system which can tell drivers where there's a free parking space.

c Masdar, UAE, is built in the desert, and solar panels provide all its energy needs.

d Songdo, a new city in South Korea, is built around a large central park with lakes.

6 LISTENING

a ▶ 07.06 Listen to Daniela and Richard talking about the cities they live in. Answer the questions.
1 Do they like living there? Why / Why not?
2 Do they think it fits the idea of a 'smart city'?

b ▶ 07.06 Which of these points do Daniela and Richard make? Listen again to check.

Daniela
1 In many American cities, people work in the centre but live outside the city.
2 The centre of Munich is quite a relaxing place to be.
3 Munich has serious problems with traffic congestion.

Richard
4 Bangkok is disorganised but full of life.
5 It's easy to find places to sit and relax in the city centre.
6 The centre of Bangkok is too expensive for ordinary people to live there.

7 SPEAKING

a Think about the town you're in now. In what ways does it fit the idea of a 'smart city'? What are the good and bad points about living there? Make notes.

b 💬 Discuss your ideas, using the expressions in 5b. Does everybody agree?

82

7B I COULD HAVE IT DONE BY A PROFESSIONAL

Learn to discuss changes to a home
- **G** Causative *have / get*
- **V** Films and TV; Houses

1 READING

a Discuss the questions.
1 What kinds of reality TV programmes are there in your country?
2 Do you enjoy these programmes? Why / Why not?

b >>> **Communication 7B** Now go to p. 131.

c Look at the photo from the article and answer the questions.
- Where is the woman?
- Why do you think she's there?
- What do you think she's doing?

d Read the article quickly. What is the main point the critic wants to make about reality TV? Choose the correct answer.
1 We no longer need stories for entertainment. Real people are more interesting.
2 Reality TV is in danger of creating unreal expectations about life.
3 A lot of the 'reality' in reality TV programmes is invented.

e Read the article again. In what way does the writer think reality is managed in these kinds of TV programmes?
- survival
- cooking
- home renovation
- garden makeover

f If what the writer says is true, … ?
- does this make the programmes less enjoyable
- are TV producers and directors being dishonest

WHO PUTS THE 'REAL' IN REALITY TV?

These days we like our entertainment to be real. We watch people go to extreme environments to see who's the most successful survivor. We can't get enough of chefs fighting it out to prove they're the best. Then there are the people who transform their homes, their gardens or even themselves in front of a TV camera. But what's really going on in these programmes?

Let's imagine someone named Julie. She isn't a real person – I've made her up – but she could be real. She's the kind of person who might appear on a reality TV programme. You know, she's someone who lives a quiet life in a small town somewhere, but then she decides to do something really extreme and dangerous on TV. Of course, it helps that she's got one or two big fears hiding under that quiet exterior – the type of thing that's going to come to the surface when, like the woman in the picture above, she's struggling to escape or survive … but, of course, we tend to forget the **crew** that's filming all this. I'm sure they're very helpful. It's also possible that the **director** asked Julie to crawl through the mud more than once – just to get a better shot.

What about those cooking programmes? They're all good cooks, aren't they? Well, yes, they are. But that's not always why they get chosen. TV **producers** want drama, so they need a range of personalities on the show. Imagine a cooking competition where the cooks all got on really well and cooperated. In other words, no conflict. Is that the kind of reality we want to watch on TV?

A NEW LIFE IN FIVE MINUTES
And then there's the makeover programmes – you know, the new home, the new garden or the new-look you. Haven't you ever stopped to wonder how people on these shows miraculously have a new kitchen after just one weekend? Remember your family's kitchen renovation? It took forever. On these programmes, they like to speed up reality a bit. While many of these programmes use professional tradespeople, others claim the renovation is all the work of the contestants. But did Julie really manage to repaint those walls between breakfast and lunch by herself? No, the director had some of it done by a professional painter. It probably would have taken Julie all weekend.

And wasn't Julie clever coming up with such a beautiful design for her garden? It's so good you would almost think that a landscape architect had done it. The chances are that's exactly what happened – the TV company got the design done by an expert.

DISASTER STRIKES … OR DOES IT?
Finally, let's not forget those little crisis moments along the way. Julie would love to be able to buy that designer fridge because it would make all the difference to her home makeover. But no, she's only got so much to spend and this just might blow her budget. Don't panic, dear **viewer**, the TV production company has lots of money, and there's nothing to stop them from increasing Julie's budget. The production company can afford to let Julie buy ten designer fridges without stopping to think about it.

TV production companies would like us to believe that what we see on TV actually happens. Well, it does, but only sort of. What we're really seeing is a kind of managed reality. Real reality on TV would probably be like real life – a little slow and boring.

83

UNIT 7

2 VOCABULARY Films and TV

a Look at the highlighted words in *Who puts the 'real' in reality TV?* With a TV programme, who … ?
1. organise(s) everything
2. tell(s) the actors what to do
3. work(s) as a technical team
4. watch(es) the programme

b Match the words in **bold** in 1–4 to definitions a–d.
1. ☐ There are only eight characters in the film – that means a small **cast**.
2. ☐ It's a very well-written film with a great **script** – there are some very funny scenes.
3. ☐ I loved everything about the film except for the **soundtrack** – too much jazz for my taste.
4. ☐ The film opens with a long **shot** of the main character walking along the edge of a cliff.

a the sounds and music
b a sequence of film from a camera
c the story the actors act out
d all the actors in a production

c ≫ Now go to Vocabulary Focus 7B on p. 160.

3 GRAMMAR Causative *have / get*

a Look at the examples from *Who puts the 'real' in reality TV?* What is the meaning of *have* and *get*? Choose the correct answer.

The director **had** some of it done by a professional painter.
The TV company **got** the design done by an expert.
1. someone arranges for another person to do something
2. someone has done something later than planned

b Complete the rule with the words in the box.

past participle   subject   noun phrase

^{1}_____ + *have/get* + object (^{2}_____) + ^{3}_____

c Change the sentences using the verbs in brackets. Begin the new sentence with the word in *italics*.

They cut her hair very short for her makeover. (have) *She* …
She had her hair cut very short for the makeover.

1. They planted a new tree for us during the ceremony. (get) *We* …
2. The director arranged for a builder to make a new cupboard. (get) *The director* …
3. An interior designer chose all the colours in the living room for the producer. (have) *The producer* …
4. Her make-up was re-done after every scene was shot. (have) *She* …
5. All their meals were cooked for them during the filming. (get) *They* …

d ≫ Now go to Grammar Focus 7B on p. 146.

e Discuss these topics. What things do you do yourself? What things do you have/get done?

personal appearance   household jobs   vehicles you own

> I have my hair cut once a month.

> My father has his car serviced twice a year.

> I always decorate the house myself.

UNIT 7

4 VOCABULARY Houses

[Handwritten annotations on image: Thatch; 1 Cottage; 2 Terraced]

a Use the words to label the parts of the picture.

| cottage | passage | attic | chimney | cellar/basement | fence |
| terrace | detached | semi-detached | terraced | bungalow |

[Handwritten: open space; só; casa térrea]

b 💬 Discuss the questions.
1. Does the house or flat you live in have a cellar or basement? What do people keep there?
2. What are different uses of attics?
3. In your country, what kinds of homes have chimneys?
4. Do you prefer fences or walls around gardens?
5. What kind of housing is most common where you live: detached, semi-detached, cottages or bungalows?
6. Is a terrace and a terraced house the same? What's the difference?
7. Where can you find passages? Are they common where you live?

5 LISTENING

a 💬 In your area, if people want to do renovations to their home, do they do it themselves or do they usually have them done by an expert?

b ▶ 07.10 Listen to Antonia and Rob talk about house renovations. Do they feel the same about renovating?

c ▶ 07.10 Tick (✓) what Antonia and Rob have done. Then listen and check your answers.

Antonia
- ☐ pulled out the original kitchen cabinet
- ☐ updated the bathroom
- ☐ uncovered the original fireplace
- ☐ repainted the kitchen
- ☐ painted the bedroom

Rob
- ☐ knocked down a wall
- ☐ bought all the supplies he needs
- ☐ hired a professional to help him
- ☐ took his kids to football matches
- ☐ discovered a place to make a playroom

d 💬 Do you know people like Antonia and Rob? What do you think about them?

6 SPEAKING

a 💬 Imagine you are a TV producer for a new home renovation programme. Rob's wife has contacted the programme to ask for help with their renovation. Think about:
- what makes your programme interesting to watch (e.g., time and budget limits)
- what you could do with Rob's new space
- what you will get Rob / professional workers to do.

b Present your ideas to the rest of the class. Decide which ideas would make the most interesting programme.

7C EVERYDAY ENGLISH
We could have a table here or something

Learn to imagine how things could be
- **P** Stress in compound nouns
- **S** Using vague language

1 LISTENING

a Look at photo a. Where are Becky and Tessa and what are they doing?

b 🎥 ▶ 07.11 Watch or listen to Part 1. Were your ideas correct?

c 🎥 ▶ 07.11 Watch or listen again and make notes on the topics below.
1. Tessa's photo
2. the photo competition
3. Tessa's feelings about the competition
4. Becky's meeting with Tom

2 PRONUNCIATION
Stress in compound nouns

a ▶ 07.12 Listen to the compound nouns and answer the questions.

A	B
estate agent	first prize
photography competition	free competition

1. Which word has the main stress, the first or the second?
2. Look at the first words. Are they nouns or adjectives?

b Complete the rules.

> If a compound noun is noun + noun, we usually stress the _____ word.
> If a compound noun is adjective + noun, we usually stress the _____ word.

c ▶ 07.13 Underline the stressed words in these compound nouns. Then listen and check. Then try saying them with the correct stress.

flower garden
front garden
nightclub
mobile phone
special offer
computer monitor
secret agent

3 SPEAKING AND LISTENING

a 💬 Think about where you live and answer the questions.
1. Is it easy to find a flat or room to rent? Why / Why not?
2. Do you think it is better to buy a flat or to rent one? Why?
3. What kind of flat or house do you live in? What kind would you like to live in?

b 🎥 ▶ 07.14 Watch or listen to Part 2. Which sentence describes what happens?
1. The estate agent is positive about the flat, and Tom and Becky like parts of the flat.
2. Tom and Becky like the flat, but they think it's too small and the estate agent agrees with them.
3. The estate agent is positive about the flat, but Tom and Becky think it's awful.

c How does the estate agent describe the flat? Choose words or phrases for each room.

cosy   a nice view   quiet   practical
good-sized   perfect   convenient

1. the living room   2. the bedroom   3. the kitchen

d According to Tom and Becky, what problems does the flat have?

e 🎥 ▶ 07.15 Watch or listen to Part 3. How is this flat different from the one in Part 2? Do Tom and Becky take the flat?

f 🎥 ▶ 07.15 Are the sentences true or false? Watch or listen to Part 3 again and check.
1. The flat has been on the market for a few weeks.
2. Becky is worried it's too expensive for them.
3. Tom and Becky start thinking about how to arrange the flat.
4. Two other people have expressed interest in the flat.
5. Tom needs time to decide what to do.

UNIT 7

4 USEFUL LANGUAGE Imagining how things could be

a ▶ 07.15 In Part 3, Tom and Becky imagine how the flat might look if they lived in it. Complete these sentences from the conversation. Use modal verbs with main verbs. Then watch or listen and check.
1 Look, this _____ _____ a kind of sitting area by the window.
2 We _____ _____ some plants and some bookshelves, or a big lamp.
3 And this _____ _____ a great dining area.
4 I _____ _____ a big TV right here.

b What does sentence 3 in 4a mean?
1 We'd need to do some work on it.
2 It could have this function.
3 It's a dining room.

c 💬 Work in small groups. Look at your classroom and try to imagine it as one of the following:
• an office   • a bookshop   • a small flat for a student.
Imagine how it might look and what might be in it. Use expressions in 4a.

d 💬 Present your ideas to other groups. Who had the most interesting ideas?

5 CONVERSATION SKILLS Using vague language

a ▶ 07.16 Listen to the conversation. Where do the speakers add the phrases in brackets?
1 I thought this could be a separate living area by the window. (kind of)
2 We could have plants and bookshelves there, or a big lamp. (and things)
3 We could have a table here and some interesting lights. (or something)

b The phrases in 5a are examples of vague language. Why do the speakers use vague language?
• because they're not sure exactly how the flat should look
• because they're in a hurry and can't think of the exact words

c **Pronunciation** Is the vague language stressed or unstressed? What do you notice about the pronunciation of *and*, *of* and *or* in the phrases?

d Look at these vague phrases. Which phrases in 5a could they replace?
1 and things like that
2 sort of
3 or something like that
4 and so on

e Add vague phrases to these sentences. Sometimes there is more than one possible answer.
1 This could be a reading corner with a bookshelf and a lamp.
2 We could use this shelf for herbs and spices and jars of jam.
3 There's a walk-in cupboard in the bedroom. We could use it for coats or shoes.
4 I could imagine a big plant over there by the window.

6 SPEAKING

a ≫ **Communication 7C** Student A go to p. 130. Student B go to p. 132.

b 💬 Show your room plans to the rest of the class. Who has designed the most interesting room?

✓ UNIT PROGRESS TEST

→ **CHECK YOUR PROGRESS**

You can now do the Unit Progress Test.

87

7D SKILLS FOR WRITING
There is a great deal of concern

Learn to write an email to complain

W Using formal language

1 SPEAKING AND LISTENING

a Discuss the questions.
1. What changes in urban development have you noticed in your local area? Think about things like new facilities (hospitals, schools), new roads, shopping centres, etc.
2. Do you think these examples of urban development are positive or negative? Why?

b ▶07.17 Listen to six people talking about a shopping centre planned for their local area. Is each person for (*F*) the plan, against (*A*) the plan or do they have mixed views (*M*)?

1 Kamal ☐   2 Susie ☐   3 Carol ☐
4 Duncan ☐   5 Miles ☐   6 Marion ☐

c ▶07.17 Listen again. What reasons does each person give for his/her point of view? Make notes. Use the words/phrases in the box to help you.

progress   living space   convenient
safe   the price you pay   part of a chain

d How would you feel if a shopping centre was planned for your local area?

2 READING

a Read Kamal's email to his friend Jun about the planned shopping centre. What does he say in the email that he didn't mention in 1b?

Hi Jun,

Thanks for your message. Great to hear from you. I'm glad your trip's going well.

The big news here is a shopping centre – would you believe it? Last Monday, the local government released their urban development plan, and it shows that a shopping centre's going to be built just across the road. My parents think it's a great idea, but I think it's going to be a disaster. It'll just mean a whole lot of the same horrible retail chains. And there'll be so much traffic!

But the thing that really makes me angry is that they aren't going to discuss this with people who live in the area. It looks like they're planning to just go ahead with building the centre. I'm sure they're not allowed to do that. Actually, I'm going to write an email to the local government and complain. I think a few people are planning to do that – maybe we can get them to change their minds.

I'd better get on with it. Hope you keep having fun!

Take care,
Kamal

UNIT 7

b Read Kamal's email to the local government. What is the main reason for his complaint?
1 the problems the local community will have when the centre is built
2 the way the local government has communicated the plan for the centre

---

Subject: Planned Riverway Shopping Centre

Dear Sir/Madam,

ᵃI am writing regarding the intention to build a shopping centre, which was outlined in the urban development plan.

ᵇIn my neighbourhood, there is a great deal of concern about the effect the centre will have on our local community. However, what worries us most of all is the fact that there has been no discussion with local residents. We understand that before a change of this nature can become part of a plan, a proposal needs to be sent out so residents can give feedback on it.

ᶜIn the past few days, I have tried to contact different local council members to find out how the plan was agreed to, but no one has returned my calls. I also visited your offices and asked to see the minutes of the meeting where the plan was discussed. I was told they were not available. The person I spoke to suggested that I should write this email.

ᵈI believe that what you are doing is against the law, and I would formally like to request that the local government withdraw the plan and put out a proposal that can be discussed with local residents.

ᵉIf I do not hear from you within two days, my next step will be to get in touch with the media. This will ensure there is a discussion of the plan in local media and also online.

I look forward to a prompt reply.

Yours faithfully,
Kamal Abadi

---

c Read the email again. Answer the questions.
1 Who has Kamal tried to speak to?
2 Who does he plan to contact next?
3 What does he want the local government to do? Why?

3 WRITING SKILLS Using formal language

a Match paragraphs a–e in Kamal's email to the local government to the summaries below.
1 ☐ describes what action Kamal has taken
2 ☐ explains his reason for writing
3 ☐ indicates why Kamal is concerned
4 ☐ says what action he will take if there's no response
5 ☐ explains what action he wants the local government to take

b Compare Kamal's informal email to Jun with his formal email to the local government. What are the differences in … ?
- greeting
- sign-off
- punctuation
- contractions

c Find more forms of these expressions in the formal email.
1 I'm just getting in touch about …
2 Everyone's worried about what the centre will be like for us.
3 We think you should have sent out a proposal.
4 I think it's illegal and I want you to …
5 Get back to me in a couple of days or …
6 I want you to …
7 I can't wait to hear from you.

d Rewrite this informal email to make it more formal.

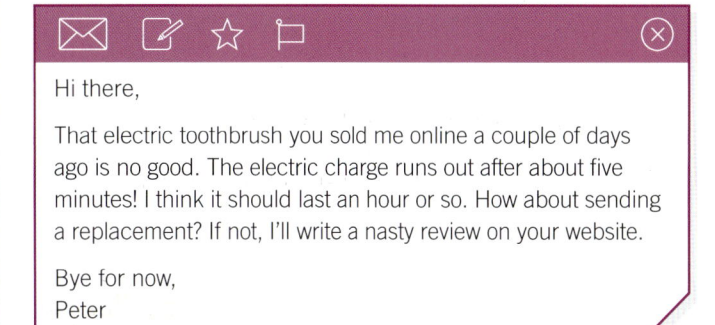

Hi there,

That electric toothbrush you sold me online a couple of days ago is no good. The electric charge runs out after about five minutes! I think it should last an hour or so. How about sending a replacement? If not, I'll write a nasty review on your website.

Bye for now,
Peter

---

e Compare with other students. Are your emails similar?

4 WRITING

a Work on your own. Choose a situation below to complain about or use your own idea.
- Your mobile phone company has changed your contract without letting you know.
- Your electricity/gas/water company has charged you too much on your last bill.

b Make notes on:
- the background to the complaint
- what actions you have already taken
- your request for action
- what you will do next if no action is taken.

c 💬 Work in pairs. Tell each other about your situation. Help each other with ideas.

d Write your email of complaint. Use the structure and expressions from 3a–c.

e Work in new pairs. Read each other's emails. Did your partner include all the points in 4b? Do you think the person receiving the email will respond to the complaint?

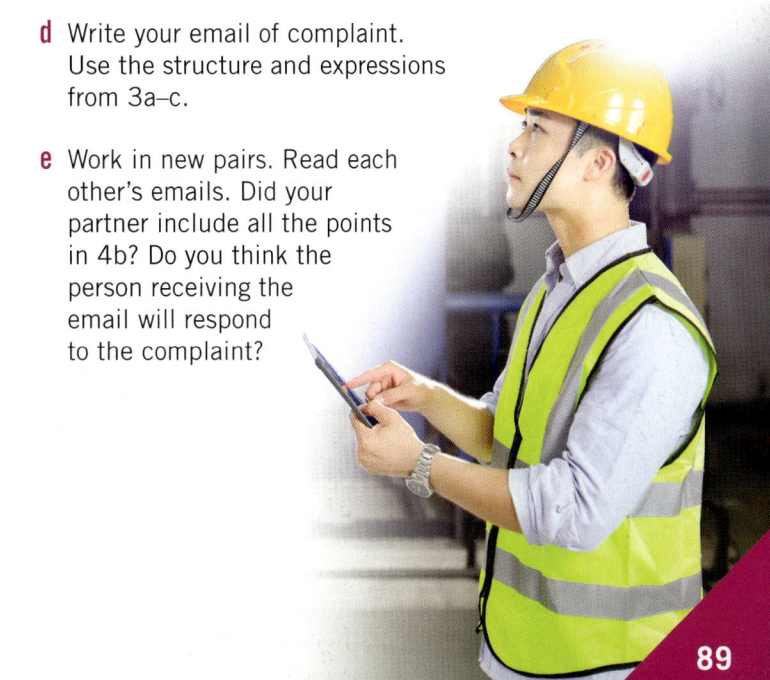

89

UNIT 7
Review and extension

1 GRAMMAR

a Rewrite the sentences, using *had* or *got* + past participle.

Sara stayed at the Excelsior Hotel on a business trip. Her boss told her the company would pay the hotel bill.
1 She decided not to eat in the restaurant. *She asked them to bring all her meals to her room.*
   She had ..*her meals brought to the room*
2 She called the laundry service. *They washed and ironed all her clothes.* *She had all her clothes washed and ironed*
3 Then she went downstairs to the hairdresser. *They cut and dyed her hair.* *She had her hair cut and dyed*
4 Then she went next door to the beautician's. *They massaged her face and manicured her nails.* *She had her face massaged and got her nails done*
5 The total cost was £3,500. *She asked them to add everything to her hotel bill.* *She had everything added to her hotel bill*

b What can you have (or get) done in these places?
1 a hairdresser's   3 a dental surgery *get my teeth whitened*
2 a garage *have my tire replaced/changed*   4 an optician's *eye doctor*

c André is unhappy about his life. Add *too*, *too much*, *too many* or *enough* to his sentences.

My faults ...
1 I don't study.   4 I'm not kind to my parents.
2 I drink cola.   5 I don't get exercise.
3 I don't go to bed early. 6 I download films.

d Connect these sentences using *so* or *such* and *that*. You may have to change some words.
1 It was a lovely day. We decided to go to the beach.
   It was such a lovely day that we decided to go to the beach.
2 There were a lot of people on the beach. We couldn't find a place to sit.
3 The water was cold. You couldn't go swimming.
4 We went to a café to eat but it was very expensive. We just ordered coffee.
5 It was very strong coffee. I couldn't drink it.

2 VOCABULARY

a Choose two words in the box for each sentence.

| space   traffic   pollution   transport |
| parking   air   congestion   public |

1 Factories are a major cause of _____ _____.
2 I don't like driving into the city because I can never find a _____ _____.
3 We want to encourage people to leave their cars at home and use _____ _____.
4 The main problem in our city is _____ _____. It takes me two hours to drive to work in the morning.

Tongs of a straightener

3 WORDPOWER *down*

a Look at the pictures. What do you think is happening?

b Match the two halves of the sentences. Which sentences go with the pictures in 3a?
1 After he got married, he decided to stop travelling and   **cut down on** the cake.
2 I've tried, but I can't find a job anywhere. It's starting to **calm down**.
3 Don't get so upset. Just have a drink of water and   **settle down**.
4 They've offered me a job in Zurich, but I think I'll have to   **look down on** everyone.
5 I love all the birthday parties, but now I need to   **turn** it **down**.
6 My new boss thinks she's so important. She seems to   **get** me **down**.

c Which multi-word verb means:
a stay in one place   d feel superior to
b relax   e refuse, say no
c make (someone) feel depressed   f decrease, lessen the amount.

d Complete the gaps with the correct forms of multi-word verbs in 3b.
1 She works ten hours a day in a factory and earns almost nothing. Sometimes it really _____.
2 We've considered your offer, but we've decided to _____ as we've already made an agreement with another company.
3 OK, everybody, there's no danger, so please just _____ and don't panic.
4 I'm trying to _____ the amount of time I spend on social media.
5 Just because they're poor and they don't have a nice car like you, there's no reason to _____.
6 You've had too many part-time jobs! It's time to _____ and choose a career.

e 💬 Work in pairs. Choose a verb and talk about it. Can your partner guess the verb?
A I don't like our new neighbours. They always criticise people. They think they're better than everyone else ...
B They *look down on* other people?

⟳ REVIEW YOUR PROGRESS

How well did you do in this unit? Write 3, 2 or 1 for each objective.
3 = very well   2 = well   1 = not so well

I CAN ...	
discuss living in cities	☐
discuss changes to a home	☐
imagine how things could be	☐
write an email to complain.	☐

CAN DO OBJECTIVES

- Discuss personal finance
- Discuss moral dilemmas and crime
- Be encouraging
- Write a review

DILEMMAS

UNIT 8

GETTING STARTED

a Look at the picture and answer the questions.
1. What do you think is happening?
2. Do you think this is real money? Who put it there? Why?
3. If you had been there, would you have taken any money? Why / Why not?

b Discuss the questions.
1. There is a common expression in English, 'Money doesn't grow on trees'. What does this mean, and when do people say it?
2. If money did grow on trees, do you think most people would be happier? Why / Why not?

8A I'D LIKE TO START SAVING FOR A HOME

Learn to discuss personal finance
G First and second conditionals
V Money and finance

1 VOCABULARY Money and finance

a Read the money facts below. Do any of them surprise you? Do you think these statistics are similar in your country? Why / Why not?

1 The UK population has a total credit card **debt** as high as £72.1 billion.

2 In the UK, the average **interest rate** on a credit card is now around 21%.

3 39% of households in the UK don't have any kind of **budget**.

4 If you take a packed lunch to work every day, your **savings** can be about £1,200 a year.

5 Over ¾ of students will never fully **pay off** their student loans.

6 The method most used by individuals in the UK to make an **investment** is through a savings account.

7 Just under 40% of households in the UK have levels of spending greater than their **income**.

8 47% of people prefer to make **donations** to charity online rather than through mail or phone donations.

b Match the definitions with the words in **bold** in 1a.
1 a financial plan
2 to repay money you owe in full
3 money you give to help people or organisations
4 money that you owe
5 a fixed amount you have to pay when you borrow money
6 the amount of money you have saved
7 money that you earn or receive
8 money you put into a bank or business to make a profit

c Complete the sentences with the collocations in the box. Use the correct verb forms.

make / living   put aside / savings   award / grant
donate / charity   debit / account   finance / project

1 The university has decided to _____ the group a _____ of £10,000 for their research project.
2 Every month, the bank _____ my _____ about £15 in fees. It feels like robbery!
3 I don't know how he _____ a _____ from his café. He never has any customers.
4 Why don't you _____ the money to a _____ like Save the Children?
5 Local businesses agreed to _____ a _____ to increase the number of trees in the city's parks.
6 Since she started work, she hasn't _____ any _____. She spends all the money she earns.

d Answer the questions and compare with other students.
- Do you or your family have a weekly or monthly budget?
- Do you or your family have a credit card? If so, do you know the interest rate?
- Do you ever donate money to charity? Do you pay in cash or online?
- Do you try to put aside savings? How often?
- Do students in your country have to pay off loans after they graduate?
- Have you ever made an investment in crowdfunding (supporting someone who is raising money for a unique goal)? Why / Why not?

UNIT 8

2 LISTENING

a ▶08.01 Listen to a radio programme about personal finance. Tick (✓) the topics you hear.
1 ☐ saving for retirement   3 ☐ investment plans   5 ☐ personal loans
2 ☐ credit card debt   4 ☐ paying off debt   6 ☐ personal spending

b ▶08.01 Listen again. Complete the table.

	Jacob	Sophie
Caller's problem		
Mia's advice		

c Work in pairs. Do you agree with Mia's advice? Why / Why not?

3 GRAMMAR First and second conditionals

a Match 1–3 with a–c to make sentences from the radio programme.
1 ☐ If you transfer your card,
2 ☐ If I did that,
3 ☐ If I were you,

a I'd use the money to pay off your student loan.
b you'll probably pay as little as 3%.
c I wouldn't be able to afford things like holidays and going out for dinner.

b Match the examples in 3a with these uses:
1 ☐ to give advice to someone
2 ☐ to talk about a situation we think is a real possibility
3 ☐ to talk about a situation that we think is imaginary or less likely to happen.

c What's the main difference between the examples in 3a and the sentences below? Choose the correct answer.

MIA If you transferred your card, you'd probably pay as little as 3%.
JACOB If I do that, I won't be able to afford things like holidays and going out for dinner.

1 Mia and Jacob are talking about a different period of time.
2 Mia and Jacob think the situations are more or less likely.

d ≫ Now go to Grammar Focus 8A on p. 148.

e Are these situations real possibilities for you or not? Make first or second conditional sentences for each one.
1 If I (get) a loan from the bank, I (be) able to buy a new car.
2 If I (put) aside £10 a week for a year, I (have) enough money to buy a new phone.
3 If I (want) to buy a new home, I (have to) borrow a lot of money from the bank.
4 If I (stop) buying my lunch for a week, I (donate) the money to charity.
5 If I (download) an app, I (have to) be careful not to make in-app purchases.

f 💬 Discuss your sentences. Did you use the same conditionals? Why / Why not?

93

UNIT 8

4 READING

a 💬 Think of things you've bought in the past week. Tell each other what you bought and the different ways you paid.

b Read *Is it time to give up on cash?* What is the writer's aim?
1 to promote the benefits of a cashless society
2 to question some of the benefits of a cashless society
3 to give a balanced view of the benefits and drawbacks of a cashless society

c Read the article again. Match the headings with paragraphs 2–6.

A sense of reality	The honesty of cash
Were they so wrong?	Better for everybody
Almost cashless now	

d Read the article again. Answer the questions.
1 What's the evidence we're already in a cashless society?
2 What costs do businesses and consumers have when they use cash?
3 Why might you spend more when you use a credit card?
4 What does the psychological test tell us about the relationship between digital payments and honesty?
5 What does the writer suggest the overall effect is of a cashless society?

5 SPEAKING

a Work on your own. What's your opinion of these statements? Make notes.

1 The reason people get into financial trouble is that they're not taught how to manage personal finance. This needs to be introduced as a subject in school.

2 Financial experts tend to oversell the need to save money. They forget that people need to enjoy life and that often means spending money.

3 There are too many financial experts saying too much about personal finance. This doesn't help – it just creates confusion and people feel too much pressure.

4 A lot of people are so obsessed with their personal wealth that they forget about giving money to charities that can help people who are less fortunate.

b 💬 Discuss the statements in 5a with other students. Explain your opinions. Do you all agree?

c Which advice do you think is the most relevant to you? Why?

IS IT TIME TO GIVE UP ON CASH?

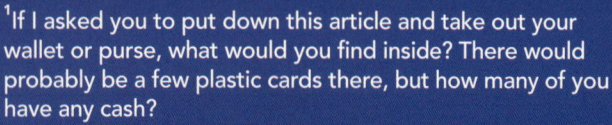

[1] If I asked you to put down this article and take out your wallet or purse, what would you find inside? There would probably be a few plastic cards there, but how many of you have any cash?

[2] For years now, economists have predicted a gradual move to what is called a 'cashless society'. Many payments are made using a card, and many more with phones or watches.

[3] So what's the attraction of a cashless world? Well, for one thing, cash is expensive. More than one in four cash machines in the UK are charging people up to £2 to withdraw their money at a time. Cash also spreads disease. Dr Peter Ender, who carried out a study looking at the bacteria on one-dollar notes, claims that 'paper money is usually full of bacteria and a dollar bill could, theoretically, be the magic carpet it rides on from one host to another'. And of course, there's always a record of digital money, so it makes it harder for people to steal it. Businesses that handle large amounts of cash usually need to pay security companies to keep their cash safe, but you don't need a security guard to help you manage digital money.

[4] However, do we really save? Some psychologists question this. They argue that waving your debit card in front of a machine doesn't give us a real sense of spending money. Furthermore, when we make a quick payment online, it's easy to forget that the credit card bill will arrive at the end of the month. There's plenty of psychological research to show that when we pay using physical notes and coins, we spend more sensibly. Basically, with a credit card we don't feel the 'pain of paying'. In a cashless society, we tend to buy more than we need to because it's easier to spend and the consequences of our spending feel separate from us.

[5] And it's certainly still possible to cheat and steal in a cashless society. If you manage to cheat someone and you never have to look them in the eye, then it's easier to take the payment. In a psychological test, people were twice as likely to accept a dishonest digital payment as a dishonest cash payment. Once again, psychologists suggest that the sense of being separate from payment in a cashless scenario increased the likelihood of dishonesty.

[6] So, while we might laugh at the idea of our grandparents with money hidden under the mattress, maybe the joke is on us. In our bright, shiny, plastic, cashless society, maybe things are not as wonderful as we think they are. Perhaps it's a society that's not quite as honest as we'd like to believe. Without a doubt, it's a world where we feel removed from the consequences of the purchases we make. Reality arrives in the form of a large credit card bill at the end of the month. So perhaps we're more efficient in our cashless society, but are we any happier?

8B I WOULD HAVE TOLD THE MANAGER

Learn to discuss moral dilemmas and crime

- **G** Third conditional; *should have* + past participle
- **V** Crime

1 READING AND LISTENING

a Read about Alena and Roberto and discuss the questions.

1 Are their experiences typical or unusual? Why do you think so?
2 Have you (or someone you know) had an experience similar to Alena's or Roberto's? Tell other students about it.

ALENA I left my bag at the bus station. The next day, I received a call from the lost-and-found office. The bag had been turned in and everything was still there – wallet, cash and cards.

ROBERTO I left my coat on a park bench with my wallet in it and when I went back, it was gone. A week later, the coat had been turned in to the police. The wallet was still in it, but someone had taken all of my money and cards.

b Read the article *The honesty experiment*. What did the researchers want to find out?

1 how honest hotel employees are
2 how honest people are worldwide
3 which cities have the highest rate of theft

c ▶08.03 Listen to three people saying what they would have done. Which person would have … ?

1 thought about keeping the money in the wallet
2 let their manager deal with the problem
3 refused to take the wallet

d ▶08.03 Listen again. What is the main point that each speaker makes? Choose a or b.

Speaker 1
a You shouldn't take money that isn't yours.
b The person who lost the money was careless.

Speaker 2
a You can't expect people in low-paid jobs to be honest.
b If you return a wallet to someone, it's OK to keep some of the money for yourself.

Speaker 3
a It could be risky to accept a wallet from a stranger.
b The police should take responsibility for stolen money.

e **Communication 8B** Go to p. 131 and find out what researchers discovered. Then answer the questions.

1 What do the results seem to show about people's honesty?
2 Why do you think people don't want to 'see themselves as a thief'?
3 Do you think this was a reliable test of honesty? Why / Why not?

The honesty experiment

Imagine you're a receptionist at a hotel. A tourist walks in and tells you they found a lost wallet outside the hotel but they're in a hurry, and they ask you take care of it. What do you do? Do you try to return the wallet to the owner and does it make a difference if the wallet has money in it?

A team of researchers recently decided to conduct an 'honesty experiment' involving more than 170,000 'lost' wallets in 335 cities in 40 different countries. The researchers handed the wallets to employees at banks, post offices, hotels and cinemas and said they had been found on the street outside. Each wallet contained a grocery list and business cards with an email address. Some of them had no money, some had about £10 in cash, and others had around £90.

So how would people react? Would they return the wallet with the money to the owner, would they keep it all, or would they take some of the money?

UNIT 8

2 GRAMMAR
Third conditional; *should have* + past participle

a Look at these examples and answer the questions.

If I'd been an employee at the hotel, I would have told the manager.
I certainly wouldn't have taken the money.

1 Are the speakers … ?
   a talking about something that really happened
   b just imagining a situation

2 Are they talking about … ?
   a the present   b the future   c the past

3 Complete the rules for the third conditional with a or b.

   With *if* clause:
   _____ + _____
   With main clause:
   would + _____ + _____
   a *have* + past participle   b *if* + past perfect

b Look at these examples and choose the correct answers.

Obviously, the person **should have been** more careful.
He **shouldn't have dropped** the wallet.

1 The **bold** expressions are used:
   a to say something was possible
   b to criticise someone.
2 The form of the **bold** expressions is:
   a *should(n't)* + present perfect
   b *should(n't)* + *have* + past participle.

c ▶08.04 **Pronunciation** Listen to these sentences. The stressed words are in **bold**.

He **shouldn't** have **dropped** the **wallet**.
You **should** have **told** me.

What do you notice about the pronunciation of the unstressed words?
Are they … ?
1 the same length as the stressed sounds
2 shorter and said more quickly

Practise saying the sentences.

d ≫ Now go to Grammar Focus 8B on p. 148.

e What would you have done if someone had given you the wallet? Would you have … ?
   • checked the contents and then contacted the owner
   • given it to your manager or boss without opening it
   • kept the money and thrown the wallet away
   • refused to take the wallet

3 SPEAKING

a Work in two pairs. You are going to read about two 'moral dilemmas'. Pair A: Read *The bribe* and answer the questions. Pair B: Go to Communication 8b p. 129.

1 Read the story and answer the questions.
   a Why was George stopped?
   b Why did they want him to sit in the police car?
   c Why did he pay them?
2 What do you think George should have done? Why?
3 What would you have done?

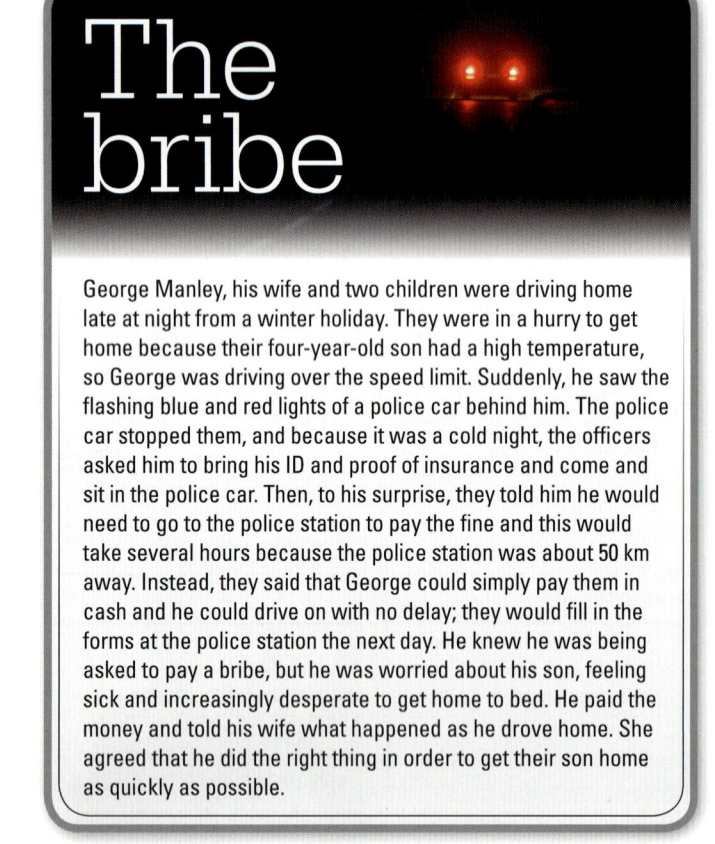

The bribe

George Manley, his wife and two children were driving home late at night from a winter holiday. They were in a hurry to get home because their four-year-old son had a high temperature, so George was driving over the speed limit. Suddenly, he saw the flashing blue and red lights of a police car behind him. The police car stopped them, and because it was a cold night, the officers asked him to bring his ID and proof of insurance and come and sit in the police car. Then, to his surprise, they told him he would need to go to the police station to pay the fine and this would take several hours because the police station was about 50 km away. Instead, they said that George could simply pay them in cash and he could drive on with no delay; they would fill in the forms at the police station the next day. He knew he was being asked to pay a bribe, but he was worried about his son, feeling sick and increasingly desperate to get home to bed. He paid the money and told his wife what happened as he drove home. She agreed that he did the right thing in order to get their son home as quickly as possible.

b 💬 Work with a student who read about the other dilemma. Take turns to talk about your stories. Do you agree with each other's ideas?

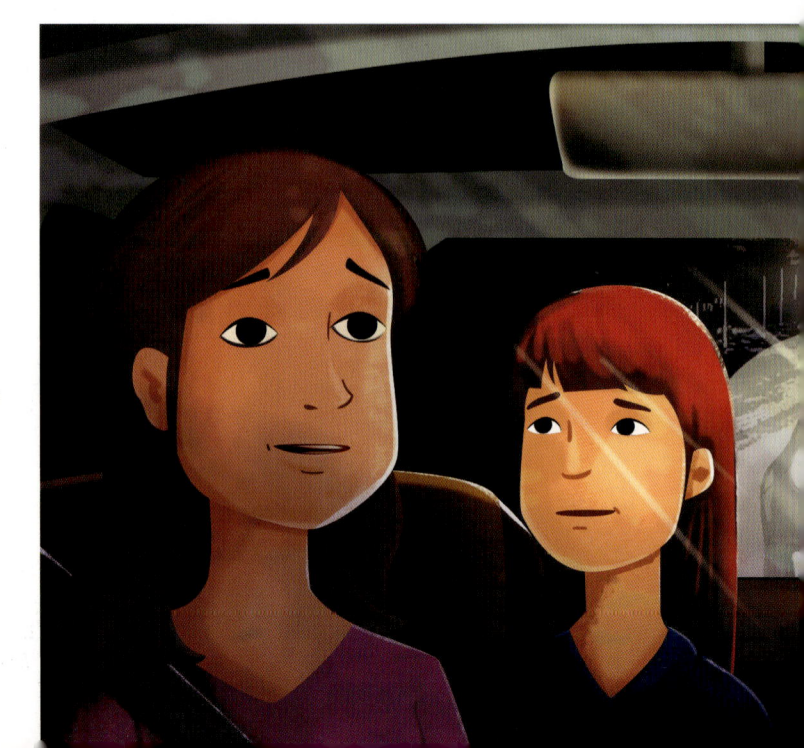

4 VOCABULARY Crime

a Which of the words in the box could you use to discuss … ?
1. the test described in *The honesty experiment*
2. the two dilemmas in 3a

burglary   theft   lying   robbery   cheating   bribery   murder

b Answer the questions about the words in 4a.
1. Which words describe … ?
   - crime
   - dishonest behaviour which is not illegal
2. Three of the words mean 'stealing money or valuable things'. Which means … ?
   a. stealing in general
   b. stealing from a home or a building
   c. stealing with violence (e.g., with a knife or a gun)

c Complete the table with the correct words in the box.

cheat   kidnapping   thief   burglary   shoplift
bribe   liar   rob   murder   kidnapper   robbery
shoplifter   murderer

Person	Behaviour/Crime	Verb
a burglar	_____	burgle
a _____	theft	steal
a robber	_____	_____
a cheat	cheating	_____
a _____	lying	lie
	bribery	_____
a _____	murder	_____
a _____	_____	kidnap
a _____	shoplifting	_____

d Read the news headlines and choose the correct word.

Bank *burglars* / *robbers* escape with $500,000 after police are forced to give up search

Car *kidnapping* / *theft* is increasing, say police

Detectives solve *murder* / *lying* mystery after years of investigating

10% of university students *cheat* / *burgle* in exams, report claims

Two teenagers sent to prison for *shoplifting* / *cheating*

***Burglars* / *Kidnappers* stole items worth more than £50,000 in three months**

e ≫ Now go to Vocabulary Focus 8B on p. 161.

5 SPEAKING

a Read the situations. What would you have done?
- 'I saw my friend stealing something in the supermarket. Of course I didn't tell anyone – she's my friend.'
- 'A colleague in my office lied about the company accounts. I was the only one who knew he was lying. I sent my manager an anonymous note.'
- 'During my final exam at university, I saw a student look at answers on a small piece of paper. I didn't say anything. It didn't have anything to do with me.'

b Which of these situations do you think is the most serious? Why?

c Do you think it's always important to be honest? Why / Why not?

8C EVERYDAY ENGLISH
You'll find somewhere

Learn how to be encouraging
- S Showing you have things in common
- P Word groups

1 LISTENING

a Discuss the situations below.
1 If a friend or family member has a bad day, how do you try to cheer that person up?
2 When was the last time you tried to cheer someone up?
   a What was the situation?
   b How did they react?

b Look at the photos of Becky and Sam. Guess the problem each person has.

1 Becky has just heard they …
   a can't afford the flat.
   b didn't get the flat.
2 Sam's about to …
   a talk to the bank manager about a loan.
   b tell Becky he can't afford to employ her any more.

c ▶08.10 ▶08.11 Watch or listen to Parts 1 and 2 and check your answers.

d ▶08.10 ▶08.11 Watch or listen to Parts 1 and 2 again. Are the sentences true or false?

Part 1
1 Another person acted more quickly to get the flat.
2 Tom tried calling Becky earlier.
3 Becky is confident they can find another place.

Part 2
4 Sam will be away from the café for about an hour.
5 He wants to buy new furniture for the café.
6 Becky thinks the changes in the café have been good.

2 USEFUL LANGUAGE
Being encouraging

a Look at these two excerpts from Part 1. <u>Underline</u> the expressions where Sam or Becky are being encouraging.

1 **BECKY** Flat hunting, you know …
  SAM Yeah, it's never easy. Don't give up hope – you'll find somewhere.
2 **SAM** I hope the bank agrees.
  BECKY I'm sure they will. Good luck.

b Look for 30 seconds at these expressions for being encouraging.

1 It might work out fine.   3 I'm sure it'll be fine.
2 Never give up hope.   4 You never know.

Now cover the expressions and complete the conversations below.

A I've got my performance review with my boss tomorrow.
B You've had a good year. I'm _____ it'll _____ fine.
A I'd like a pay rise, but I don't think I'll get it.
B Well, you _____ know.

C It's our final game of the season tomorrow and two members of our team can't play. We're bound to lose.
D It _____ work _____ _____.
C But they're our two best players.
D Never _____ up _____.

c ▶08.12 Listen and check.

d Work in pairs. Take turns to have short conversations like in 2b. Use expressions to be encouraging.

Student A: Tell your partner about a grammar test you've got tomorrow. You're worried that you haven't studied enough.
Student B: Tell your partner about a speaking test you've got next week. You don't think your pronunciation is good enough.

3 LISTENING

a ▶08.13 Watch or listen to Part 3. Sam and Tom meet by chance. How have their experiences been similar?

b ▶08.13 Watch or listen again and answer the questions.
1 How does Sam feel about his meeting at the bank?
2 What's Tom's reaction to his visit to the estate agent's?
3 What was Sam's experience of finding the right place for the café?
4 How do Sam and Tom respond to each other in this scene?

UNIT 8

4 CONVERSATION SKILLS
Showing you have things in common

a 🎥 ▶08.13 In Part 3, Sam and Tom sympathise with each other by saying they have things in common. For example, Tom says:

The same thing happened to me.

Watch or listen again and find two more expressions that show they have things in common.

b Look at the expressions below. Do we use them before or after someone mentions his/her experience?
1 The same thing happened to me.
2 I've just had a similar experience.
3 I know the feeling.
4 It was just like that when …
5 It was the same with me.
6 That's just like when …

c Cover 4b and correct the mistakes.
1 It was same with me.
2 I've had the similar experience.
3 I know a feeling.
4 It was just so when …

d 💬 Tell each other about your experiences learning English. Say when you have something in common.

5 LISTENING

a 🎥 ▶08.14 When Tom returns to his office, he finds a voicemail message. Watch or listen to Part 4 and answer the questions.
1 Who's the message from?
2 What's it about?
3 What's the telephone number?

6 PRONUNCIATION Word groups

a ▶08.15 Listen again to Katie's message. Add // where she pauses.

Hello, Tom. It's Katie here from Barkers Estate Agents. Thanks for coming in earlier. Something interesting's just come up. Can you call me back on 249 456?

b Why does Katie use pauses? Choose the correct description.
1 She needs to stop and think about what she's going to say next.
2 She wants to make sure the information in her message is clear.

c Work alone. Think of a message you can leave for your partner. Decide where you need to pause to make the message clear.

d 💬 Work in pairs.
Student A: Give a telephone message to Student B.
Student B: Listen and write Student A's message.
Swap roles.

7 SPEAKING

a Think of a hope you have but are worried about. For example, it could be:
- a holiday
- a job
- a study goal
- a place to live.

b 💬 Take turns to talk about your hopes. Encourage your partner and show him/her you have something in common if they talk about similar experiences.

> I don't know whether I can afford to go to both Rome and Florence.

> Yeah, never easy. But you can stay in a hostel.

> I've heard the job interviewing process is quite hard.

> Yes, I know the feeling. But you're good at interviews …

✓ UNIT PROGRESS TEST
→ CHECK YOUR PROGRESS

You can now do the Unit Progress Test.

8D SKILLS FOR WRITING
I really recommend it

Learn to write a review
W Organising a review

1 SPEAKING AND LISTENING

a What TV programmes do you enjoy watching? What do you like about them? What don't you like?

b The credit card statement below was the focus of a crime that was featured on a reality TV crime programme. What do you think could have happened?

CREDIT CARD STATEMENT

ACCOUNT NUMBER
256-6658-1153

DUE DATE
01/07

TRANSACTION DATE	DESCRIPTION	AMOUNT
02/06	Bus pass	36.00
03/06	Groceries	69.00
04/06	Dentist	25.00
05/06	Jewellery	150.00
05/06	Handbag	120.00
05/06	Women's clothing	300.00
05/06	Women's shoes	220.00
06/06	Women's clothing	130.00
07/06	Women's clothing	280.00
	TOTAL:	1,330.00

c 08.16 Listen to Paul and Zoe talk about the TV programme. Were any of your ideas in 1b correct?

d 08.16 Listen again. Are the sentences true or false?
1 Paul thinks the programme shows people how to commit crimes.
2 The man's niece went looking for the credit card statement.
3 Zoe isn't sure the niece did the right thing.
4 The man talked about how frightened he was by the theft.
5 Paul didn't like the attitude of the presenter.
6 Zoe thinks the programme could be seen as useful advice.
7 Paul thinks the presenter had an original point of view.

e Discuss the questions.
- Do you know of any crimes similar to this? Or any famous crimes? What happened?
- Do you think these TV programmes show people how to commit crimes? Why / Why not?

Crime with a Smile

2 READING

a Read the book review *Crime with a smile*. Is the series fact or fiction?

b Read the review again and complete the table.

author	
characters	
setting	
kind of story	
reason for liking	
why it's recommended	

Janet Evanovich

¹I like a good crime story, but sometimes they are too serious. They often take you into the mind of the criminal and can be too intense. So, I was delighted to find a crime novelist who makes me laugh. Janet Evanovich is a best-selling author whose Stephanie Plum series is hilarious. If you enjoy classic crime stories that are also humorous, you must read this series.

²Stephanie Plum is a bounty hunter who hunts down criminals and then gets a reward for finding them. Sometimes, she gets asked to do very unusual jobs. I've just finished reading book 25 in the series, *Look Alive Twenty-Five*, and it's my new favourite. Stephanie and her business partner, Lula, take over running a delicatessen. Why? The last three managers vanished, leaving behind only one shoe each. Stephanie has to figure out what happened while making sure she doesn't disappear, too. Lula is on hand to help and so is Stephanie's on-again, off-again boyfriend, cop Joe Morelli.

³One of the things I really like about *Look Alive Twenty-Five*, and the whole series, is the way the story revolves around great characters. There is the key group – Stephanie, Lula, Joe, Vinnie, Stephanie's boss who's always in a bad mood, as well as her live-in grandmother, Grandma Mazur, who refuses to grow old. They're all funny and lovable. Each book introduces more characters who are equally entertaining. The other thing I like about the series is that the crime doesn't always involve a murder. People don't need to die to create a sense of mystery and excitement. Evanovich is great at building the action, so you are pulled into the story and you can't put the book down.

⁴So if you're looking for a break from the typical crime story and you want to read crime-with-a-smile, I highly recommend *Look Alive Twenty-Five*.

3 WRITING SKILLS
Organising a review

a Read the book review again. Choose the correct endings for the descriptions of paragraphs 1–4.
1. ☐ This introduces the book and gives …
2. ☐ This outlines the plot and introduces …
3. ☐ This outlines the key strengths of the book and the reviewer's …
4. ☐ This is a summary of the review and a final …

a positive recommendation.
b personal opinion.
c information about it.
d the main characters.

b Underline phrases in the review in 2a that show the writer's positive opinion of the book.

c Notice how the words and phrases in the box are alternatives to the language used in the review. Complete the sentences with the words and phrases in the box. Sometimes more than one answer is possible.

| love | should | enjoy |
| really | number one | |

1 … you _____ read this series.
2 This is my new _____.
3 One of the things I really _____ about *Look Alive Twenty-Five* is the great characters.
4 The other thing I _____ about the series is that the crime doesn't always involve a murder.
5 I _____ recommend it.

4 WRITING

a Think of a book, film or TV programme that you like and would recommend. Make notes using the table in 2b.

b Work on your own. Write your review. Organise the review clearly, using the advice in 3a. Include your positive opinions, using language in 3b and 3c.

c Work in pairs. Read each other's reviews and check that each paragraph has a clear purpose and the paragraphs are in the right order. Check the correct use of positive expressions.

d Swap your review with other students. Would you like to read the book or watch the film or TV programme you read about?

UNIT 8
Review and extension

1 GRAMMAR

a Complete the sentences with your own ideas.
1 If I go out tonight …
2 If I went to a very expensive restaurant …
3 If I buy some new clothes this weekend …
4 If I bought a new IT device …
5 If I download some new music …

b 💬 Discuss your sentences.

c Read about Sam's disastrous night out.

As he went out, he forgot to lock the front door and some burglars stole all of his electronic equipment. He didn't put any petrol in his car, so he ran out and had to pay for a taxi home. He didn't check the name of the club he was going to, so he couldn't meet his friends. He put his phone in his back pocket and it was stolen.

Imagine a different night out for Sam with sentences beginning with *if*. For example:

If he'd remembered to lock his front door, he wouldn't have been burgled.

d Make sentences criticising Sam. Begin each sentence with *He should/shouldn't have* …

2 VOCABULARY

a Put the letters of the underlined words in the correct order.
1 Every month I work out the <u>dteugb</u> for household expenses.
2 My weekly <u>ceinmo</u> is just over £500, and I don't think it's nearly enough.
3 They borrowed money from the bank and have a <u>bdte</u> of £8,000.
4 I've got a new credit card that has a very low <u>eernitts eatr</u> on payments.
5 Last year, I made a total of 12 <u>oonndasti</u> to different charities.
6 We've just <u>daip fof</u> a loan from my parents so we can start saving for a home.

b Write the correct noun form of the verbs in brackets in the gaps.
1 There have been a lot of _____ (burgle) in our neighbourhood lately.
2 Police charged the man with _____ (steal) and sent him to prison to wait for a trial.
3 She's a _____ (cheat) and is always copying my ideas and work.
4 There was a real problem with _____ (bribe) and corruption in the local government.

3 WORDPOWER *take*

a Join a sentence from 1–6 to another from a–f.
1 ☐ There seems to be no one who's responsible for the project.
2 ☐ You may not believe what the adverts say, but this chocolate tastes great.
3 ☐ My friends tell me not to worry about the exam.
4 ☐ I love the food she makes because she's such an enthusiastic cook.
5 ☐ It's done nothing but rain since we arrived. It's making me feel so depressed.
6 ☐ I didn't read the conditions on the ticket carefully.

a You can tell she takes pleasure in what she makes.
b I took it for granted that we could get a refund easily.
c But I take all assessments seriously and make sure I study hard.
d Take my word for it.
e I can't take it for much longer.
f I'm more than happy to take charge.

b Answer the questions about the *take* expressions.
1 Which word can be replaced with the word *control*?
2 What preposition follows these expressions: *take an interest*, *take pride*, *take pleasure*?
3 What's the problem with this example? *We take seriously all security matters.*
4 What's the problem with this example? *Please believe me – take the word for it.*
5 Which expression is followed by *that* + clause?

c Add a *take* expression where you see ^. Think about the verb form and word order.

I always ^ that my friends ^ in the hiking trips I used to organise. I was happy to ^ of all the preparation. However, one of my friends, Julia, admitted that no one was really that interested in going hiking except me. Julia was very diplomatic when she said that it was important to ^ people's different interests. However, another friend, Shelley, was far more direct. She said, 'I'm sorry, but I ^ it any longer – I've had enough of hiking!' Well, we won't be going hiking ever again – ^ !

d 💬 Discuss your answers to the questions.
1 What do you take pleasure in?
2 Are you someone who likes to take charge? Why / Why not?
3 What's something you take seriously?

🔄 REVIEW YOUR PROGRESS

How well did you do in this unit? Write 3, 2 or 1 for each objective.
3 = very well   2 = well   1 = not so well

I CAN …	
discuss personal finance	☐
discuss moral dilemmas and crime	☐
be encouraging	☐
write a review.	☐

CAN DO OBJECTIVES

- Discuss new inventions
- Discuss people's lives and achievements
- Express uncertainty
- Write an essay expressing a point of view

UNIT 9

DISCOVERIES

GETTING STARTED

a Look at the picture and answer the questions.
1 What is the person at the computer doing?
2 What do you think this robot is capable of?

b Discuss the questions.
1 Imagine you could have a robot built for you. What would you want it to do? Why?
2 Do you think new inventions and discoveries always lead to an improved quality of life? Why / Why not?
3 Do you think there are things people will always want to do themselves (instead of machines)? Which ones? Why?

103

9A WHAT REALLY SHOCKS ME IS THAT IT COSTS €250,000

Learn to discuss new inventions
- G Relative clauses
- V Health

1 READING

a Read *Medical science or science fiction*? Do you think the inventions are fact or fiction?

b Read the article *Too good to be true?* Which of the inventions in 1a are real?

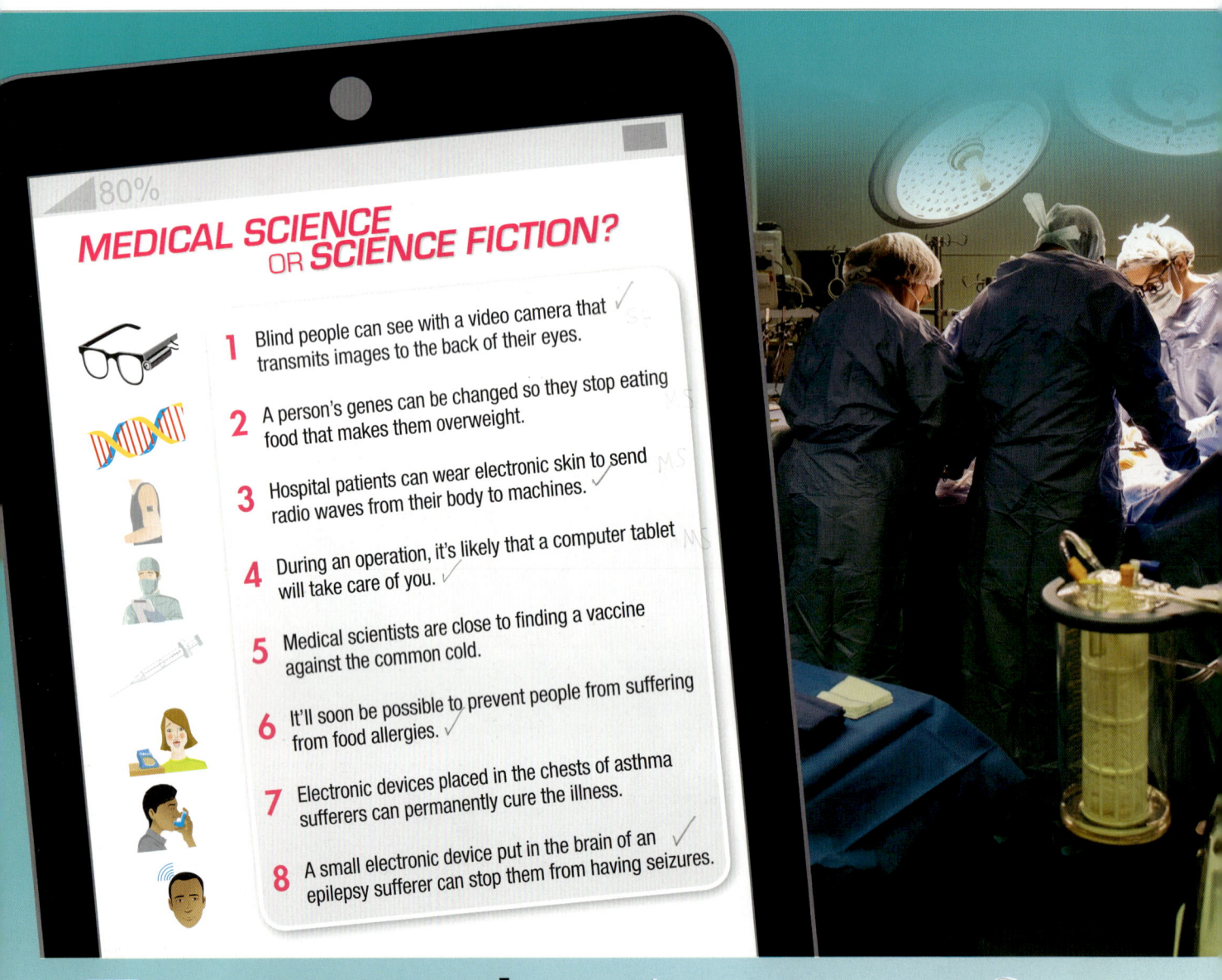

MEDICAL SCIENCE OR SCIENCE FICTION?

1 Blind people can see with a video camera that transmits images to the back of their eyes.

2 A person's genes can be changed so they stop eating food that makes them overweight.

3 Hospital patients can wear electronic skin to send radio waves from their body to machines.

4 During an operation, it's likely that a computer tablet will take care of you.

5 Medical scientists are close to finding a vaccine against the common cold.

6 It'll soon be possible to prevent people from suffering from food allergies.

7 Electronic devices placed in the chests of asthma sufferers can permanently cure the illness.

8 A small electronic device put in the brain of an epilepsy sufferer can stop them from having seizures.

Too good to be true?

We're always hoping for the next medical miracle – like a simple pill that can cure cancer. Often we hear of breakthroughs in medical science that sound almost too good to be true. However, sometimes they really are as good as they say they are. Here are five inventions from the world of medical science. If they sound like science fiction, that just means that the future is here – now.

1 Black and white

Wouldn't it be great if people who had lost their sight could see again? This is already happening for some blind people. A small device is put in the back of a blind person's eye. They then wear special sunglasses with a camera, which transmits images to the device. It isn't a perfect system, but it's enough for them to be able to walk down the street or to know the difference between black and white socks.

UNIT 9

c Read the article again. Are the sentences true or false?
1 Anyone who's blind is able to get sight back with the new glasses and see perfectly. F
2 Electronic skin can be used to monitor patients and speed up the healing process. T
3 The tablet now means that the anaesthetist can leave the patient once the operation begins. F
4 Scientists hope that it will be possible to turn off other allergies in the future. T
5 The epilepsy device has two functions: prediction and prevention. T

d Discuss the questions.
1 Which of the inventions do you think is the biggest breakthrough in medical science? Why?
2 Imagine a medical invention you would like to exist. What would it do? Why would you like it to be real?

2 VOCABULARY Health

a Underline the medical verb in each example. Then match the verbs with definitions 1–3.

… simple pill that can cure cancer.
It can also be used to help heal wounds …
… a computer tablet will take care of you.

1 treat a disease and make healthy again
2 provide treatment
3 treat an injury and make healthy again

b Complete the sentences with the correct form of the verbs in the box.

get   develop   strain   come   treat

1 I feel terrible. I've _____ down with the flu.
2 His doctor _____ his throat infection with antibiotics and that helped.
3 I can't stand up for very long because I've _____ my back.
4 I don't want to go out yet. I'm still _____ over a bad cold.
5 People who eat too much fatty food are likely to _____ heart disease.

2 It's all about comfort
In hospital, patients often complain about all the uncomfortable cables and wires that connect them to monitors. It's now possible to get rid of all this wiring simply by putting on electronic skin. This piece of 'skin' is very small and very thin. It's about the size of a postage stamp and as thick as a piece of human hair. It's made of silicon and is attached using water in the same way that a fake tattoo is. Despite being extremely small and thin, the skin contains electronic circuits that can receive and send radio waves to and from monitors. It can also be used to help heal wounds by sending out heat that speeds up the repair process.

3 Under the care of three
During an operation, there's always a surgeon in the operating theatre and an anaesthetist, whose job is to check the patient constantly. In the past, the anaesthetist had to watch the patient carefully, but these days they are also likely to use a touchscreen computer like a tablet. This tablet monitors key functions like breathing and heart rate, but more importantly, it can send the anaesthetist warnings and suggest how medication should be altered during the operation. It also keeps a record of everything the surgeon does. So these days, when you have an operation, you're under the care of three 'professionals': the surgeon, the anaesthetist and the tablet.

4 Sometimes a matter of life and death
It's surprising how many people are allergic to different kinds of food. Sometimes this can be life-threatening, for example, for people who are allergic to peanuts. Scientists at Northwestern University in Chicago have found a way to turn off an allergy to peanuts. They attached some peanut protein to blood cells and reintroduced them into the body of someone suffering from the allergy. This makes the body think that peanuts are no longer a threat and there's no allergic response. Scientists think this approach could be used with a wide range of food allergies.

5 Warning signs
People who suffer from epilepsy never know when they are going to have an attack. This lack of certainty can be very stressful. Researchers have now created a device that makes an epileptic seizure predictable. These very small devices are planted in the brain. They're able to tell if an attack is about to happen, and they can then send out electrical signals to other parts of the brain that can stop the seizure.

UNIT 9

c Match verbs 1–5 with the pictures a–d. Two verbs describe one picture.

1 cough	2 faint	3 sneeze
4 pass out	5 shiver	

d 💬 Discuss the questions.
- When did you last come down with the flu?
- What do you think is the best way to treat a sore throat?
- Have you ever fainted? What happened?
- Have you ever strained a muscle? Which muscle? How did it happen?
- What serious disease or illness are people in your country most likely to develop?

e ⏵⏵ Now go to Vocabulary Focus 9A on p. 162.

3 LISTENING

a ▶09.03 Listen to Toby and Rosie talk about inventions. Which medical invention and which food invention do they talk about?

b ▶09.03 Listen again and answer the questions.
1. What did the scientist do with the meat?
2. Why's this meat better for the environment?
3. What does Toby suggest that Rosie do to reduce the amount of land used for crop production?
4. What does Toby say about the taste of the meat?
5. Why does Rosie think it's strange that Toby's worried about global warming?

c Whose point of view do you agree with more, Toby's or Rosie's?

4 GRAMMAR Relative clauses

a Underline the relative clause in each sentence and circle the relative pronouns.
1. ☐ Yeah, there's this laboratory where they're growing meat.
2. ☐ There was that scientist who made his own burger and ate it online.
3. ☐ But all these tiny pieces of meat that they have to push together just to make one burger.
4. ☐ And the end result is something that costs €250,000 to make!
5. ☐ There's no fat or blood in it, which means it would taste different.
6. ☐ I mean, these scientists, who are sort of like Dr Frankenstein, how can they justify that?

b Look at the descriptions of two kinds of relative clause.
- Defining relative clauses: they give essential information about the noun and make it more specific.
- Non-defining relative clauses: they just give extra information.

Which clauses in 4a are examples of each type? Write D (defining) or ND (non-defining) in the boxes in 4a.

c Look at the pronouns you circled in 4a.
1. In which sentences could you replace the pronoun with …?
   - which
   - that
   - no pronoun
2. In one sentence, the pronoun tells us more about a fact, not just a single noun. Which sentence is it?

d ⏵⏵ Now go to Grammar Focus 9A on p. 150.

e Read the text about 'Impossible Foods'. In the gaps, use the notes in brackets to add defining or non-defining relative clauses. Add commas if necessary.

Most burger restaurants offer customers a choice between burgers ¹which are made of beef or chicken (made of beef or chicken) and veggie burgers ² _____ (usually made of beans or soya). Unfortunately, a veggie burger simply doesn't taste as good as a beefburger ³ _____ (a problem for vegetarians), especially for those ⁴ _____ (like the taste of meat). But a company called Impossible Foods ⁵ _____ (based in California) has found a way to solve the problem. They discovered that the red colour and taste of meat is due to a molecule called 'heme' ⁶ _____ (found in meat), but ⁷ _____ (also found in many plants). By using this molecule, they were able to create a burger ⁸ _____ (has plant-based ingredients) but ⁹ _____ (tastes exactly like beef). Their burger ¹⁰ _____ (called 'Impossible Burger') was first sold in the USA ¹¹ _____ (burgers are very popular), but now you can buy them all over the world. Most people ¹² _____ (try it) say they can't tell it's not made from meat.

5 SPEAKING

a ⏵⏵ Communication 9A Student A: Go to p. 132. Student B: Go to p. 131.

b 💬 Put the inventions in order of usefulness from 1–4 (1 = very useful, 4 = completely useless). Discuss your ideas with the class.

9B THEY HAD NO IDEA IT WAS A FRAUD

Learn to discuss people's lives and achievements

- **G** Reported speech; Reporting verbs
- **V** Verbs describing thought and knowledge

1 READING

a Look at the reports and discuss the questions.

> The airport was closed after a bomb scare, but it turned out to be a **hoax**.
> They thought it was painted by Monet, but it was a **fake**.
> The manager of the company was arrested for **fraud**.
> If you receive an email asking you to check your bank account, it's almost certainly a **scam**.

1. What do all the statements have in common?
2. What do the words in **bold** mean?
3. How common do you think fraud is in your country? What forms does it take?

b Read the article *The Rise and Fall of Barry Minkow* and answer the questions.

1. What was Barry Minkow's job?
2. How did Minkow 'rise'?
3. How did Minkow 'fall'?

c Read the article again and make brief notes on the following:

- how Barry Minkow made money at the beginning
- the second company Minkow set up
- the people and organisations that Minkow made money from

Compare your notes with another student. Did you write the same things?

d Read the sentences about what happened to Barry Minkow later. Three of the sentences are true. Which do you think they are? Give reasons for your choice.

1. He stayed in prison less than 10 years.
2. He completely changed his character.
3. He became a pastor in a church.
4. He was sent to prison again.

e ≫ **Communication 9B** Now go to p. 132. Did you guess correctly?

The Rise and Fall of Barry Minkow

At the age of 16, Californian Barry Minkow launched his own carpet cleaning company from his parents' garage. He was so successful that, only four years later, the company was listed on the American stock market with a value of $280 million, making Barry Minkow a multi-millionaire and also the youngest CEO of a public company in American history. But a few years later, he resigned from the company and was sentenced to 25 years in prison. So what went wrong and how did his phenomenal success turn to disaster?

The answer is that although Barry Minkow seemed like a successful entrepreneur, he wasn't able to run a profitable business. Instead he focused on getting money for his company in any way he could.

When he started his carpet-cleaning business, called *ZZZZ-Best*, he raised money by engaging in credit card fraud, stealing his grandmother's jewellery and even arranging fake 'robberies' at his office to get insurance money.

Later he set up a second company, which specialised in restoring buildings damaged by flooding or fire, with the work paid for by insurance companies. In fact the company was a fake: the buildings didn't exist and the documents and contracts were forged. However, he convinced the banks that he was running a successful business and got them to lend him more money, which enabled him to expand *ZZZZ-Best* and turn it into a public company. But Barry Minkow's past was finally catching up with him.

An article in the *Los Angeles Times* claimed that Minkow had been involved in false credit card charges and that only those who had noticed the false charges had got their money back. Shortly after that, investigators reported that his second company was a fake and that its 'restoration' jobs didn't actually exist. After Minkow suddenly resigned 'for health reasons', the new directors discovered that he had stolen $230 million from the company before he left.

A year later he was charged with fraud and sentenced to 25 years in prison.

UNIT 9

2 GRAMMAR Reported speech; Reporting verbs

a Look at these examples of things people said.

> Minkow **was** involved in false credit card charges.

> Only those who **noticed** the false charges **got** their money back.

> His second company **is** a fake.

> Its 'restoration' jobs **don't** actually **exist**.

These statements are reported in the sentences below using reporting verbs. Complete the sentences with the correct form of the verbs in brackets. Then check your answers in the text.

1 An article in the *Los Angeles Times* <u>claimed</u> that Minkow _____ (be) involved in false credit card charges.
2 The article also <u>claimed</u> that only those who _____ (notice) the false charges _____ (get) their money back.
3 Shortly after that, investigators <u>reported</u> that his second company _____ (be) a fake.
4 They also <u>said</u> that its 'restoration' jobs _____ (not/actually/exist).

b Complete the rule with the correct answers.

> Because the reporting verbs (*said, claimed, reported*) are in the *present / past*, what the people said moves 'one tense back' into the *present / past*.

c Look at these examples of questions people asked or thought.

> Is he really the reformed character that he claims to be?

> What's going on?

> Where is our money really going?

Complete the reported questions with the correct form of the verbs in brackets. Check your answers in the text.

1 Very few people questioned whether he _____ (be) really the reformed character that he claimed to be.
2 Some people began to wonder what _____ (be) going on and where their money _____ (really/go).

> Choose the correct word to complete the rule:
> In reported questions, *use / don't use* question word order.

d ⟫ Now go to Grammar Focus 9B on p. 150.

e Correct the mistakes in these sentences.

1 Investigators weren't sure whether Barry Minkow is telling the truth.
2 They asked him if he can show them the company accounts.
3 People at the church didn't understand why did he steal money from them.
4 Customers were asking will they ever get their money back.

3 LISTENING

a Imagine you receive the email subject below.

From: health@importantinfo.gov
Subject: WARNING! Dangerous bananas

How would you react? Would you think … ?
1 That sounds serious and I eat bananas. I'd better see what it says.
2 It sounds like a hoax, but it could be serious.
3 It's probably a scam. I'll delete it without opening it.

What do you imagine the email might say?

b ▶09.07 Listen to two people talking about the email. Tick (✓) the topics that they mention.

☐ poison ☐ bacteria ☐ Central America
☐ restaurants ☐ monkeys ☐ supermarkets
☐ chat shows

How are the topics you chose connected?

c ▶09.07 Listen again and answer the questions.
1 Is the Centers for Disease Control and Prevention a real organisation?
2 In what sense were the bananas supposed to be 'man-eating'?
3 Why did the news about the bananas spread so quickly?
4 What effect did this have?
5 How common is necrotizing fasciitis?
6 How was the story in Africa different from the one in the USA?

108

4 VOCABULARY
Verbs describing thought and knowledge

a Look at the sentences from the discussion. Which verbs in the box can you use instead of *thought* or *knew* to make the meaning more precise? Put them into the correct form.

> assume   come to the conclusion
> have no idea   realise   suspect

1 Maybe they *thought* it was a hoax but they weren't sure. (= think or believe something is true but be uncertain about it)
2 People *didn't know* what necrotising fasciitis was. (= not know at all)
3 They started discussing it on TV chat shows and eventually people *thought* it was just a hoax. (= decide after thinking about it)
4 It sounded like a reasonable story, so I guess people just *thought* it was true. (= believe something is true without questioning it)
5 So everyone stopped eating bananas from South Africa for a while, until they *knew* it was all a hoax. (= suddenly understand)

b ▶ 09.08 Listen and check your answers.

c Write possible continuations to these sentences. Think carefully about the correct verb form to use.

1 After getting to know her better, I came to the conclusion …
2 It was already 5:30. He realised …
3 After working for the company for six months, I started to suspect …
4 Our next-door neighbour seemed very ordinary. We had no idea …
5 You didn't answer when I called, so I assumed …

5 SPEAKING

a Think of an example of a hoax, scam or case of fraud that you know about. It could be:
- a hoax designed just for fun
- an email or Internet scam
- a case of fraud that happened in your country or in another country.

b 💬 Work with a partner. Think about how you will describe what happened and make brief notes. Try to include reported speech and verbs from 4a.

c 💬 Tell other students about your topic.

9C EVERYDAY ENGLISH
What's the big secret?

Learn how to express uncertainty
- P Linking and intrusion
- S Clarifying a misunderstanding

1 LISTENING

a Discuss the questions.
1 When was the last time you had a surprise?
2 Was it a good or bad surprise? What happened?
3 Do you usually like surprises? Why / Why not?

b Look at photo a and answer the questions.
1 Who has organised a surprise?
2 How does Becky feel about it?
3 Do you think Becky knows where she is?

c 09.09 Watch or listen to Part 1. Check your ideas in 1b.

d What do you think the surprise is?

2 USEFUL LANGUAGE
Expressing uncertainty

a 09.10 Read the conversation below. Is it what Becky and Tom said? Listen and check.
BECKY I don't know where we are.
TOM Just wait and see.
BECKY Where are we going?
TOM Wait and see.

b In which version does Becky express herself more strongly? Why does she do this?

c Becky talks about a place: 'I've no idea where we are.'

Look at these expressions for talking about a thing.
1 I've (really) (got) no idea what that is.
2 I haven't got a clue what that is.
3 What on earth is that?
Change expressions 1–3 to talk about a person.

d ▶ Communication 9C Student A: Go to p. 133.
Student B: Go to p. 131.

3 LISTENING

a Look at photo b and answer the questions.
1 What has Tom done?
2 How does Becky feel about it?

b 09.11 Watch or listen to Part 2 and check your ideas in 3a.

c 09.11 Watch or listen to Part 2 again. Answer the questions.
1 How did Tom manage to get the flat?
2 What did Tom do earlier in the afternoon?
3 Why's Becky a bit annoyed?
4 What things does Becky like about the flat?
5 Why didn't Becky guess?
6 What two documents do Tom and Becky have to sign?

UNIT 9

4 PRONUNCIATION Linking and intrusion

a ▶ 09.12 Listen to an excerpt from the conversation. Pay attention to the underlined phrases. Do they sound like separate words or one word?

TOM You're not too annoyed?
BECKY No. In fact, <u>not at all</u>.
TOM You did say it was the perfect flat.
BECKY <u>And it is</u>.

BECKY I've no ^ idea where we ^ are. I've never seen this street before.
TOM Just wait and see.
BECKY Where ^ on earth are we going?
TOM Wait and see.

b Why do the sounds join together? Choose the correct description.
1 All the vowel sounds in these words are short sounds.
2 Final consonant sounds are followed by vowel sounds.
3 There is no stress in any of these phrases.

c ▶ 09.13 Listen to the excerpt. Notice the phrases with ^. Where are the sounds in the box added?

/j/ /r/ /w/

d Why do we add the sounds in 4c? Choose the correct explanation.
1 The main stress is on the word that comes after each added sound.
2 The consonants in the two words are voiced.
3 The last sound in the first word and the first sound in the following word are both vowels.

e ▶ 09.14 Using the rules from 4b and d, predict where the speaker is going to use linking and intrusion. Then listen and check.

Here at work, I've just received a gift from my aunt. I've got no idea what it is. I'm going to open it when I get home this evening.

5 CONVERSATION SKILLS Clarifying a misunderstanding

a ▶ 09.15 Listen to part of Tom and Becky's conversation. Which two expressions does Becky use to clarify a misunderstanding? (Both expressions begin with *but*.)

b Look at the exchanges. Which are social situations? Which are work situations? <u>Underline</u> the expressions in B's replies used to clarify misunderstandings.
1 **A** I'm off to the movies now.
   B I thought that you were going to go to a football game.
2 **A** Our next meeting's in two weeks.
   B I understood that we were going to meet once a week.
3 **A** Here's your ticket. It's £50.
   B Did I get this wrong? I thought it was free.
4 **A** By the end of this month, you'll be able to take a week's holiday.
   B Have I misunderstood something? I thought I could take two weeks' holiday.
5 **A** How about if I make the starter and you make the dessert?
   B Didn't we say that I'd make the starter?

c What could you say in the situations below? Write your ideas and compare with your partner.
1 You're in a restaurant. Your friend told you he/she wasn't hungry but has ordered a starter, a main and dessert.
2 You stay in a hotel. When you pay the bill, you're surprised to find breakfast is extra.
3 A friend offers you a lift to the station. When you get in the car, he/she starts driving in the opposite direction.

6 SPEAKING

a ≫ **Communication 9C** Student A: Go to p.131. Student B: Go to p.130.

UNIT PROGRESS TEST
→ CHECK YOUR PROGRESS
You can now do the Unit Progress Test.

9D SKILLS FOR WRITING
People argue that it is no use at all

Learn to write an essay expressing a point of view

W Presenting a series of arguments

1 SPEAKING AND LISTENING

a 💬 Discuss the questions.
1. Do you think alternative treatments really work or do you think people just imagine that they work?
2. What kinds of alternative medicine are common in your country?
3. If you were ill, would you try alternative medicine? Why / Why not?

Alternative medicine Kinds of medical treatment that use different methods from standard Western medicine (also called *conventional medicine*). Examples of alternative medicine are homeopathy, radionics and acupuncture.

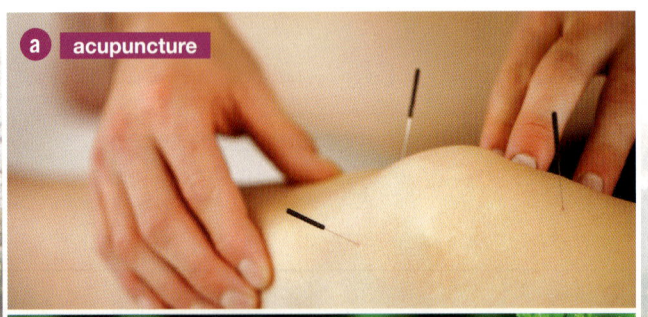

b ▶ 09.16 Listen to people talking about four alternative treatments. What treatment does each person talk about? Match them with photos a–d.

c ▶ 09.16 Listen again and answer the questions for all the speakers.
1. Why did the person try this treatment?
2. What did the doctor/therapist do?
3. Does the speaker feel positive or negative about it?
4. Do we know if the treatment worked?

2 READING

a Read Alicia's opinions in her essay, *The value of alternative medicine*. Which sentence best summarises her argument?
1. Conventional medicine is more effective, but alternative medicine may be useful sometimes.
2. Alternative medicine is often more effective than conventional medicine, so it should be used more widely.
3. Conventional and alternative medicine work in different ways and both of them are important.

a acupuncture
b homeopathy
c radionics
d hypnosis

The value of alternative medicine

People often have extreme points of view about alternative medicine. People who believe in conventional medicine often argue that alternative medicine is of no use at all, and supporters of alternative medicine sometimes claim that it can replace conventional medicine completely.

There are several good reasons for taking alternative medicine seriously. First, many forms of alternative medicine, such as acupuncture and herbal medicine, have a very long tradition and are widely used

b Look at the points that Alicia makes in her essay. Which are about conventional medicine and which are about alternative medicine? Write conventional (C) or alternative (A).

1. ☐ It has been used for a very long time and in many different countries.
2. ☐ It is often cheaper.
3. ☐ It may have harmful side effects.
4. ☐ We can't show scientifically that it works.
5. ☐ People who use it often say it works.

3 WRITING SKILLS
Presenting a series of arguments

a Alicia's essay in 2a has five paragraphs. What is the purpose of each one? Complete the sentences.

1. In the first paragraph, she outlines …
2. In the next three paragraphs, she presents …
3. In the final paragraph, she summarises …

b Find the expressions in Alicia's essay which introduce arguments and points of view.

People often argue that …

c Alicia uses linking words and phrases to show how her ideas are connected. Find words and phrases that mean:

1. also (x2)   2. but   3. so   4. although
5. finally

d Choose one of the topics below and think about your point of view. Write three sentences about the topic, using expressions from 3b and 3c.

- Are zoos cruel to animals?
- Can dieting be unhealthy?
- Do video games cause bad behaviour in young people?
- Should cars be banned from city centres?
- Should smoking be made illegal?

4 WRITING

a Think again about the topic you chose in 3d. Plan an essay using the structure in 3a. Think about:

- how you will introduce the topic
- what arguments you will present and what examples you will give to support them
- what conclusion you will give.

b Write the essay in around 200 words.

c Swap essays with your partner. Read the essay. Does it … ?

- have a clear introduction and conclusion
- present the arguments clearly, with a separate paragraph for each main idea
- include examples to support the arguments
- use appropriate expressions to introduce the arguments

d 💬 Work in new pairs. Read another student's essay. Then say if you agree with his/her point of view and why.

---

in many parts of the world. It's important not to ignore traditional knowledge that has been used and developed for centuries.

In addition, unlike the drugs and antibiotics used in conventional medicine that can be harmful to the human body, most alternative therapies are completely harmless. Homeopathic treatments, for example, have few or no side effects, and consequently the worst that can happen is that they have no effect at all.

One argument against alternative medicine is that there is very little scientific evidence to prove that it is effective. Yet, in spite of the lack of scientific evidence, people who use alternative therapies generally say that they work. This suggests that alternative therapies may perhaps work in ways that we do not yet fully understand. Furthermore, people are often willing to spend a lot of money on alternative treatment, despite the fact that it is often not covered by insurance, so it can be more expensive than conventional medicine.

In conclusion, I believe that conventional medicine and alternative therapies should exist side by side. They work in completely different ways and are often effective for different kinds of illnesses, so they should both be seen as a useful way to keep us healthy.

UNIT 9
Review and extension

1 GRAMMAR

a Join the sentences using a relative clause. Use a relative pronoun if it's necessary. Cut any unnecessary words.

1 The bandage is like a piece of skin. The bandage is very small and thin.
2 The skin contains electronic circuits. The circuits can communicate with monitors.
3 An operating theatre is a sophisticated environment. Patients require extra care in an operating theatre.
4 People with severe peanut allergies have to check the ingredients for everything they eat. Some people are severely allergic to peanuts.

b Tell the story, changing the parts in *italics* into indirect speech, using reporting verbs.

I was on a business trip, and I had a terrible time getting back home. My flight was at 12:30. But when I arrived at the airport, they announced: ¹'*There has been a delay to the incoming flight, so the flight will be delayed by about an hour.*' After an hour, we still hadn't heard anything and I started to wonder, ²'*What's happening?*' I asked one of the flight attendants, ³'*Do you know when the flight will leave?*' She told me, ⁴'*I haven't heard anything.*' I waited for two more hours. At about 5:00, they told us, ⁵'*The flight has been cancelled.*' I realised, ⁶'*I'll have to spend the night in an airport hotel, and I probably won't be home for another 18 hours.*'

2 VOCABULARY

a Choose the best word in these sentences.

1 Some scientists *estimate / realise* that there are 100 billion stars just in our galaxy.
2 I'm sorry I didn't say anything. I didn't *assume / realise* it was your birthday.
3 I followed you because I *doubted / assumed* that you knew the way.
4 I *wonder / come to the conclusion* how much she earns in a month. It must be at least €10,000.
5 As I left the flat, I *doubted / was aware* that someone was following me, and I was fairly sure I knew who it was.

b Add words from the box to the gaps.

| patients | strained | feel | back | lost | dizzy |
| scar | care | consciousness | heals | | |

1 I _____ _____. I think I'm going to faint.
2 It hurts when I try to stand up. I think I've _____ my _____.
3 She's a student nurse. She takes _____ of _____ in hospital and she also has to study for exams.
4 They hit me on the head and I _____ _____.
5 When the wound _____, it will probably leave a _____.

3 WORDPOWER *come*

a Match the sentence beginnings and endings.

1 Her dream was to see the sea, and last month her dream **came**
2 I think we should go to the cinema, unless you can **come**
3 Look, there's a photo of you in the paper. I **came**
4 The restaurant was rather expensive – the bill **came**
5 I thought about buying the car for ages, but I **came**
6 We were talking about who to ask, and your name **came**

a **across** it this morning
b **true**.
c **to** more than €250.
d **up** as a possible person.
e **to the conclusion** that I couldn't afford it.
f **up with** a better idea

b Match the expressions in **bold** in 3a with the definitions.

a see something by chance   d add up to
b think of   e reach a decision
c be mentioned   f really happen

c Choose the correct words or phrases.

1 'OK – two coffees – that comes *to / up* £9.50.'
2 At the meeting, we came up *to / with* lots of new ideas.
3 Nuclear power is a topic that often comes *true / up* in students' essays.
4 We thought about going to Paris, but we came *to / across* the conclusion that Rome would be nicer.
5 I came *across / to* a fascinating article in this magazine. It might interest you.
6 I always wanted to own a BMW, and now my dream has finally come *true / across*.

d Complete each question with one word.

1 Do you know anyone whose dream came _____?
2 Have you ever been given a bill that came _____ more than you could afford?
3 Have you ever come to the _____ that something you bought was a waste of money?
4 How do you feel if someone says, 'Your name came _____ in our conversation'?
5 Many people come _____ with new ideas when they're falling asleep or going for a walk. Is that true of you?
6 Have you ever come _____ a bargain in a shop or at a market that you couldn't resist?

e 💬 Ask and answer the questions in 3d.

⟳ REVIEW YOUR PROGRESS

How well did you do in this unit? Write 3, 2 or 1 for each objective.
3 = very well   2 = well   1 = not so well

I CAN ...	
discuss new inventions	☐
discuss people's lives and achievements	☐
express uncertainty	☐
write an essay expressing a point of view.	☐

114

CAN DO OBJECTIVES

- Speculate about the past
- Discuss life achievements
- Describe how you felt
- Write a narrative

UNIT 10

POSSIBILITIES

GETTING STARTED

a Look at the picture and answer the questions.
1. What has just happened to this man?
2. What is he thinking? What is he feeling?

b Discuss the questions.
1. When people have high ambitions, what kinds of expectations do they have of themselves?
2. Do you think people are sometimes unrealistic in setting goals for themselves? Why?
3. What are the positive and negative consequences of having high expectations of yourself?

115

10A IT MIGHT NOT HAVE BEEN HIS REAL NAME

Learn to speculate about the past

G Past modals of deduction
V Adjectives with prefixes

1 READING

a You are going to read a story about Dan Cooper, who mysteriously disappeared in 1971. Look at the pictures of people and events in the story. Can you guess what happened?

b Read *The man who disappeared* quickly. How similar is it to your ideas?

c Find sentences in the story that show:
1 the flight from Portland to Seattle was a short one
2 we're not sure if Dan Cooper was the man's real name
3 the passengers didn't know about the note or the bomb
4 Cooper told the pilots to fly towards Mexico as slowly and as low as possible
5 the pilots didn't want to leave the rear door open
6 the pilots knew when the rear door was opened.

d Discuss the questions.
- What questions would you like answered that are not explained in the text?
- Do you think Cooper survived? What would you prefer to believe, that he survived or that he didn't survive? Why?

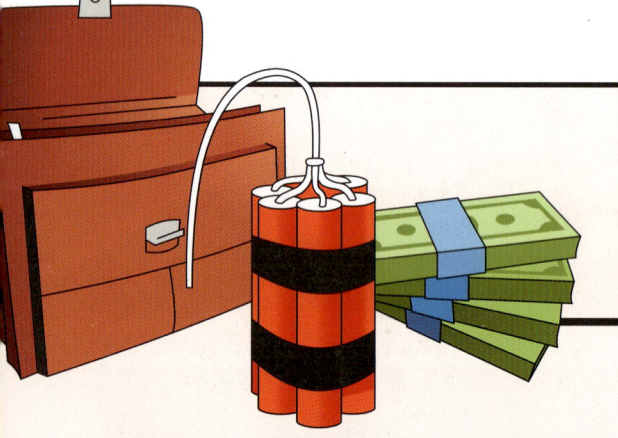

The man who DISAPPEARED

Flight attendant Florence Schaffner was sitting in her seat during takeoff. A man in a seat near her passed her a note. It read, 'I have a bomb in my briefcase. I will use it if necessary. Sit next to me.'

It was 2:50 pm on 24 November, 1971, on Flight 305, a 30-minute flight from Portland to Seattle in the northwest of the USA. And it was the beginning of one of the strangest stories in the history of plane travel – a mystery that remains unsolved to this day. The man's name – or at least, the name he gave when he bought his plane ticket – was Dan Cooper. Of course, this might not have been his real name; no one really knows for sure.

Schaffner quietly got up and sat next to the man. He opened his briefcase slightly, and she glimpsed eight red sticks inside before he closed it again. Then Cooper made his demands: $200,000 (a huge amount of money in 1971), four parachutes and a fuel truck ready at Seattle Airport to refuel the plane. The attendant told the pilot, who passed the demands on to the airline company, and they agreed to them. The other passengers were told there was a 'technical difficulty' and the plane circled for almost two hours over the sea to give the airline time to get the money and parachutes ready.

Cooper was told that his demands had been met, and the plane landed at Seattle-Tacoma airport at 5:45 pm. The money (in $20 notes) and the parachutes were delivered and the passengers and Schaffner left the plane. Cooper talked to the pilots and ordered them to fly towards Mexico at minimum speed and altitude, with a refuelling stop in Reno. The plane, a Boeing 727, had a door at the back that opened downwards –

Cooper ordered the pilots to leave it open all the time. They objected, so Cooper said that he would open it himself when they were in the air.

After refuelling, the plane took off at approximately 7:40, with Cooper and four crew members on board. After take-off, Cooper told the lone flight attendant to go to the cockpit. As she went, she saw him tie something around his waist, which may have been the bags of money. At eight o'clock, a warning light went on in the cockpit, so they knew that he must have opened the rear door. The plane landed in Reno at 10:15, with the rear door still open. Police searched the plane immediately, but they quickly confirmed that Cooper was gone.

Cooper was never seen again, dead or alive. No one has even found out if he really was Dan Cooper. And many people say that he can't have survived the jump (if indeed he jumped – he could have hidden on the plane and then escaped later) but no body or parachute was ever found. A bag with almost $6,000 of the money was found in a river, but the rest never showed up. The money might have belonged to Cooper, but even that wasn't certain.

Fifty years later, the crime remains unsolved – and it will probably remain that way forever.

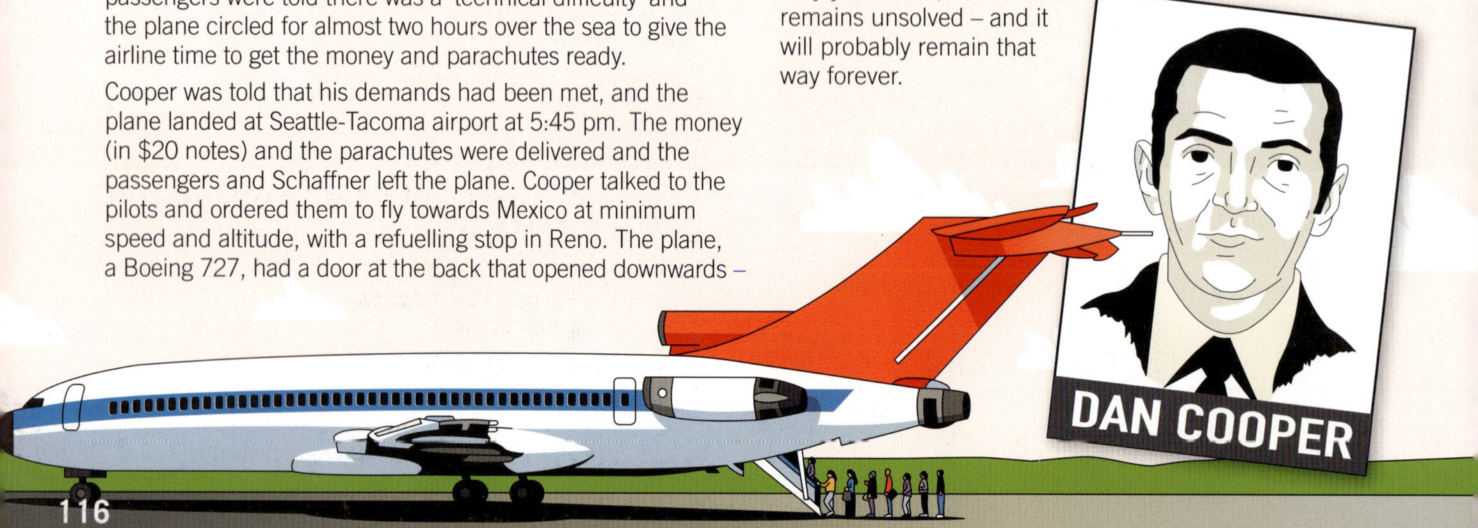

DAN COOPER

2 GRAMMAR Past modals of deduction

a Match sentences 1–5 with meanings a–d.
1. ☐ He tied something around his waist, which **may have been** the bags of money.
2. ☐ Many people say that he **can't have survived** the jump.
3. ☐ It **might not have been** his real name.
4. ☐ He **could have hidden** on the plane.
5. ☐ A warning light went on in the cockpit, so they knew that he **must have opened** the door.

a It seems certain that this was the case.
b It seems certain that this was not the case.
c It's possible that this was the case. (x2)
d It's possible that this was not the case.

b Look at the examples in 2a again.
1. Complete the rule with the modal verbs in the box.

must   may   might   can't   could

To speculate about things in the past:
- we use _____ or _____ + have + past participle to talk about things we think are certain.
- we use _____, _____ or _____ + have + past participle to talk about things we think are possible.

2. Choose the correct answer, a or b.
- *must* and *can't* mean a) the same b) the opposite
- *may*, *might* and *could* mean a) the same b) the opposite

3. In the examples, *have* is:
   a part of the present perfect tense
   b an infinitive form which always stays the same.

c ▶10.01 **Pronunciation** Listen to the sentences. Underline the stressed syllables in each sentence.
1. He can't have survived the jump.
2. It might not have been his real name.
3. He must have opened the door.

Practise saying the sentences.

d ▶▶ Now go to Grammar Focus 10A on p. 152.

e Read these situations. What do you think happened? Use past modals of deduction to discuss each one.

1. Renato Nicolai was in his garden in the south of France when he heard a whistling sound and saw what he thought was an experimental aircraft. He watched as it dropped out of the sky, hovered about two metres off the ground, then rose into the sky and disappeared. When experts studied the place where it had come down, they found a 'black material' on the ground that was not oil.

2. A ship called *The Joyita* disappeared in the Pacific without sending a call for help. It was found a month later floating in the ocean with no one on board. The lifeboats and the food were missing. There was a hole in the side, but it wasn't serious and the engines weren't damaged. The crew were never found.

3 LISTENING

a ▶10.03 Listen to an interview about Dan Cooper's disappearance. Number the topics in the order you hear them. There is one extra topic that you do not need.

the river ___
Dan Cooper's 'wife' ___
airport security ___
the pilot of the Boeing 727 ___
the parachute ___
the money ___

b ▶10.03 What evidence is there for the opinions below? Listen again and check.
1. Dan Cooper wasn't his real name.
2. He worked in the aircraft industry.
3. He survived the jump.
4. He didn't survive the jump.
5. Someone helped him.

c What do you think might have happened?

UNIT 10

4 READING

a 💬 What famous event is shown here? What's happening in the picture?

b Read the blog *Ten amazing coincidences* and answer the questions.
1 Which came first, the *Titanic* disaster or the book *The Wreck of the Titan*?
2 What is unusual about the book?

c Read the blog again. Which of these features of the book were similar to the *Titanic* disaster? Write Yes (*Y*), No (*N*) or Don't know (*DK*).
1 the name of the ship ___
2 the type of ship ___
3 the number of passengers ___
4 the description of the ship ___
5 where and when it sank ___
6 the reason it sank ___
7 how many people were rescued ___

d 💬 Discuss these three opinions about the blog. Which do you agree with the most? Why?

> It's amazing. Morgan Robertson must have been able to see into the future in some way.

> It might have been just a coincidence, but it's very difficult to explain it.

> It's not so extraordinary. Morgan Robertson must have known that large ships were being built and that icebergs were a danger.

5 VOCABULARY
Adjectives with prefixes

a Find adjectives in the blog in 4b which mean:
1 you can't believe it (x2)
2 it's not likely
3 it's not possible
4 it didn't sell many copies
5 it's not part of the main point.

What do all these adjectives have in common?

b ≫ Now go to Vocabulary Focus 10A on p. 163.

6 SPEAKING

a ≫ **Communication 10A** You are going to read two more stories from the series *Ten amazing coincidences*. Student A: Go to p. 130. Student B: Go to p. 133.

| BLOG | REVIEWS | GIVEAWAYS | ABOUT |

Ten amazing coincidences
The Wreck of the Titan
by Morgan Robertson

Morgan Robertson writes about the *Titanic* … 14 years early!

A hundred years before James Cameron made the film *Titanic*, American author Morgan Robertson wrote an unsuccessful book called *The Wreck of the Titan* about the sinking of an ocean liner. It's a story that's been told many times and 13 films have been made about it.

The incredible thing is …

Robertson's *The Wreck of the Titan* was published in 1898; that's 14 years before the *Titanic* was even built.

The similarities between Robertson's work and the *Titanic* disaster are really improbable. The *Titan*, like the *Titanic*, was described as 'the largest craft afloat', 'like a first class hotel', and 'unsinkable'. Both ships were British-owned steel vessels, they were both around 800 feet long, and they both sank after hitting an iceberg in the North Atlantic, in April, 'around midnight'.

What's even more unbelievable

In the novel, the *Titan* crashed into an iceberg 650 kilometres from the coast of Canada at 25 knots. The real-life *Titanic* crashed into an iceberg 650 kilometres from the coast of Canada at 22.5 knots. If you think of the size of the Atlantic, about 65 million square kilometres, that's such a close guess it seems impossible that Robertson didn't know in advance what was going to happen.

The weirdest thing of all

But maybe the weirdest thing about the *Titan* were details that were irrelevant to the story but match what happened to the *Titanic*. For example, both the *Titan* and the *Titanic* had too few lifeboats to take every passenger on board. But it's an odd point to mention in the book when you consider that lifeboats had nothing to do with the story. In the book, when the *Titan* hit the iceberg, the ship sank immediately – so why did Robertson mention the lifeboats? Was it just coincidence or did he somehow know what was going to happen?

b 💬 Tell each other your stories. Do you think the events are coincidences, or is there some other explanation for what happened? Do you know any other stories like these?

10B I'VE MANAGED TO MAKE A DREAM COME TRUE

Learn to discuss life achievements
- **G** Wishes and regrets
- **V** Verbs of effort

1 LISTENING

a Read quotes a–c about believing in your dreams. Which one do you like the most? Why?

a 'Work hard and dream the biggest dream you can – you'll see amazing things happen!'

b 'Dreams are all about what's going to happen tomorrow. Don't let your dreams get in the way of being the best person you can be – right here, right now.'

c 'You need dreams when life gets boring or difficult – they're what get you out of bed in the morning and keep a smile on your face.'

b 💬 What do you think is the most important ingredient in realising your dreams? Why?

believing in yourself   hard work   knowing the right people   luck   money

c ▶ 10.05 Listen to Louise and Terry. They both decided to pursue their dreams. Match the speakers with the photos. They both made one change that was the same. What was it?

d ▶ 10.05 Listen again. What reasons do Louise and Terry give for making their change?

e 💬 What do you think happened next to Louise and Terry?

f ▶ 10.06 Listen to the second part of their stories. Were your predictions correct?

g ▶ 10.06 Listen again. Complete the table.

	What problems did he/she experience?	What regrets does he/she have?
Louise		
Terry		

h 💬 Would you do what Louise and Terry did? Why / Why not?

119

UNIT 10

2 GRAMMAR
Wishes and regrets

a Look at these examples from Louise and Terry's conversation. Who says each one?
1 If only I'd applied for his job when it became free.
2 I found it a bit crowded. I wish I'd checked this before leaving.
3 I should have checked out other companies.

b What are the speakers doing in the examples in 2a? Are they … ?
1 wishing for a change in their life
2 expressing regrets for things they have done
3 expressing regrets for things they didn't do

c Complete the rule.

> To express regret about the past, we use:
> 1 *I wish* or *if only* + I + ___
> 2 *I should have* + ___

d ▶ 10.07 **Pronunciation** Listen to the examples in 2a. Notice the linking sounds. Which two words in each example are stressed?
1 If only I'd applied for his job.
2 I wish I'd checked this.
3 I should have checked out other companies.

e ▶ Now go to Grammar Focus 10B on p. 152.

f Think of something you did in the past with mixed results (some parts were good, but others weren't). What would you do differently now? Make notes.

g 💬 Tell each other about your past experiences and regrets.

3 READING

a Do you agree with the statement below? Why / Why not?

> If you want a personal dream to come true, you need to focus on yourself and not think about other people. You will only be successful if you are determined in this way.

DREAM TO HELP

Many people have a dream or a goal in life. However, some dreams include the idea of helping other people. Meet two people who have done just that.

Kotchakorn Voraakhom

What was her dream?
Kotchakorn Voraakhom's dream was quite ambitious. She wanted to save Bangkok, the city she was born in. Her dream involved two connected ideas: reducing heavy flooding and creating more green spaces in the city.

How did her dream come about?
Kotchakorn is a landscape architect. She first studied at Chulalongkorn University in Bangkok, then pursued graduate studies at Harvard University in the USA. Having completed her studies, she worked on landscape projects in Las Vegas and Aspen in the USA that gave her a greater awareness of the importance of ecology in landscape architecture. She realised it wasn't just a question of making things look nice.

In 2011, Kotchakorn returned to Bangkok and not long after that, there was severe flooding in Thailand as a result of heavy rains during the monsoon season. Bangkok was badly affected because what was once agricultural land that absorbed water is now a cityscape. This means water has nowhere to go. Kotchakorn also believes that Bangkok needs green spaces that encourage its inhabitants to change their way of living and give them a greater understanding of the idea of sustainability.

How did she achieve her dream?
When her old university, Chukalongkorn, asked for submissions to design a park for its 100-year anniversary, Kotchakorn saw an opportunity to realise her dream. The first difficulty she had to overcome was creating an outstanding design. With colleagues at LANDPROCESS, she worked on a submission that was not only innovative but ecologically sustainable. It was a clear winner.

The four-hectare park uses gravity so that rain falling on higher sections of the park runs down to a wetland area where some of the water is absorbed and cleaned by plants. The rainfall ends up in a large pond that can hold 3.8 million litres of water. This water can be used to irrigate the park when the weather is dry.

Kotchakorn has also stuck with her idea of having more green spaces in Bangkok. She has designed large rooftop gardens on top of Siam Square shopping centre and Ramathibodi Hospital. The one she created on top of Thammasat University is the largest rooftop garden in Asia. It uses a traditional system of terraces which is similar to a rice field. This allows water to run off the building more slowly and the water is used in gardens that grow food for the university canteen.

In following her dream, Kotchakorn has become famous around the world. She has been invited to give a TED talk and often appears on lists of influential and important women in the world. While she may not have completely saved Bangkok from floods, her work has made a significant difference and has helped change the way people think about the growth of cities. They are now more aware of the environmental consequences of non-stop development.

b Work in two groups and read the introduction. Group A reads about Kotchakorn Voraakhom and group B reads about Michelle Javian. Decide with your group if you think Kotchakorn or Michelle would agree with the statement in 3a.

c Read the text again and make notes about your person.

d Work with a student from the other group. Tell each other about your person. Decide which person you admire the most. Give a reason.

e Both individuals in the article made a dramatic change to follow their passion. How important do you think it is to do that? What type of person does it take?

What was her dream?
Michelle Javian wanted to set up and run a non-profit organisation that helps heart patients and their families. She wanted to be able to offer these people practical help during critical times in their illness.

How did her dream come about?
In 2008, Michelle's father had a heart transplant. She spent hours at his bedside in hospital. During this time, she began to realise how difficult life is for families who have someone in cardiac care, particularly if they have to travel from out of town.

Sadly, Michelle's father passed away. She felt that the best way to honour his memory and cope with her sadness was to set up a non-profit organisation that gives practical support to families of people who are unwell because of heart disease.

How did she achieve her dream?
While looking after her father in hospital, Michelle made friends with Yuki Kotani, whose father was also having a heart transplant. They talked to doctors and social workers and got a lot of ideas for the best way they could help people in similar situations. The health professionals suggested that providing affordable housing for the families of heart patients was the most effective way of reducing the stress of patients and their families. This led to Michelle and Yuki setting up a charity called Harboring Hearts.

Michelle had given up her job in the corporate world to jump into non-profit work. She didn't have previous experience in that area, so it was a huge challenge for Michelle to tackle. She quickly realised that the best way to raise money was by talking to people and telling her story. Donations began to come in, and before long she was able to help a family with four-year-old twin boys who both needed heart transplants.

In the beginning, it was extremely hard for Michelle because she hadn't got over her father's death. She felt as if she was just managing to put one foot in front of the other. However, thinking about her father also gave her the energy to not give up.

Harboring Hearts now works with a range of partner hospitals in New York and they help up to 140 families a year. They have also begun organising community events where heart patients can connect with and get support from people in the community who have been through a similar experience.

Michelle is very proud of what she has achieved – founding a charity organisation that has such a positive impact on heart patients and their families. It's a real safety net for families who need it.

UNIT 10

4 VOCABULARY Verbs of effort

a Notice the **bold** verbs in these examples from *Dream to help*. They are connected with the idea of making an effort to do something. Match the verbs with their meanings.

1. ☐ She first studied at Chulalongkorn University in Bangkok, then **pursued** graduate studies at Harvard University in the USA.
2. ☐ The first difficulty she had to **overcome** was creating an outstanding design.
3. ☐ With colleagues at LANDPROCESS, she **worked on** a submission …
4. ☐ Kotchakorn has also **stuck with** her idea of having more green spaces in Bangkok.
5. ☐ She felt that the best way to honour his memory and **cope** with her sadness was to set up a non-profit organisation.
6. ☐ She didn't have previous experience in that area, so it was a huge challenge for Michelle to **tackle**.
7. ☐ However, thinking about her father also gave her the energy to not **give up**.

a to succeed in controlling difficult circumstances
b continue trying hard to do something difficult
c try to achieve something, usually over a longer period of time
d spend time doing something to improve it
e try to do a difficult task
f stop doing something
g manage to live with something even though it's difficult

b Replace the verbs/phrases in *italics* with the correct form of the **bold** verbs/phrases in 4a.

1. When was the last time you had to *succeed in controlling* a difficult work or study problem?
2. What's something that you do regularly and wouldn't want to *stop doing*?
3. In your free time, is there something you're *spending time to improve*?
4. What's a personal goal in your life that you are *trying to achieve over time*?
5. How well do you *manage* in emergency situations?
6. What's a work or study problem you *tried hard to solve*?
7. Do you have a difficult task you're *trying to do* at the moment?

c Ask and answer the questions in 4b.

5 SPEAKING

a Think of someone you know who has done something you think is brave or amazing.

He/She could be:
- a relative
- a family friend
- a colleague
- someone well known in your country.

Make notes on this person's background and his/her achievement.

b Tell each other about the people you chose. What similarities are there between them?

10C EVERYDAY ENGLISH
Two things to celebrate today

Learn to describe how you felt
- P Consonant clusters
- S Interrupting and announcing news

1 LISTENING

a Discuss the questions.
1 When was the last time you celebrated something?
2 Was the celebration for yourself or for someone else?
3 How did you celebrate?

b Look at the photo. The tutor wants to speak to Tessa in his office. Why do you think he wants to see her?

c ▶ 10.10 Watch or listen to Part 1. Check your ideas.

d Answer the questions with the adjectives in the box.

delighted   pleased   surprised   worried

1 How does Tessa feel at first?
2 How does she feel after she hears the news?
3 How does the tutor feel? Why?

e ▶ 10.11 Watch or listen to Part 2. Which of these things are they celebrating?
1 It's Sam's birthday.
2 Tom and Becky have got married.
3 Tom and Becky have found a flat.
4 The café is making more money.
5 Emma has got a job.

f ▶ 10.11 Answer these questions. Watch or listen to Part 2 again if necessary.
1 What was Tom's 'quick decision'?
2 Why does Sam thank Emma and Phil?

2 PRONUNCIATION Consonant clusters

a ▶ 10.12 Look at the words below. The underlined consonant sounds are pronounced together. We call these 'consonant clusters'. Listen and repeat.

prize   pleased   celebrate

b ▶ 10.13 Underline the consonant clusters in the words below. Then practise saying the words. Listen and check.

flat   dreams   brilliant   crazy   frightened   flight
agree   Africa   glasses   asleep   climate

c ▶ 10.14 Look at the words with three consonant sounds together (three sounds, but not always three letters). Listen and underline them.

asked   balanced   scream   sixth   text   strength
lamps   hands   watched   spread

d Practise saying the words in 2b and 2c that are difficult for you.

3 LISTENING

a In Part 2, Becky said, 'There's something else we have to celebrate.' What do you think she'll say next?

b ▶ 10.15 Watch or listen to Part 3 and check. They celebrate three more things. What are they?

c Which person … ?
1 invites everyone to a celebration
2 cuts the cake
3 offers to buy everyone coffee
4 admires Phil's novel
5 admires Tessa's photos

122

UNIT 10

4 USEFUL LANGUAGE
Describing how you felt

a ▶10.16 Complete what Tessa says with the words in the box. Then listen and check.

| get | believe | can't | surprised | so | over | couldn't |

I _____ _____ it. I was _____ _____. First prize! I still _____ _____ _____ it.

b 💬 Discuss the questions.
1 How does Tessa say she felt?
   a happy   b disappointed   c surprised
2 Which word has the main stress in each sentence? Practise saying the sentences.

c Here are some more ways to describe how you felt.
1 I wasn't expecting it.   3 I was really pleased.
2 It was quite a blow.   4 I was expecting it.

Which mean … ?
a I was surprised.   c I was happy.
b I wasn't surprised.   d I was shocked or disappointed.

d Choose one of the situations below. Make notes to describe how you felt and why, but don't mention what happened! Use expressions in 4a and 4c.
1 Your boss called you into his office and said that you were fired.
2 You have won £10,000 on the lottery.
3 You didn't prepare for the exam and you failed it.
4 Your best friend told you he/she is getting married.
5 Someone stole your wallet.
6 You were promoted.

e 💬 Read out your sentences. Can other students guess the situation?

> I really wasn't expecting it.

> I was so surprised because I only bought one ticket.

> I still can't believe it.

5 CONVERSATION SKILLS
Interrupting and announcing news

a 📹 ▶10.15 Watch or listen to Part 3 again. Complete the remarks.
1 Hold _____.
2 There's something _____ we have to celebrate.
3 Hang _____ a minute.
4 I know you won't _____ this …
5 Just a _____.
6 One more _____.

b Which remarks … ?
1 are ways to stop people ending a conversation
2 are ways to show you are about to say something important

c Answer these questions.
1 At the end of each remark, does the voice … ?
   a stay high
   b go down
2 Does this show the other person … ?
   a that you've finished speaking
   b that you haven't finished speaking

d Practise saying the remarks.

6 SPEAKING

a Work in groups of four (A, B, C and D). You're in a restaurant. You each have an important piece of news to tell your group.

Student A: You've just been offered a new job.
Student B: You've won a free trip to Paris for two weeks.
Student C: You're getting married.
Student D: You've won a prize in a poetry competition.

Work alone and decide:
- what details you will give
- which expressions you will use in 4a, 4c and 5a.

b 💬 Have a conversation. Take it in turns to announce your news. Then continue talking until the next person interrupts.

✓ UNIT PROGRESS TEST
→ CHECK YOUR PROGRESS
You can now do the Unit Progress Test.

10D SKILLS FOR WRITING
I forced myself to be calm

Learn to write a narrative
W Making a story interesting

1 SPEAKING AND LISTENING

a Discuss the questions.
1 Have you ever performed activities like these in public? If so, what was it like? If not, how do you think it would feel?
2 What preparation is required to perform in public?
3 What do you think it takes to be successful in these activities?

b ▶10.17 Listen to Rosa speak to her teacher Kurt and answer the questions.
1 What is Rosa learning to play?
2 What's her ambition?
3 Does Kurt mention any of the ideas you discussed in 1a?

c ▶10.17 Listen again and make notes about the following topics.
1 Rosa's level of motivation
2 the three choices Kurt outlines
3 the way he suggests she could deal with pressure

d Discuss the questions.
1 What do you think Rosa should do? Give reasons for your answer.
2 Do you know of someone who has tried to excel in a demanding activity or job? What was their experience?
3 Do you think the sacrifices these people often need to make are worth it? Why / Why not?

ROSA'S DIARY

THE ULTIMATE GOAL

I sat in the dressing room and sighed. The moment had arrived. After months of hard practice, I was about to go on stage and perform in my first major competition. I looked at myself in the mirror. I looked like I could be a classical music pianist, but did I feel like one? There was a difference between the image I saw and what I felt when I closed my eyes.

I put my hands on my knees, breathing slowly to calm down. I repeated everything Kurt had told me, 'You've practised, you are well-prepared and you can do this.' But the thought that I would soon have to play for such a large audience was unnerving.

There was a knock at the door. It was the stage manager. Time for me to go on stage. I left the dressing room, feeling the butterflies in my stomach flutter more insistently. I walked along the corridor to the steps that led to the wings of the stage. As we walked slowly up the stairs, the stage manager wished me good luck. 'Can luck help me now?' I asked myself.

I stood in the wings, staring at the floor of the stage. I could hear the murmur of the audience – a wall of sound standing between me and the music. 'Ladies and gentlemen,' said the announcer. The murmur dissolved and there was quiet. My name was announced, and I stepped into a flood of light.

I took one step and was almost blinded by the stage lights. Where is the piano? I can't see anything! My heart was racing. But we had practised this at the rehearsal yesterday. You know the way. You know where to go and what you have to do.

I began to cross the space between the wings of the stage and the piano stool. The audience applauded and this wave of sound seemed to draw me across the stage. I tried to smile, but I'm not sure if I did. I eventually reached the piano and remembered to bow to the audience. I slowly took my seat on the stool, trying to keep my breathing regular. I forced myself to be calm. Silence. A moment of complete concentration.

I raise my hands and they float above the piano keys. I feel the adrenalin running through my body. Remember the final words of advice: go with the music, don't worry about mistakes and stay in the moment, stay in the music.

My fingers touch the piano keys and I begin to play. I still feel the adrenalin, but it's working for me. Everything is falling into place. The notes float from my hands and the warmth of the audience embraces me.

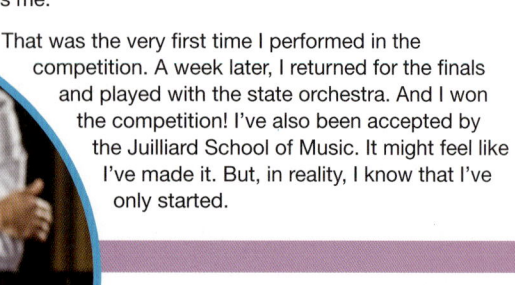

That was the very first time I performed in the competition. A week later, I returned for the finals and played with the state orchestra. And I won the competition! I've also been accepted by the Juilliard School of Music. It might feel like I've made it. But, in reality, I know that I've only started.

Rosa and Kurt

124

2 READING

a Read an excerpt from *Rosa's diary* and answer the questions.
1. What event does Rosa describe?
2. What is the dominant feeling?
3. What is the outcome?

b Read the diary again. Make notes about Rosa's thoughts, feelings and sensations at each of the following steps.
1. in the dressing room
2. from the dressing room to the wings
3. in the wings
4. moving across the stage
5. sitting at the piano

c Tell your partner about a time you had to do something that made you feel nervous.

3 WRITING SKILLS
Making a story interesting

a The writer uses various ways to make the story interesting. Find one more example of these in the story.
1. short sentences to describe Rosa's thoughts and feelings
   The moment had arrived.
2. questions to show what she was thinking
   … but did I feel like one?
3. phrases with verb + *-ing* to describe actions and events
   I put my hands on my knees, breathing slowly to calm down.

b Match the beginnings in A to the endings in B to make more sentences from 'first time' stories.

A
1. ☐ She dived into the water,
2. ☐ He stood up in front of the meeting,
3. ☐ She couldn't stop tuning the guitar,
4. ☐ He walked onto the football pitch,
5. ☐ She peered into the microscope,

B
a. looking down and pretending the crowd wasn't there.
b. playing nervously with his slide clicker.
c. hoping she'd be able to see more of the sample.
d. breathing in deeply before she jumped.
e. humming the first few notes of the song repeatedly.

c Choose one of the beginnings in A. Continue the story, using a new phrase with verb + *-ing*.

d Swap stories with a partner. Continue their story by adding a sentence of your own. Read the story back to your partner.

e Look at these examples. What verb tenses does the writer use?

I repeated to myself everything Kurt had told me …
My heart was racing. But we had practised this at the rehearsal yesterday.

Which tense does the writer use … ?
1. to tell the main events of the story
2. to refer to an earlier event that explains what happened

f Continue these sentences with your own ideas, using the past perfect tense.
1. When I opened the PowerPoint presentation on my laptop, all the slides were blank.
2. I opened my mouth to sing, but the microphone wasn't working.
3. When I hit the ball, it went sailing up into the crowd.
4. As I stepped onto the ice, I realised I wasn't wearing gloves.

4 WRITING

a Make notes about the first time you did something. It can be the same situation you talked about in 2c or a different situation. Use these ideas to help.
- where the event took place
- preparation for the event
- different steps you had to go through
- your feelings before and during the event
- any problems/obstacles you encountered
- the outcome

b Write your story. Remember to use …
- short sentences
- direct questions
- verb + *-ing*
- past perfect to explain the background actions.

c Read other students' stories.
1. Did they use all the writing skills suggested in 4b?
2. Which story was … ?
   - the most unusual
   - the greatest challenge
   - the most nerve-wracking
   - the most amusing

UNIT 10
Review and extension

1 GRAMMAR

a Complete the conversation using the verbs in brackets with a past modal of deduction.
   A Who left those flowers for us?
   B It ¹_____ (be) Rachel – she's away at the moment.
   A Janet ²_____ (leave) them – she occasionally surprises us like that.
   B Actually, it ³_____ (be) Elaine. She called this morning and said something about a surprise for us.
   A Well, whoever left them – they're beautiful.

b Imagine different past possibilities for the following situations. Make notes.
   1 You check your online bank account and find someone has deposited £100 into the account.
   2 You arrive home and find the front door wide open.
   3 You receive a parcel addressed to you containing a brand-new tablet and an anonymous card saying, 'Enjoy!'

c 💬 Discuss your different ideas.

d Put the verbs in brackets in the correct form.
   1 My business degree wasn't very interesting or useful when it came to finding a job. I wish I _____ (study) history at university instead.
   2 She didn't start studying Mandarin until she went to China. She should _____ (do) a course about six months before going there.
   3 In his new job, he has to interpret a lot of statistics. If only he _____ (pay) more attention in maths classes at school.

2 VOCABULARY

a Correct the adjective prefixes.
   1 She's very good with young children, but she can get a bit inpatient with teenagers.
   2 He left without saying goodbye – that's very unpolite.
   3 They made an inexpected visit to the children's hospital. It was a nice surprise for the patients.
   4 We were extremely missatisfied with the level of service we experienced during our stay.

b Complete the sentences using the correct verbs in the box.

   work   overcome   cope   tackle

   1 When I lived in Northern Australia, I found it easy to _____ with the heat.
   2 On Sundays I like nothing more than to _____ a really difficult crossword puzzle.
   3 He managed to _____ his shyness and make friends at university.
   4 My grammar's quite good – I just need to _____ on my pronunciation.

3 WORDPOWER way

a Match the *way* expression in 1–6 with the correct meanings in a–f.
   1 ☐ I'm sorry, but *there's no way* I can sign that contract – the conditions aren't clearly described.
   2 ☐ *One way or another,* we have to know all that vocabulary for the test.
   3 ☐ I thought it would be cheaper to go by bus than train, but it was *the other way round.*
   4 ☐ After a quick dinner, *we made our way* to the concert.
   5 ☐ I ran *all the way* around the park and I'm exhausted.
   6 ☐ *In some ways*, it would be easier to not go abroad on holiday this year.

   a We can't avoid it.
   b I can't do it.
   c We went there.
   d It's partly true.
   e the complete distance
   f the opposite

b Replace the incorrect *way* expressions. Tick (✓) the ones that are correct.
   1 ☐ We travelled in some ways to the end of the island.
   2 ☐ I thought she'd be nicer than her brother, but it was one way or another.
   3 ☐ I don't feel well and there's no way I can go out.
   4 ☐ All the way, it might be easier to talk to him than send an email.
   5 ☐ If you hear an alarm, please make your way towards the exit as quickly as possible.

c Answer the questions. Make notes.
   1 What's something that you would never do?
   2 When did you last go the whole distance somewhere?
   3 What's something you think is partly true?
   4 What's a situation where you found that the opposite was true?

d 💬 Discuss the situations in 3c. Use a *way* expression with each example.

⟲ REVIEW YOUR PROGRESS

How well did you do in this unit? Write 3, 2 or 1 for each objective.
3 = very well   2 = well   1 = not so well

I CAN ...	
speculate about the past	☐
discuss life achievements	☐
describe how I felt	☐
write a narrative.	☐

COMMUNICATION PLUS

2B

a Read the texts and check your answers to 1f on p. 24.

Wolf
If you see a wolf before it sees you, walk away silently. If the wolf sees you, back away slowly and avoid eye contact. Wolves see eye contact as a challenge. If the wolf runs towards you, don't run away because wolves are faster than you. Instead, turn to face the wolf. If the wolf attacks you, curl up in a ball or defend yourself with a stick. A wolf's nose is very sensitive, so if you hit it on the nose it will probably run away. Wolves are also easy to distract with food, so if you have some food, throw it to the wolf, then move slowly away, still facing the wolf.

Shark
Don't lie on the surface of the water in areas where there are sharks because this makes you look like a seal. Instead, try to stay vertical in the water. Sharks normally won't attack unless they smell your blood or they think you're food. So if a shark comes towards you, keep still or swim slowly towards the shark. As long as you don't panic, it will probably swim away. If the shark bites you, hit it in the eye.

Bear
In bear country, always wear a bell or hit trees with a stick to make a noise. This will make any bears that are near go away. If a bear comes towards you, lie on the ground and 'play dead'. Provided you stay absolutely still, the bear will lose interest. If you are on a hill, run away downhill, going from side to side. Bears find it hard to run fast downhill because they are so heavy and they can't turn quickly.

b Imagine that you had to encounter one of these three animals. Which would you choose? Why?

c ≫ Now go back to p. 24.

4A PAIR A

a Read about Rupesh Thomas. Use these questions to help you focus on the main points.
1 What was Rupesh's childhood like?
2 What was his dream?
3 What did he do at university and after he graduated?
4 What jobs did he have in London?
5 How did meeting Alexandra change his life?

Rupesh Thomas

Rupesh Thomas grew up in Kerala, in the south of India. Although he came from a humble background, he had a happy childhood. Still, ever since he was a young boy, he had always dreamed of travelling abroad, and especially of going to England. His father used to travel for his work and he once gave him a picture of London. He kept it in his room and as a child he would often look at it and dream of living there. When he was 18, he went university to study engineering, but he never wanted this to become his career so after graduating, he instead decided to follow his dream. He sold his motorbike, which was his only valuable possession, for £600 and used the money to buy a single ticket to London. Once he was in England, it took a long time and a lot of hard work to become successful. His first job was at McDonalds, where he earned £4 an hour. He also worked as a carer for elderly people and as a door-to-door salesman. Through hard work, he gradually worked his way up to become the manager of a sales company and it was there that the second event that changed his life happened. He met his wife, Alexandra, who loved drinking chai made in the traditional way with real tea leaves and spices. She used to make it herself and she would often drink ten cups of it a day. At that time, it wasn't available in London, and this gave them the idea of producing it themselves. So, they invested all their savings in a company, which they called TukTuk Chai. It has become so popular that it is now sold in shops all over the UK and internationally and has won several international awards.

Rupesh used to think that to be successful it was enough to follow your dream. He was right, but he is living proof that you also have to work hard to achieve what you want.

b ≫ Now go back to p. 44.

4C STUDENT A

a Prepare to give an opinion on one of the topics below. Plan what you will say about it.
- a recent sporting event
- a famous person
- your classroom

b 💬 Tell Student B your opinion about the topic you have chosen.

c 💬 Listen to Student B's opinion about their topic. Express careful disagreement. Use language in 4c on p. 51.

d ≫ Now go back to p. 51.

127

4C STUDENT A

a Look at the photos of Bogotá, Colombia. Imagine you visited this place. Prepare to present your photos to other students. Decide:
- what the photos show
- what you will say about them
- which expressions in 2a on p. 50 you can use.

Notes: The photos show Plaza de Bolívar in the heart of Bogotá, a cycling tour of city murals and your favourite café.

A

B

C

b Now go back to p. 50.

5C

a You're opening a café in your town. You want it to be different from other cafés. Make notes about:
- furniture
- food and drinks
- music and entertainment
- special things you could offer.

b Explain your ideas and respond to other students' ideas. Use language from 6a and 6c on p. 63.

c Now go back to p. 63.

4A PAIR B

a Read about Mark Pearson. Use these questions to help you focus on the main points.
1. What was Mark Pearson's childhood like?
2. How did winning the cookery competition change his life?
3. How did he get his idea for myvouchercodes.co.uk?
4. What did he do after he sold the company?
5. How did he spend his money?

Mark Pearson

Mark Pearson grew up in poverty in a small flat in Liverpool with his mother and younger sister, and he often used to get into trouble at school. It was only after he left school at sixteen and went to catering college that his life began to change for the better. He won a nationwide cookery competition, and this made it possible for him to leave Liverpool and get a job in a luxury hotel in London. A few years later, he was managing his own small chain of restaurants and was able to save £10,000 – an amount which seemed huge to him at the time. Using this money, he decided to start up his own web-based company, but he needed an idea. One day on a visit to his grandmother, he noticed she had an old fridge in her kitchen. She would save vouchers which offered discounts on things you could buy, and she would stick them on her fridge, so the fridge was covered in these vouchers.

This was a time when e-commerce was only just beginning, and his grandmother's fridge gave him his idea – instead of paper vouchers he could set up a company offering vouchers online. With the help of a programmer in India, he set up a website offering discount vouchers for products, which he called myvouchercodes.co.uk, and within a few years the site was earning over £10 million a year. A few years later, at the age of 32, he was able to sell his company for £55 million. Although he no longer needed to work, he decided to set up an investment company supporting young people who wanted to start a business. He remembered that when he was young, he used to be afraid that he would never find a good job, so now he wanted to show people that they could start up their own business too. And of course, his mother and sister don't live in a small flat any more – one of the first things he did with his money was buy them each a new house.

b Now go back to p. 44.

3C STUDENT A

a You need to buy a new jacket. You'd like Student B to come with you after class, because you need someone's advice on the best jacket to buy. You're not sure if Student B is keen on shopping. Perhaps suggest doing something nice as well, for example having a coffee together. Make careful suggestions and try to agree on what you can do after class.

b Now go back to p. 39.

Communication Plus

3C STUDENT B

a 💬 You'd like to go somewhere fun with Student A after class. You're not very keen on shopping unless it means going to a shop or department store that sells video games. It might be fun to go to a new juice bar that opened last week. You could also go to the cinema. Make careful suggestions and try to agree on what you can do after class.

b ⟫ Now go back to p. 39.

4C STUDENT B

a Prepare to give an opinion on one of the topics below. Plan what you will say about it.
- a film or book
- a café or restaurant
- the town/city you're in now

b 💬 Listen to Student A's opinion about their topic. Express careful disagreement. Use language in 4c on p. 51.

c 💬 Tell Student A your opinion about the topic you have chosen.

d ⟫ Now go back to p. 51.

5B

a Read the text and check your answers to the quiz in 1b on p. 59.

Antarctica is the fifth largest continent in the world and is completely surrounded by the Southern Ocean. It is approximately the size of the USA and Mexico. About 98% of Antarctica is covered by ice that averages 1.6 km in thickness. It is the coldest, driest and windiest continent in the world. Temperatures reach minimums of between –80 °C and –90 °C in the winter. The landscape is considered a kind of desert because there is very little rainfall. There are mountains, glaciers and rivers, but no trees or bushes. There is a variety of animal life on the continent, but the two most well known are penguins and seals. The continent is positioned around the southernmost point of the planet, the South Pole. The first person to reach the South Pole was the Norwegian Roald Amundsen.

b ⟫ Now go back to p. 59.

8B PAIR B

a Read the story and answer the questions.
1 Why was the art teacher given the job?
2 What was wrong with his CV?
3 Why did the head teacher fire him?

The Art Teacher

A school was looking for a new art teacher. They had received several applications, including one from a well-known local artist who also had many years' teaching experience. He made a good impression in the interview, so they offered him the job.

On his CV, he had listed an MA in art history. After the school employed him, they discovered that he had started an MA course but never finished it. His CV was clearly wrong.

The head teacher called him into her office and asked him about it. He explained that he hadn't finished the MA because he'd had to spend a year in the army. He had intended to write 'Course work completed for MA' – it was just a simple mistake.

The head teacher of the school was faced with a difficult decision. She didn't believe the art teacher, but he had already started working and he was doing a good job. However, after thinking it over, she decided to fire him.

b What do you think the head teacher should have done? What would you have done?

c ⟫ Now go back to p. 96.

5A

a Are you an optimist or a pessimist? Read the descriptions below to find out.

Your answers are mostly on the *Optimist* side of the scale.
You expect things to turn out well for you, and when you encounter problems, you believe you can overcome them. When things go well, you usually see it as the result of your own ability or hard work. When things go badly, you see it as just bad luck and expect it to be better next time.

Your answers are mostly on the *Pessimist* side of the scale.
You don't always expect things to turn out well for you, and when you encounter problems, you believe you are generally unlucky. When things go well, you usually see it as the result of chance or what other people have done. When things go badly, you see it as a result of your own weaknesses.

b ⟫ Now go back to p. 56.

6B PAIR A

a Prepare for a discussion. You believe that everything in the world changes and languages naturally die out. There's no point in trying to stop that from happening, and it doesn't really matter.

Use these arguments or prepare your own:
- In the modern world, everyone needs to speak a major world language.
- A lot of tribal languages are not adapted to modern life. They belong to a way of life that is dying.
- If young people speak a major language, they can travel and get jobs.
- Languages die because young people don't want to speak them. It's wrong to try to force them.

b ⟫ Now go back to p. 73.

9C STUDENT B

a 💬 Have two conversations.

Conversation 1
Your partner has got a surprise for you. Try to find out what it is. You like going to classical music concerts and the opera, but you're not very keen on the theatre. Try to be polite and grateful.

Conversation 2
Tell your partner you've got a surprise for them to do with a sports game. Make them try and guess. Eventually tell them it's free tickets for them to go to a basketball game. If your partner looks a little disappointed, check that they like basketball – you're sure they told you they did.

b ⟫ Now go to p. 112.

10A STUDENT A

a Read the story.

Separated twin boys with almost identical lives
Stories of identical twins are often incredible, but perhaps none more so than those of identical twin boys born in Ohio. They were separated at birth and grew up in different families. Unknown to each other, both families named them James. The boys grew up not even knowing each other, but they both became police officers and both married women named Linda. They both had sons, who one named James Alan and the other named James Allan. They both got divorced and then married again to women named Betty. They both owned dogs they named Toy. They met for the first time after 45 years.

b ⟫ Now go back to p. 118.

7C STUDENT A

a Imagine what you would do with the room shown in the picture. Think about:
- how you could use different parts of it (e.g., sleeping, working, watching TV)
- what furniture you might put in it
- where you could put different items (e.g., pictures, a TV, a computer).

b Draw a rough plan of the room to show what you would do. Think how you could use:
- expressions for imagining from 4a on p. 87.
- vague phrases from 5a and 5d on p. 87.

c 💬 Show Student B your plan and tell him/her how you imagine the room. Then listen to Student B and ask questions about his/her room.

d ⟫ Now go back to p. 87.

4C STUDENT B

a Look at the photos of Moscow, Russia. Imagine you visited this place. Prepare to present your photos to other students. Decide:
- what the photos show
- what you will say about them
- which expressions in 2a on p. 50 you can use.

Notes: The photos show Moscow State University, built in 1953.

b ⟫ Now go back to p. 50.

Communication Plus

8B

The researchers expected employees to be more likely to contact the wallet's 'owner' if it contained no cash, but might keep the wallets that did contain cash. They were surprised to find that the opposite happened. People were more likely to return the wallet when it contained more money: 71% of the wallets with the most cash were returned, 51% of those with a small amount of cash, and 40% of the wallets without cash. Also, people returned all the money and didn't keep any for themselves. Fear of being found out didn't seem to be a factor, as it made no difference whether or not there were surveillance cameras.

The researchers suggest two explanations for this. One is that we care about people losing things, and the more money they have lost, the more we care. But another explanation is that people don't want to see themselves as a thief, and the more money there is in the wallet, the more it would 'feel like stealing' if they didn't return it.

So it seems that people are more honest worldwide than you might think, and also that they care more about each other than you might expect.

⟫ Now go back to p. 95.

9C STUDENT B

a   Have two conversations.

Conversation 1
Student A is going to draw a picture in four steps. After each step use expressions in 2c (p. 110) to show that you're unsure what the picture is. Get Student A to explain or add more detail to the picture until you can guess what it is.

Conversation 2
Look at the guide to drawing a penguin. Follow the steps to draw your own penguin. Student A will try and guess what you are drawing. Be prepared to explain or add more detail.

What in the world is that?

I haven't got a clue what that is.

b   ⟫ Now go back to p. 110.

9C STUDENT A

a   Have two conversations.

Conversation 1
Tell your partner you have a surprise for them to do with entertainment. Make them try and guess. Eventually tell them it's free tickets for them to go and see *Hamlet*. If your partner looks a little disappointed, check that they like the theatre – you're sure they told you they did.

Conversation 2
Your partner has got a surprise for you to do with a sports game. Try to find out what it is. You like going to tennis games and football matches, but you're not very keen on basketball. Try to be polite and grateful.

b   ⟫ Now go to p. 112.

7B

a   This is a picture from a reality TV programme. Talk about the questions. What do you think? 
- Is the woman really suffering or is she acting?
- Would you like to be in her situation? Why / Why not?

b   ⟫ Now go back to p. 83.

9A STUDENT B

a   Describe your invention to Student A, but don't tell him/her what it is. Ask him/her to guess what the invention is. Use these expressions to help you.

This thing's made of …
You can hold it in your hand.
You can put it …
You can put something in it.
You can maybe find one in …
It might be useful after/when …

Portable Oxygen Booster
This portable oxygen booster increases available oxygen from 20% or lower up to 30%. You can use this in the office, while exercising or anywhere you feel the need for a bit of extra air.

Ultraviolet Steriliser 
This is an ultraviolet steriliser that can keep you from getting sick. You can use it to sterilise everyday things from computer keyboards to kitchen items and even beds. It uses ultraviolet radiation to kill bacteria. It's ideal for any home.

b   ⟫ Now go back to p. 106.

131

9A STUDENT A

a 💬 Describe your invention to Student B, but don't tell him/her what it is. Ask him/her to guess what the invention is. Use these expressions to help you.

You can hold it in your hand.
You can put it …
You can put something in it.
You can maybe find one in …
It might be useful after/when …

Anti-Snoring Pillow

This pillow uses a sensor to detect snoring and then responds by vibrating. Tests show that this is efficient in reducing snoring. In addition, the pillow has an internal recording device that allows you to record your snoring and monitor the effectiveness of the pillow.

Ear Dryer

You can use this to dry the inside of your ear after you've had a shower, bath or swim. You place the device in your ear and it blows hot air. The makers suggest you use it after you have dried your ears with a towel.

b ≫ Now go back to p. 106.

7C STUDENT B

a Imagine what you would do with the room shown in the picture. Think about:
- how you could use different parts of it (e.g., sleeping, working, watching TV)
- what furniture you might put in it
- where you could put different items (e.g., pictures, a TV, a computer).

b Draw a rough plan of the room to show what you would do. Think how you could use:
- expressions for imagining from 4a on p. 87.
- vague phrases from 5a and 5d on p. 87.

c 💬 Listen to Student A and ask questions about his/her room. Then show Student A your plan and tell him/her how you imagine your room.

d ≫ Now go back to p. 87.

9B

a Read the final part of the story about Barry Minkow.

While he was in prison, Barry Minkow became a new person (or so it seemed). He trained as a pastor and he wrote a book about his life, with the profits going to the people he owed money to. He was released from prison after only seven years.

After coming out of prison, Barry Minkow worked as a pastor. He also gave talks in schools about the mistakes he had made. He became well-known as a fraud expert, often appearing on TV, and he set up a company which investigated company fraud. At the time, very few people questioned whether he was really the reformed character that he claimed to be. It later turned out that he was making huge amounts of money from buying and selling shares in the companies he was 'investigating.' He was sentenced to five more years in prison.

While he was a pastor, he was very good at persuading people to donate money to the church, but after a while, some people began to wonder where their money was really going. Later, investigations showed that he had opened false bank accounts and tricked people into making donations to the church, which had actually gone into his own pocket. He was sentenced to five more years in prison for stealing more than $3 million from church members.

b ≫ Now go back to p. 107.

6A STUDENT B

a Read about the two tourist destinations. Make notes about them. Think about which you prefer and why.

b 💬 Tell Student A about the destination you prefer. Try to agree on which of your two destinations to visit. Use your notes from **a** to persuade your partner to visit your place.

HAMPI

This small village in South West India offers the chance to discover a whole new culture. Until 500 years ago, it was the capital of the Vijayanagara Empire. There's an astonishing number of monuments and ruins that belonged to this ancient civilisation. Perhaps the most impressive is the Virupaksha Temple. Hampi is a cultural experience like no other.

Rotorua

This small city in New Zealand is surrounded by a series of stunningly beautiful lakes and forests. But what makes it so special is all its geothermal activity. You can see hot steam shoot from the ground in the form of a geyser, while nearby a pool of mud boils away. Rotorua is dramatic and unique – it's well worth a visit.

c ≫ Now go back to p. 70.

Communication Plus

9C STUDENT A

a 💬 Have two conversations.

> **Conversation 1**
> Look at the guide to drawing a panda. Follow the steps to draw your own panda. Student B will try to guess what you are drawing. Be prepared to explain or add more details.

> **Conversation 2**
> Student B is going to draw a picture in four steps. After each step, use expressions in 2c (p. 110) to show that you're unsure what the picture is. Get Student B to explain or add more details to the picture until you can guess what it is.

What in the world is that?

I haven't got a clue what that is.

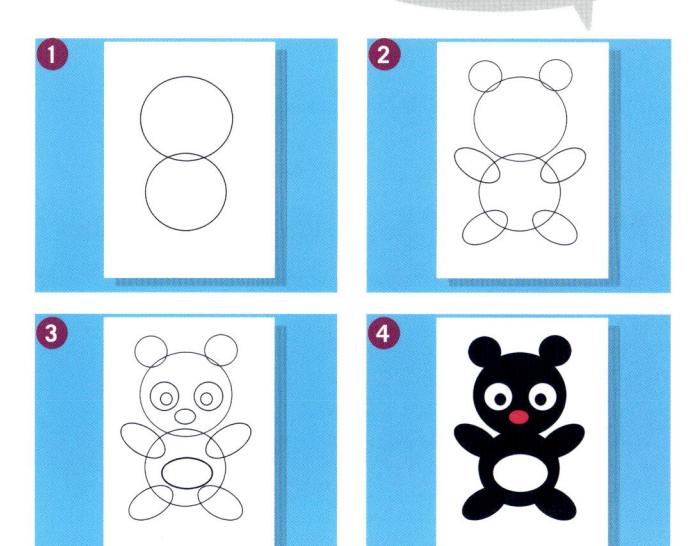

b ⟫ Now go back to p. 110.

6B PAIR B

a Prepare for a discussion. You believe that it's important to stop languages dying out. Every time we lose a language, we lose part of our culture.

Use these arguments or prepare your own:
- There's no reason why people shouldn't speak several languages: their own language and one or two 'bigger' languages.
- Languages die out because people feel ashamed of them. It's important to educate people to respect and value minor languages.
- The world needs variety – the world would be very boring if people all spoke one language.
- Many tribal languages contain knowledge about plants, medicines and the environment that could be very useful. We need to preserve this knowledge.

b ⟫ Now go back to p. 73.

6A STUDENT A

a Read about the two tourist destinations. Make notes about them. Think about which you prefer and why.

b 💬 Tell Student B about the destination you prefer. Try to agree on which of your two destinations to visit. Use your notes from **a** to persuade your partner to visit your place.

> **Dominica**
> A small but beautiful Caribbean island with superb beaches and tropical rainforests filled with exotic bird life. Dominica's biggest attraction is a boiling lake. After a three-hour trek through a stunningly beautiful forest, you come to a lake that is hot and steaming. No one knows about it yet, so go there before everyone else does!

> **Bornholm**
> Bornholm is Denmark's secret island in the Baltic Sea. You can get there easily by ferry or plane. Bornholm has a unique coastline with dramatic rock formations in the north, picturesque historic towns and dense forests. The island boasts the largest medieval fortification in Northern Europe as well as Denmark's tallest lighthouse.

⟫ Now go back to p. 70.

10A STUDENT B

a Read the story.

> **A falling boy caught twice by the same man**
>
> In Detroit, sometime in the 1930s, a baby fell from a window. But it fell onto a passerby, a man named Joseph Figlock. He broke the baby's fall and it survived unharmed.
>
> A year later, the same baby fell from the same window again. Once again, Joseph Figlock happened to be passing by. The baby fell on him again and the same thing happened!

b ⟫ Now go back to p. 118.

GRAMMAR FOCUS

1A Review of tenses

▶ 01.01

Present simple
We use the **present simple**:
- for habits, repeated actions, facts and things which are generally true
  I usually **do** my homework in the evening.
  She **writes** crime stories.
- with state verbs for short-term states, verbs of preference and verbs of the senses
  I **want** to go home.

Present perfect
We use the present perfect:
- for experiences in our life without saying when they happened
  I**'ve seen** this film three times.
- to focus on present states which started in the past and have continued up to the present
  I**'ve lived** here since I was a child.
- with *yet* in a question to ask if something is complete
  Have you **sent** it **yet**?
- with *already* in positive statements to show that something is complete, often before we expected
  I**'ve already posted** your parcel.
- to focus on past completed actions which are recent (often with *just*) or which have a connection with the present
  I**'ve just spoken** to Mark.

Present continuous
We use the **present continuous**:
- for actions in progress now (at the moment of speaking) or around now
  Sorry, I can't talk now – I**'m doing** my homework.
  She**'s writing** a book about her life.
- for temporary situations
  I**'m studying** English in Cambridge this summer, but normally I work in Milan.

Past simple
We use the past simple:
- to talk about completed past actions and states. We often specify the time in the past with the past simple
  I **lost** my phone last week, but then I **found** it in my car.

Past perfect
We use the past perfect:
- for actions and events that happened before a particular moment in time
  I decided to walk home because I **had forgotten** my bus pass.

Past continuous
We use the past continuous:
- to describe actions that were in progress at a particular moment in the past
  I **was writing** my essay at the start of the lesson.
- for actions or events in progress at the time of a shorter, past simple action (often with *while*, *when* and *as*)
  He phoned while I **was doing** my homework.

1B Questions

▶ 01.12 Positive and negative questions

Most questions have an auxiliary verb (e.g., *be*, *do*, *have* or modal verb) before the subject. The auxiliary verb can be positive or negative:
How **do** you spell that?   Why **isn't** my computer working?

Prepositions usually come at the end of questions.
Where are you **from**? NOT ~~From where are you?~~

In very formal questions they can go at the beginning.

> 💡 **Tip** We can make short questions from *who/what/where* + preposition:
> **A** I'm going to a party tonight. **B** Who with?
> **A** Can I borrow your phone? **B** What for? (= Why?)

We use negative questions to express surprise:
Haven't they **finished** yet? (= I'm surprised)

When we ask about the subject of a sentence, the word order doesn't change and we don't use an auxiliary verb.
Somebody wrote this book. → **Who** wrote this book?
NOT ~~Who did write this book?~~

▶ 01.13 Indirect questions

We use indirect questions to sound polite. Start indirect questions with *Can you tell me… / Do you know….* We don't use an auxiliary verb and the word order doesn't change. Use *if* in indirect *Yes/No* questions:
Why **did she become** famous? → **Do you know why** she became famous?
Do you like foreign films? → **Can you tell me if** you like foreign films?

We can also use indirect questions in sentences starting with:
I'm not sure … I know / don't know … I wonder … I can't remember … etc.
Is this answer correct? → **I'm not sure** if this answer is correct.
Where have they been? → **I wonder** where they've been.

> 💡 **Tip** We use **which** + **noun** when there is a limited number of options and **what** + **noun** when there are many possibilities:
> We can have our meeting at 10:00, 12:15 or 2:30. **Which time** would you prefer?
> I'm free all day. **What time** do you want to meet?

134

Grammar Focus

1A Review of tenses

a Correct the mistakes in the sentences. Think about spelling, tense and form.
1 I'm ~~studing~~ hard at the moment because ~~I try~~ to pass my final exams.   _studying, I'm trying_
2 Electric cars become more and more popular these days.
3 We looking for new members for our group. Do you want to join?
4 This food is tasting a bit strange. I think I prefer food from my own country.
5 We think of buying a new car, but they're costing a lot of money.
6 I write to apply for the job of sales assistant. I attach my CV with this email.

b Complete the sentences with the correct form of the verbs in brackets.
1 When I _____ (arrive) home yesterday, Sally already _____ (leave).
2 While my brother _____ (cook) yesterday evening, I _____ (watch) television.
3 I _____ (wait) for the plumber yesterday morning when he _____ (phone) me to cancel.
4 I _____ (be) to Istanbul twice in my life.
5 Robert _____ (stay) in my flat both this summer and last summer.
6 I _____ (move) to Singapore in 2014 to work abroad for a year.

c ⟫ Now go back to p. 9.

1B Questions

a Choose the best word or phrase to complete each question.
1 Where *we are / are we* going to eat?
2 What *you thought / did you think* of the film? Did you enjoy it?
3 We have cheese sandwiches and egg sandwiches. *What / Which* one do you prefer?
4 Why *you didn't / didn't you* call me?
5 I hear you're a musician. *What / Which* kind of music do you play?
6 **A** I got this watch for my birthday. **B** *Who from? / What from?*
7 What *happened / was happened* to the window?

b Write questions about the underlined words and phrases.
1 _____Who discovered pulsars?_____   <u>Jocelyn Bell-Burnell</u> discovered pulsars.
2 _____   She's interested in <u>classical</u> music.
3 _____   <u>Over 2,000</u> people watched the game.
4 _____   They haven't started yet <u>because they're waiting for you</u>.
5 _____   My <u>left</u> foot hurts.
6 _____   She heard the news from <u>Ralph</u>.

c Rewrite the sentences and questions using the prompts.
1 What do you want?
  I don't know _____what you want._____
2 Why didn't they come back?
  I wonder _____
3 Where are they going?
  Where do you think _____
4 Have you ever met him?
  Can you tell me _____
5 Who wrote this story?
  Do you know _____
6 Does this pen work?
  I wonder _____
7 What's your sister's name?
  Can you tell me _____
8 When will it be ready?
  When do you think _____

d ⟫ Now go back to p. 13.

135

2A Narrative tenses

We use narrative tenses to tell stories about what happened in the past. The most important narrative tenses are past simple, past continuous, past perfect and past perfect continuous.

▶ 02.05
We use the past simple for completed past actions and states which happened at a specific time in the past:
We **spotted** them on the mountain, so we **rescued** them and **took** them to hospital.

We use the past continuous for activities (not states) in progress at the time of the main events in the story. They often provide background description:
When we spotted them, they **were standing** next to some stones. They **were waving** their arms, but we couldn't hear what they **were shouting**.

We use the past perfect / past perfect continuous for events and activities that happened before the main events in the story and to give explanations or reasons. It often occurs after *because*:
We spotted them because they **had built** the word 'HELP' out of stones.
We finally spotted them after we **had been searching** for over a week.

Past perfect or past perfect continuous?

We use the past perfect:
- to focus on the results of an earlier completed action
  We **spotted** them (result) because they**'d built** a big sign (earlier action).
- to talk about 'time up to then' with a <u>state</u> verb (e.g., *know, have, be*)
  When we found them, they**'d been** on the mountain for a week.

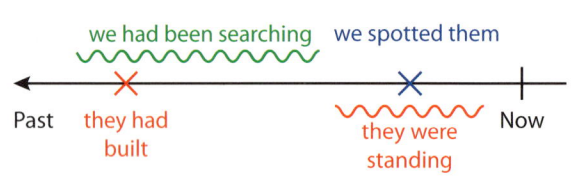

We use the past perfect continuous:
- before a result in the past to show the effect of an earlier activity
  They **were tired** (result) because they**'d been building** a big sign (earlier activity).
- to emphasise the duration of time with an <u>action</u> verb (e.g., *wait, search, drive*)
  We found them after we**'d been searching** for a week.

After we**'d been searching** for them for over a week, we finally **spotted** them on the mountain. They **were** standing next to the word 'HELP', which **they'd built** out of stones.

2B Future time clauses and conditionals

We use future time clauses to talk about future possibilities, future plans or to give advice. We can normally use *will*, *be going to* or the imperative in the main clause.

We normally use a present tense in the subordinate clause with words like *if*, *when*, *as soon as*, *unless*, *as long as*, *provided*, *in case*. We can also use the same time clauses to talk about facts and things which are generally true. In these sentences we often use a present tense verb in the main clause.

▶ 02.06
When we **go** hiking next weekend, we'll try a new path.
If you **see** a bear, don't run.
It won't attack you **provided** you**'re standing** still.
Unless you know the way well, **bring** a map.
Always bring a snack **in case** you **get** hungry.
As soon as it **gets** too cold, we'll go home.

> **Tip**
> When *if* means *whether*, we normally need *will* or *going to* to refer to the future:
> I don't know **if/whether** I**'ll** see any wild animals when I'm on holiday.
> NOT … ~~if I see~~ …

▶ 02.07 *as soon as*
As soon as shows that something will happen immediately after another thing:
  As soon as I get home, I'll email you.

> **Tip**
> We can use present simple or present perfect after words like *as soon as* or *when* to talk about completed processes in the future. There is little difference in meaning:
>   We'll leave **when / as soon as I finish** my work. (Or: … **I've finished** …)

▶ 02.08 *if*, *unless*, *as long as*, *provided* and *in case*
Unless means *if not*. The verb after *unless* is usually positive:
You won't see any animals **unless** you **stay** quiet.
(= You won't see any animals if you don't stay quiet.)

As long as and *provided* are similar to *only if*:
We'll be safe **provided** / **as long as** we stay here.
(= But only if we stay here.)
You can go out tonight **as long as** you're back by 10. (= But only if you're back by 10.)

We use *in case* to talk about preparations for possible future situations:
Take your keys **in case** we're out when you get home.

Don't worry! She **won't** attack you **unless** she **thinks** you're scared.

Grammar Focus

2A Narrative tenses

a Complete the sentences with the past simple or past continuous form of the verbs in brackets.

1. While he __was walking__ (walk) in the forest, he __tripped__ (trip) and __cut__ (cut) his knee.
2. I __didn't notice__ (not / notice) what the thief __was wearing__ (wear) because I __was hiding__ (hide) under the desk the whole time. [had been hiding]
3. When I __got__ (get) home, everyone __was watching__ (watch) TV. Nobody __even said__ (even / say) 'Hello'.
4. **A** Where __were you__ (you / be) when you __heard__ (hear) the news?
   B I __was__ (be) on the bus – I __was travelling__ (travel) to work.
5. Fortunately, I __didn't hurt__ (not / hurt) myself when I __fell__ (fall) because I __was wearing__ (wear) a helmet.
6. **A** What page number __did ... say__ (the teacher / just / say)?
   B Sorry, I __wasn't / didn't hear__ (not / hear) anything. I __didn't ... listening__ (not / listen).

b Choose the best verb forms.

1. She was out of breath because *she'd run* / *she'd been running*.
2. It was sad to sell my old car – *I'd had* / *I'd been having* it since I was a student.
3. The party was great. *They'd planned* / *They'd been planning* it for months.
4. We were really pleased because *we'd finished* / *we'd been finishing* our project.
5. The race was cancelled because it *had rained* / *had been raining* for days and the streets were flooded.
6. How long *had they known* / *had they been knowing* each other when they decided to get married?
7. They weren't very happy because *they'd waited* / *they'd been waiting* for six hours.
8. I didn't watch the film because *I'd already seen* / *I'd already been seeing* it four times.

c Choose the best verb forms.

It [1]*happened* / *had happened* on the last day of our holiday. We [2]*were getting* / *got* up and [3]*saw* / *were seeing* that, at last, the sun [4]*was shining* / *had shone*. We [5]*were leaving* / *left* the hotel and [6]*were starting* / *started* walking along the narrow cliff path. Then, after [7]*we'd been walking* / *we walked* for about two hours, the path [8]*was suddenly becoming* / *suddenly became* much narrower – it was no more than 10 cm wide. There [9]*had been being* / *had been* a storm the previous night, and the sea [10]*had washed* / *was washing* part of the path away.

The cliff wasn't very high, so [11]*we'd decided* / *we decided* to keep going, along the narrow path. I [12]*went* / *was going* first, and [13]*had made* / *made* it safely to the other side. But then I [14]*was hearing* / *heard* a shout and a splash. Mike [15]*had fallen* / *fell* into the sea below. There were sharp rocks all around him, but luckily [16]*he'd landed* / *he'd been landing* safely in the water, and [17]*wasn't hurting* / *hadn't hurt* himself. So I [18]*climbed* / *was climbing* down the cliff to help him to safety.

Later, back at the hotel, he [19]*had been explaining* / *explained* what had gone wrong: [20]*he'd been trying* / *he tried* to take a selfie at the time of his fall.

d ≫ Now go back to p. 22.

2B Future time clauses and conditionals

a Tick (✓) the correct sentences. Correct the mistakes.

1. ☐ I'll send you a postcard when ~~we'll be~~ on holiday.   incorrect   we're
2. ✓ We'll come out as soon as we finish dinner.
3. ☐ My parents don't mind if I go out as long as I'll tell them where I'm going.
4. ☐ You won't pass the exam unless you don't study harder.
5. ☐ If it's still raining when you'll finish work, I'll pick you up.
6. ☐ I'm going to leave my laptop at home in case it'll get damaged.
7. ☐ I lend you my car provided you won't drive too fast.

b Join the sentences using the words in brackets.

1. Maybe I'll see Joseph. I'll tell him to call you. (if)   I'll __tell Joseph to call you if I see him.__
2. She'll finish university. She wants to be a teacher. (when)   She _____.
3. They'll be late if they don't hurry up. (unless)   They'll _____.
4. I'll check your work. Then I'll send it back to you immediately. (as soon as)   I'll _____.
5. You can take photographs but you mustn't use a flash. (provided)   You _____.
6. You should take some money because you might need to take a taxi. (in case)   You _____.
7. He won't bite you, but you must be careful. (as long as)   As _____.
8. You'll only understand if you listen very carefully. (unless)   You _____.

c ≫ Now go back to p. 24.

137

3A Multi-word verbs

▶ 03.03 Multi-word verbs consist of a verb and one or two particles:
We **came up with** some good ideas and decided to **try** them **out**.

Sometimes the meaning of the multi-word verb is clear from the meaning of the verb and the particle (e.g., *sit down*), but often you have to learn the meaning of each multi-word verb.

Transitive and intransitive multi-word verbs
- Transitive multi-word verbs need an object. The object can come before the particle (e.g., *throw **sth** away*) or after the particle (e.g., *look after **sb***), depending on the type of multi-word verb.
- Intransitive multi-word verbs don't have an object, e.g., *go away* NOT *go somebody away*.

Type 1 has no direct object (intransitive): verb + particle	wake up; go away; fall down; stay up; break up; sit down; take off; calm down
Type 2 has an object (transitive): verb + noun/pronoun + particle OR verb + particle + noun/pronoun	wake sb up; take sth off, calm sb down; try sth out; figure sth out; make sth up; throw sth away; pick sth up; let sb down
Type 3 has an object (transitive): verb + particle + noun/pronoun	look into sth; focus on sth; believe in sth; live for sth; be into sth; look after sb
Type 4 has two particles and always has an object: verb + particle 1 + particle 2 + noun/pronoun	come up with sth; look down on sb; look up to sb; run out of sth; fall out with sb; go on about sth; get away with sth

💭 **Tip** Many multi-word verbs are both transitive and intransitive (e.g., *wake up*; *give up*; *take off*; *calm down*):
When you **wake up** (intransitive), try not to **wake the dog up** (transitive) too!
After the plane **took off** (intransitive), I **took my shoes off** (transitive).
Use a dictionary to find out if a multi-word verb is transitive or intransitive.

Type 2 multi-word verbs
When the object is a long noun phrase, it normally comes after the particle:
Please throw away those old shoes that are nearly falling apart!
When the object is a pronoun (e.g., *it, me, sb*), it almost always comes before the particle:
Those shoes are really old. Please throw them away! NOT *Please throw away them!*
When the object is a short noun phrase (e.g., up to three words), it can come before or after the particle:
Please throw those old shoes away. / Please throw away those old shoes.

3B Present perfect and present perfect continuous

▶ 03.08 We use the **present perfect**:
- to talk about experiences without saying when they happened
  He's tried to run a marathon four times in his life.
- for experiences during any present period of time
  What have you learnt so far this year?
- with superlatives
  She's the nicest person I've ever met.
- for recent completed actions which have a result in the present
  Oh no! I've broken my key.
- with *already, just* and *yet*
  I've already done the shopping, I've just put the food in the oven, but I haven't laid the table yet.
- to talk about *how long* with state verbs (with *for/since*)
  I've known them for years, but I haven't seen them since January.
- with *how many, how much* and *how often* to talk about experiences
  How many essays have you written?

We use the **present perfect continuous**:
- when a recently completed action has a result now
  She's tired because she's been training hard.
- to describe repeated activities which started recently
  I've been going to the gym a lot recently.
- to talk about unfinished activities using *how long* and *for/since*
  We've been walking since the sun came up.

Grammar Focus

3A Multi-word verbs

a Choose the correct sentences. Sometimes more than one sentence is correct.
  1 a I don't **believe in** these new language learning techniques.
     b I don't **believe** these new language learning techniques **in**.
     c I don't **believe in** them.
     d I don't **believe** them **in**.
  2 a Do you want **to** try the new guitar I got for my birthday **out**?
     b Do you want to **try out** the new guitar I got for my birthday?
     c Do you want to **try out** it?
     d Do you want to **try** it **out**?
  3 a We've **fallen out** with our neighbours.
     b We've **fallen with** our neighbours **out**.
     c We've **fallen** them **out with**.
     d We've **fallen out with** them.
  4 a Did you **make up** that story?
     b Did you **make** that story **up**?
     c Did you **make up** it?
     d Did you **make** it **up**?

b Rewrite these sentences replacing the words in **bold** with multi-word verbs.
  Use a verb from A and one or two particles from B.

  A
  ~~come~~ be go take look let figure run

  B
  ~~up~~ into out off about of ~~with~~ into out down on

  1 How did you **invent** a name for your shop?   _How did you come up with a name for your shop?_
  2 Have you **investigated** the cause of the accident?   _Have you looked into the ...?_
  3 I've **liked** jazz since I was at university.   _I've been into jazz ...?_
  4 I hope we don't **use all of** this food.   _I hope we don't run out of food._
  5 I hate to **disappoint** you.   _I hate to let you down._
  6 I can't **understand** it.   _I can't figure it out._
  7 I know I was wrong. Stop **repeating** it!   _... Stop going on about it_
  8 Do you think this product will **be successful**?   _Do you think this product will take off?_

c ⟫ Now go back to p. 34.

3B Present perfect and present perfect continuous

a What are the most likely combinations? Match the sentence halves.
  1 ☐ I'm really proud of myself because …   a I've been building a wall in my garden.
  2 ☐ I'm exhausted lately because …   b I've built a wall in my garden.

  3 ☐ They've been on holiday …   a three times this year.
  4 ☐ They've been going on holiday …   b to the same place for 20 years.

  5 ☐ I've written …   a six emails already.
  6 ☐ I've been writing …   b emails all morning.

  7 ☐ She's been playing …   a tennis twice this week.
  8 ☐ She's played …   b a lot of tennis recently.

b Tick (✓) the correct sentences. Correct the mistakes.
  1 ✓ How long have you worked here?
  2 ✗ Please don't come in – we ~~haven't been finishing~~ yet.   _haven't finished_
  3 ☐ Have you ever been sailing?
  4 ☐ We've been giving three presentations this week.
  5 ☐ This room has been empty since our son left home.
  6 ☐ I've been watching a lot of films lately … maybe too many.
  7 ☐ I haven't been hearing that old song since I was a child.
  8 ☐ Those people have been calling me five times today.

c Complete the sentences with the correct form of the verbs in brackets. Use the present perfect or the present perfect continuous.
  1 I _'ve just spent_ (just / spend) over £200 on tennis lessons for you, and now you're saying you don't like tennis!
  2 Can you hurry up? We _____ (wait) for ages!
  3 How long _____ (you / study) to become a doctor?
  4 She _____ (not / say) a word all day – I think she's angry with me.
  5 _____ (you / clean) the car yet, or is it still dirty?
  6 A Your eyes are red. _____? (you / cry) B No, I _____ (chop) onions!

d ⟫ Now go back to p. 37.

139

4A used to and would

▶ 04.01 **used to and would**
We often use *used to* to describe past situations. In general, these situations continued for a long time and are not true now. They can be states (e.g., *like, live, have*) or habits (= repeated actions):
*When I was a child, I **didn't use to** like vegetables, but now I love them.*
*When we were students, we **used to** go dancing every week.*

We can also use *would* to describe past habits. Don't use *would* for past states:
*When we were students, we**'d go** dancing every week.*

We often use a mixture of *used to, would* and the past simple when talking about our past:
*When I was young, we never **used to** go on holidays. Instead, we**'d spend** the whole summer playing in the fields near our house. We **loved** it.*

> **Tip** To make negative and question forms of *used to*, remember to drop the final *-d* ending from *used*.
> *He didn't **use to** drink black coffee.* NOT *He didn't used to…*
> *Did you **use to** live in London?* NOT *Did you used to…*

▶ 04.02 **no longer and any more**
We use *no longer* before a positive verb or after *be*:
*We **no longer** go to the old forest. It's **no longer** there.*
We use *any more* at the end of a sentence with a negative verb:
*We **don't** go to the old forest **any more**. It's **not** there **any more**.*

▶ 04.03 **Comparing the past and the present**
Don't confuse *used to* with *be/get used to*. They have very different meanings:
*I **used to** study for many years.* (= This was my habit in the past.)
*I'm **getting used to** working in an office.* (= It's becoming normal for me now.)
*I'**m used to** the job now.* (= It's normal for me. It's not difficult.)
After *be/get used to*, we use a gerund or a noun phrase.

> **Tip** We can also use *usually* + the present simple to talk about habits in the present tense:
> *I **usually get up** at 6:30 am.*

Before I made my fortune, I'd cycle to work every day. I really miss that.

4B Obligation and permission

▶ 04.10

	Making rules / Giving advice	Describing someone else's rules	
		Present	**Past**
Strong positive obligation	You **must** wear a helmet. I won't let you ride without one.	You **have to / need to** wear a helmet. It's the law.	We **had to / needed to** wear a helmet to go on the motorbike.
Strong negative obligation	You **must not / mustn't** remove your helmet. It's dangerous.	We're **not allowed to / can't** remove our helmets. The instructor says so.	We **weren't allowed to** remove our helmets.
Mild obligation	I think you **should / ought to** give the money back.	I'**m supposed to** give the money back, but I don't want to.	I **was supposed to** give the money back, but I forgot.
No obligation	You **don't have to / don't need to / needn't** buy a ticket.		You **didn't have to / didn't need to** buy a ticket.
Permission	Yes, it's OK, you **can** go home.	I **can / I'm allowed to** go home now.	I **could / was allowed to** go home before 5 pm.
No permission	No, I'm sorry. You **cannot / can't** go home yet.	I **can't / I'm not allowed to** go home yet.	I **couldn't / I wasn't allowed to** go home early.

- *must* and *mustn't* are very strong. In most situations, it's more natural to use *have to, need to, needn't, can't, be not allowed to*, etc. Questions with *must* are very rare.
- *should* is much more common than *ought to*. Questions and negatives with *ought to* are very rare.
- *Need to* has a similar meaning to *have to*: *You don't need to show your passport at the border but you need to have some kind of ID with you.*

▶ 04.11 **make and let; be forced to and be allowed to**
make and *let* are special because they are followed by an object + infinitive without *to*:
*They **made** me **pay** extra.* NOT *They made me to pay extra.*
*They **let** me **come** in for free.* NOT *They let me to come in for free.*
We often use the verbs *force* and *allow* in passive constructions. Both are followed by *to* + infinitive:
*I **was forced to pay** extra.* (Less common: *I **was made to pay** extra.*)
*I **was allowed to come in** for free.* NOT *I was let come in for free.*

Grammar Focus

4A used to and would

a Tick (✓) the possible forms in the sentences. More than one answer is sometimes possible.
1 She _____ good at maths when she was little.
   a ✓ used to be   b ☐ would be
2 Laura was my best friend – we _____ for hours every day.
   a ✓ used to talk   b ✓ would talk
3 I _____ five swimming competitions when I was at school.
   a ✓ won   b ☐ would win
4 Our teacher, Mr Williams, was very strict. He _____ allow us to speak at all during class.
   a ☐ didn't use to   b ✓ wouldn't
5 I'll never forget the time I _____ my leg. I couldn't walk for weeks!
   a ☐ used to break   b ✓ broke
6 We _____ a dog, but he died about five years ago.
   a ✓ used to have   b ☐ would have

b Choose the correct forms.
1 I *used to* / would be really good at football when I was young, but now I'm terrible at it.
2 I *didn't use to* / didn't used to like jazz, but now it's my favourite kind of music.
3 I used to / *'m used to* living on my own. It was strange at first, but now it's fine.
4 I don't think I'll ever *get used to* / get use to writing on a tablet computer – it's much easier on a laptop.
5 Where did you *use to go* / used to go on holiday when you were a child?
6 How long did it take you to *get used to* / used to working from home?

c ⟫ Now go back to p. 45.

4B Obligation and permission

a Rewrite the sentences using the words in brackets.
1 You can wear whatever you want. (need to)   _____ You don't need to wear _____ a uniform.
2 I think you should write to them. (ought)   I think _____.
3 They made me give them my phone. (forced)   They _____.
4 They won't let you park there. (allowed)   You aren't _____.
5 You don't have to stay here. (can)   _____ if you like.
6 They advised us to bring strong shoes. (supposed)   We _____.
7 I wasn't allowed to use a dictionary. (let)   They _____.
8 It was raining so we were forced to stop. (made)   The rain _____.

b Look at the rules for a computer training course. Andy explains the rules to his friend Dan. Complete the conversation with one word or a contraction (e.g., *can't*) in each gap.

- All users must change their passwords after first logging in.
- You are not allowed to access the computer system without a new password.
- You can choose your own password.
- Your new password must be at least 20 characters long.
- Your password should be easy to remember, but it shouldn't be easy to guess.
- You must not tell anyone else your password.

Dan: So how was the course?
Andy: It was OK, but the security was really tight. We ¹ _had / needed_ to change our password straight away.
Dan: Why?
Andy: They said we ² _____ access the system without a new one. We were ³ _____ to choose our own passwords, but it ⁴ _____ to contain at least 20 characters.
Dan: Wow … that's long!
Andy: Yes, but it was ⁵ _____ to be something that's easy to remember.
Dan: OK, so the name of your football team then?
Andy: No, it was ⁶ _____ to be something that's not easy to guess.
Dan: So what was it?
Andy: I ⁷ _____ tell you! We're not ⁸ _____ to tell anyone else!

c ⟫ Now go back to p. 49.

141

5A Future probability

We use a wide range of modal verbs, adverbs, adjectives, etc. to describe what we think is the probability of future events.

Degree of probability	Modal verbs and adverbs	Other expressions	Adjectives
100% high	We **will** go. We **will certainly** go.	I'**m sure** we'll go.	It's **certain** that we'll go.
	We **will probably** go. We **will likely** go. We **could well** go.		It's (very) **likely** that we'll go.
50% medium	We **could** go. We **may** go. We **might** go.	There's a (good) **chance** that we'll go.	It's **possible** that we'll go.
	We **probably won't** go.	I **don't think** we'll go. I **doubt if** we'll go.	It's (very) **unlikely** that we'll go.
0% low	We **won't** go. We **certainly won't** go.	There's **no chance** that we'll go. I **can't imagine** that we'll go.	

▶ **05.06** **Positive and negative forms**
In positive sentences, we can use *may*, *might* or *could*. In negative sentences, we can use *may not* or *might not*:
We **may / might / could** go out on Friday. (= Perhaps we'll go out.)
We **may not / might not** go out on Friday. (= Perhaps we won't go out.)
Don't use *couldn't* here. *Couldn't* usually refers to things we weren't able to do in the past:
We **couldn't** go out on Friday. (= We weren't able to go out last Friday.)

Position of adverbs
Adverbs like *certainly* and *probably* come after *will* but before *won't*:
It'**ll probably** be a nice day today, but it **probably won't** be nice tomorrow.

▶ **05.07** **Adjective + *to* + infinitive**
With the adjectives *sure/likely/unlikely/certain/bound* we can use the pattern *be + adjective + to + infinitive*:
They'**re sure to be** late. (= I'm sure that they'll be late.)
He'**s certain/likely/unlikely to see** you.
They'**re bound to know** the answer. (= I'm sure someone knows the answer.)
 99% chance

5B Future perfect and future continuous

▶ **05.09** **Future perfect**

Positive	Negative	Question	Short answer
We'**ll have left**.	She **won't have left**.	**Will** they **have left**?	Yes, they **will**. / No, they **won't**.

We use the future perfect to describe what we expect to happen before a specific time in the future:
*I don't know exactly when somebody will buy my car. I hope I'**ll have sold** it by the end of the month.*

> **Tip** We often use future perfect with *by*.
> We'**ll have finished by Friday / by the time** they get here.

▶ **05.10** **Future continuous**

Positive	Negative	Question	Short answer
He'**ll be driving**.	We **won't be driving**.	**Will** you **be driving**?	Yes, I **will**. / No, I **won't**.

We use the future continuous for activities that will be in progress around a particular time in the future:
*Don't phone me at 5 pm. I'**ll** still **be driving** home from work at that time.*

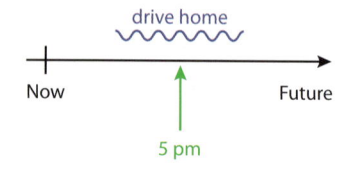

We can also use the future continuous to talk about actions that will be future routines:
*It'll be tough in my new job – I'**ll be getting** up at 4 am every day.*

A third use of the future continuous is to talk about planned actions in the future:
*I'**ll be staying** at my grandparents' house over the holidays.*

*I don't know exactly when somebody will buy my car. I hope I'**ll have sold** it by the end of the month.*

Grammar Focus

5A Future probability

a Complete the sentences with the words from the box. Use each word once.

> can't chance if likely may no probably doubt think sure

1. I'll _probably_ get up at about 8 am tomorrow.
2. I don't _think_ I'll ever see them again.
3. It's very _likely_ that you'll get a better job soon.
4. I _can't_ imagine that they'll move to another country.
5. There's _no_ chance that we'll win, but we can try.
6. That _may_ well be the best idea.
7. I'm _sure_ you'll have a brilliant time.
8. I _doubt_ if many people would be interested.
9. There's a good _chance_ that I'll be back before 10.
10. I doubt _if_ they'll be able to fix my printer.

b Rewrite the sentences using the words in brackets. Keep the meaning the same as the original.

1. It's certain that he'll pay you. (to)
   He's _certain to pay you._
2. It's very unlikely that we'll leave. (probably)
   We _probably won't leave_.
3. He'll certainly win a medal. (bound)
   He's _bound to win a medal_.
4. These new phones are probably not going to sell well. (unlikely)
   It's _very unlikely that these new phones will sell well_.
5. It's possible that she won't notice. (might)
   She _might not notice_.
6. I'm sure there'll be another chance. (to be)
   There's _going to be another chance_. _sure_

c ▶▶ Now go back to p. 58.

5B Future perfect and future continuous

a Tick (✓) the correct sentences. Correct the mistakes.

1. ☐ I'd prefer to visit you in August because I'll be finishing my exams then. — _incorrect I'll have finished_
2. ✓ I don't want to be late – they'll have eaten all the food before we get there!
3. ☐ I can't take you to the airport at 10 because I'll have attended a very important meeting at that time. — _be attending_
4. ☐ The presentation is scheduled for the 15th, so I'm sure I'll be writing it then. — _I'll have written_
5. ☐ Thursday is the best day to call me at home because I'll have worked from home then. — _I'll be working_
6. ✓ I can pass the message on to Arthur – I'll be seeing him tomorrow at university.
7. ☐ A How will I recognise you at the airport?
   B I'll have carried a sign with your name on it. — _I'll be carrying_
8. ✓ A I can't access the Internet right now.
   B Try again in ten minutes – hopefully it'll be working again then.

b Look at Christina's calendar for tomorrow. Complete her conversation with Zofia with the future continuous or future perfect form of the verbs in brackets.

ZOFIA   So, what time can I come and visit you tomorrow? How about 8:30?
CHRISTINA   No, sorry, ¹ _I'll still be taking_ (I / still / take) the kids to school at that time.
ZOFIA   OK, so maybe when you're back home. ² _____ (you / get) back by 9:30?
CHRISTINA   Yes, probably. But ³ _____ (I / still / deal) with my emails then. I have some urgent emails that I need to reply to. But you could come at about 11. I'm sure ⁴ _____ (I / finish) by then. Does that suit you?
ZOFIA   Er … not really. Could we make it a bit later? How about 2:00?
CHRISTINA   Yes, that's fine, but it'll only give us an hour. ⁵ _____ (I / leave) at 3:00 to pick the kids up from school.
ZOFIA   OK, yes, an hour should be perfect. Oh, one thing. Can you lend me that book you were telling me about?
CHRISTINA   Well, Hannah's got it at the moment. She wants to read it tonight. But ⁶ _____ (I / see) her tomorrow, so I can ask her to bring it. ⁷ _____ (she / finish) it by then.

Monday
8:00 – 9:00 Take children to school
9:00 – 10:45(?) Deal with emails
12:30 – 2:00 Meet Hannah
3:00 – 4:00 Pick up children from school

2. Will you have gotten back?
3. I'll still be dealing
4. I'll have finished
5. I'll be leaving
6. I'll be seeing
7. She'll have finished

c ▶▶ Now go back to p. 61.

143

6A Infinitives and -ing forms

▶ 06.03 verb + -ing
We use verb + -ing:
- as (part of) the subject of a sentence
  Swimming is good for you. / **Meeting** you last week was a real pleasure.
- after some verbs
  I **enjoy swimming** in cold water.
  Do you **mind carrying** my suitcase?
- after prepositions (e.g., about, by, without, of, etc.)
  I worry too much **about making** mistakes.
  They escaped **by digging** a tunnel under the wall.
- In time phrases, after before, after, when and while
  Before leaving the house, I checked I had my key with me.
  (= Before I left ...)
  Be careful to look both ways **when crossing** the road.

▶ 06.04 to + infinitive
We use to + infinitive:
- after adjectives (e.g., happy, pleased, easy, difficult, dangerous, safe, possible)
  It's **easy to find** your way into the city centre, but it's very **difficult to get** out again.
- after some verbs
  She **wants to work** for an aid organisation, but she doesn't **expect to earn** much money.
- to express purpose (what a person wants to achieve)
  We're going to the beach **to lie** in the sun. (= because we want to lie in the sun)
  To watch the clip again, click 'replay'. (= if you want to watch it again)

> **Tip** Be careful with verb forms after to. The word to is sometimes a preposition and sometimes part of to + infinitive.
> I'm looking forward **to seeing** you.
> I hope **to see** you. (NOT I hope to seeing)

▶ 06.05 verb + verb
There are many verbs that are followed by verb + -ing (e.g., I **enjoy painting**) and many that are followed by to + infinitive (e.g., I **want to watch**). There are also a few that allow both patterns with a change of meaning:
- try + to + infinitive
  I **tried to talk** to him, but he didn't answer his phone. (= I attempted to do it)
- try + verb + -ing
  I **tried talking** to him, but he's still angry. (= I did it but it didn't work)
- remember / forget + to + infinitive
  Please **remember** / don't **forget to buy** some milk. (= a task for the future)
- remember / forget + verb + -ing
  I **remember** / I'll never **forget hearing** that tune for the first time. (= an experience in the past)
- go on + to + infinitive
  After explaining the theory, I'll **go on to describe** some examples. (= stop one thing and start the next)
- go on + verb + -ing
  The professor **went on talking** for over an hour. (= didn't stop)

> **Tip** stop can be followed by verb + -ing or an infinitive of purpose:
> I **stopped drinking** coffee. (= I don't drink it now.)
> I **stopped to drink** coffee. (= I stopped because I wanted to drink coffee in a café.)

▶ 06.06 Sense verbs
Verbs connected with senses can be followed by an object and verb + -ing. (e.g., look at / see / watch / notice / observe / hear / listen to / feel / smell / taste):
I **watched** the people **walking** around.
I could **smell** something **burning**.

6B The passive

▶ 06.14 We can use the passive:
- when we don't know who did something / what caused something, or when this is not important
  These words **were written** thousands of years ago.
- when the agent (the doer) is very obvious
  Which languages **are spoken** in your family?
- when the main thing we are talking about is the object of the action
  I read a really interesting article today. It **was written** by someone who spent a year living in a jungle. (= We're talking about the article, not about the person in the jungle.)

The passive is formed with the verb be in the appropriate tense + past participle.

	Active	Passive
Present simple	They **use** it.	It **is used**.
Past simple	They **used** it.	It **was used**.
Present continuous	They **are using** it.	It **is being used**.
Past continuous	They **were using** it.	It **was being used**.
Present perfect	They **have used** it.	It **has been used**.
Past perfect	They **had used** it.	It **had been used**.
Future	They **will use** it.	It **will be used**.
	They **are going to use** it.	It **is going to be used**.
Infinitive (e.g., after modal verbs)	They **can use** it.	It **can be used**.
	They **might use** it.	It **might be used**.

▶ 06.15 Prepositions after made
We can use a range of prepositions after passives with made:
- made + by + method
  These cakes are **made by hand** / **by mixing** cornflakes with chocolate.
- made + with + tool
  I think these marks were **made with a knife**.
- made + of + material
  The wings are **made of very strong plastic**.
- made + from / out of + original object
  Our table is **made from** / **out of** an old door.

Our table **is made from** / **out of** an old door.

Grammar Focus

6A Infinitives and -ing forms

a Underline the correct verb forms.
1. I was looking forward to *hear* / *hearing* your ideas.
2. We need to make an appointment to *see* / *seeing* them again.
3. I'm still getting used to *be* / *being* a manager.
4. Riding an elephant is similar to *ride* / *riding* a horse.
5. He doesn't find it easy to *talk* / *talking* to anyone.

b Match the sentence halves.
- C 1 Oh, no! I forgot …
- J 2 I'll never forget …
- F 3 Why don't you try …
- A 4 We're going to try …
- H 5 Can you please stop …
- E 6 You'll have to stop …
- B 7 Did you remember …
- J 8 I don't remember …
- G 9 Start with the easy questions and then go on …
- D 10 We started in the morning and went on …

a to win the match. It'll be hard, but we've still got a chance.
b to turn off the lights before you went out?
c to pay the phone bill. I'm really sorry.
d playing until it was dark.
e to buy some petrol. You're going to run out soon.
f restarting the computer? That usually works for me.
g to try the ones that are left.
h making that noise? I can't concentrate.
i meeting the President – it was the most memorable day of my life.
j buying these shoes. Are you sure they're mine?

c Complete the sentences with the correct form of the verbs in brackets.
1. I'll be happy __to help__ (help) you find somewhere to stay.
2. He spent two years without __speaking__ (speak) to another person.
3. __Living__ (live) in another country is the easiest way of __learning__ (learn) a foreign language.
4. Can I borrow your laptop __to check__ (check) my emails?
5. Suddenly, I noticed a young man __running__ (run) towards me.
6. I'm afraid of __being__ (be) alone in the dark.
7. __To avoid__ (avoid) the risk of misunderstandings, I'll explain everything twice.
8. Would it be possible __to leave__ (leave) five minutes early?
9. __Spending__ (spend) a year as a volunteer teacher was one of the best experiences of my life.
10. As he waited for his results, he could feel his heart __beating__ (beat) in his chest.

d ⟫ Now go back to p. 69.

6B The passive

a Complete the sentences with the correct passive form of the verbs in brackets.
1. The local people are angry because these old trees ____are going to be cut____ (cut) down next week.
2. The first email between two organisations _____ (send) in 1971.
3. Currently, English _____ (use) as an official language in almost 60 countries.
4. I promise that you _____ (inform) as soon as your bags arrive.
5. The thief _____ (not / catch) yet, but I'm sure they'll catch him soon.
6. When we got to the cinema all the best tickets _____ (sell), so we had to sit right at the front.

b Rewrite the sentences in the passive.
1. I wrote that report. That report ____was written by me____.
2. My sister told us about this restaurant. We _____.
3. We can only dream of the technology of 2100. The technology of 2100 _____.
4. Someone had already built this bridge 1,000 years ago. This bridge _____.
5. You can't always depend on Martina. Martina _____.
6. I'm sure they'll look after you well. I'm sure you _____.

c Complete the sentences with the correct prepositions.
1. Jam is made __out of / from__ fruit.
2. This toy car was made _____ an old shoe box.
3. I can't believe this music was made _____ a computer.
4. If you want a perfect paper plane, it must be made _____ scissors and glue.
5. Windows in a plane are made _____ special glass, so they don't break easily.
6. All our clothes are made _____ local wool and _____ local people.

d ⟫ Now go back to p. 73.

145

7A too / enough; so / such

▶ 07.01 **too and enough**

We use *too* to say that something is more than we like or want.

We use *too* and *(not) enough* with nouns, adjectives and adverbs.

We use *too* before adjectives and adverbs, and *too much/many* before nouns.

We use *(not) enough* after adjectives and adverbs but before nouns.

*It's **such** a beautiful city, but there are **too** many people! It's **such** a shame!*

	More than the right amount / number	The right amount / number	Less than the right amount / number
With adjectives	It's **too** warm to play tennis.	It's warm **enough** to go to the beach.	It is**n't** warm **enough** to have a picnic.
With adverbs	You answered **too** quickly.	My English is improving quickly **enough**.	I did**n't** write quickly **enough** in the test.
With countable nouns	There are **too many** people. I can't see anything.	There are **enough** people for a game of volleyball.	There are**n't enough** people for a game of football.
With uncountable nouns	I spend **too much** time in Internet chat rooms.	I have **enough** time to bake a cake.	There is**n't enough** time to go shopping.

▶ 07.02

💡 **Tip** After *too* and *enough*, we often use *to* + infinitive:
*It's **too** late **to walk** home, but I don't have **enough** money **to pay** for a taxi.*

▶ 07.03 **so / such**

- *so* + adjective or adverb: *Why are you **so** happy?* (= Why are you as happy as you are?)
- *so* + *much/many* + noun: *There were **so many** people at the gym.*
- *such* + *(a/an)* + noun: *It was **such a** waste of money.*
- *such* + *(a/an)* + adjective + noun: *It's **such a** beautiful day!* (= It's a very beautiful day!)
- *such* + adjective + plural noun: *They're **such** friendly people!*

💡 **Tip** We can use *such a* + noun to express a positive or negative opinion:
*It's **such a pity/shame** you missed the beginning!* (= I'm so sorry/sad.)
*You're **such a genius**!* (= You're so clever!)
*The meal was **such a waste** of money!*
*It's always **such a pleasure** to talk to you.*

▶ 07.04

After *so / such*, we often use a *that* clause:
*It was **such** a nice place **that** we decided to stay another week.* (= We decided to stay because it was extremely nice.)
*I ate **so** much food **that** I felt ill.*

7B Causative *have / get*

We use the structure *have/get* + object + past participle to talk about things that we arrange or pay for but don't actually do ourselves. *Have* is slightly more formal than *get*.

▶ 07.08

	have / get	Object	Past participle
They're	having	their kitchen	painted.
When are you going to	get	your hair	cut?
I've	had	my car	fixed.
She wants to	have	her book	published.

We can mention the agent (the person who did the action) after *by*:
*She had her dress made **by a top designer**.*

▶ 07.09

💡 **Tip** We use a reflexive pronoun (e.g., *myself, herself, ourselves*) to emphasise that we **didn't** arrange or pay for somebody else to do something:
*I wanted to get my trousers shortened, but it was too expensive, so I did it **myself**.*

We can use the structure *have* + something + past participle to talk about experiences that are caused by other people. These experiences are usually negative:
*He **had his phone stolen**.* (= He experienced the situation where somebody stole his phone.)

We can use the structure *get* + something + past participle to focus on the end results of an activity rather than the activity itself:
*I don't care how you do it – just **get this work done**!* (= finish it or pay for somebody to finish it)

*I wanted to **get** my trousers **shortened**, but it was too expensive, so I did it myself.*

Grammar Focus

7A too / enough; so / such

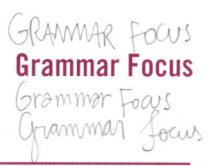

a Complete the sentences with words in the box. Use each word or phrase twice.

| enough | too | too many | too much |

1. She speaks quite quickly but she makes _too many_ mistakes.
2. Oh, no! We haven't got _____ milk. Can you go to the shop and buy some?
3. They're nice children, but they make _____ noise.
4. We wanted to go out, but it was _____ cold.
5. They spend _____ time watching TV. It's not healthy!
6. Your project isn't brilliant, but it's good _____. You don't need to do it again.
7. You should take a bus – it's _____ far to walk.
8. _____ people attended the meeting. Everyone was talking at the same time and they couldn't make any decisions.

b Match the sentence halves.

1. ☐ They're so …
2. ☐ It was such a …
3. ☐ You've read that book so many …
4. ☐ Watching reality TV is such a …
5. ☐ There was so much …
6. ☐ They're such …

a. times that you must know every word by now.
b. waste of time.
c. nice people that I'm sure you'll like them!
d. boring film that we left halfway through.
e. lazy that they never do any homework.
f. food that we couldn't eat it all.

c Rewrite the second sentence so that it means the same as the first. Use the words in brackets and *so*, *such*, *too* or *enough*.

1. They went by plane because they're rich. (that)
   They're _so rich that_ they went by plane.
2. I'm so sorry that we didn't see you. (pity)
   It's _such a pity_ that we didn't see you.
3. He's too young to be a doctor. (old)
   He isn't _old enough to_ be a doctor.
4. I didn't go out because I was so tired. (too)
   I was _too tired to_ go out.
5. That player's so good that he plays for his national team. (such)
   He's _____ he plays for his national team.
6. It was such a serious situation that they had to call the police. (so)
   The situation _____ they had to call the police.

d ≫ Now go back to p. 81.

5. such a good player that
6. was so serious that

7B Causative have / get

a Match the sentences with reasons A–C for using causative *have/get*.

1. ☐ Did you get your hair done? It looks lovely.
2. ☐ My boss isn't very good at getting his team motivated.
3. ☐ I've had my heart broken too many times – I don't want to fall in love again.
4. ☐ I need to get my eyes checked. I can't see very well.
5. ☐ My neighbours had their car stolen last week.
6. ☐ I just want to get this work done quickly so I can relax again.
7. ☐ I had my portrait painted by a wonderful artist.
8. ☐ Last time I went to the dentist, I had to have two teeth taken out.

A. The subject arranges or pays for somebody to do something.
B. The subject has a bad experience caused by someone else.
C. The speaker focuses on the end result rather than the activity itself.

b Rewrite the phrases in **bold** with causative *have/get*. Don't include the words in brackets.

1. I'm going to **(pay sb) to clean my flat**.
2. I'll **(arrange for sb) to install the new programs**.
3. Can you try to **finish the project** as quickly as possible?
4. **(sb) stole my email password** last week.
5. Robert, would you like to **start the meeting**?
6. We **really need to paint the flat** – the walls are so dirty.

c ≫ Now go back to p. 84.

147

8A First and second conditionals

▶ 08.02 We can use both first and second conditionals to talk about future possibilities.

The first conditional
The future real conditional describes possible or likely future events and the expected results of those events:
if + present simple, *will* + infinitive
If I save a little every month, **I'll be able to afford** a new car soon.

The second conditional
We use the second conditional to talk about present and future situations that are not real. The speaker thinks they are either not possible or not very likely to happen:
if + past simple, *would* + infinitive
If I had £1 for every time I've heard that, **I'd be** a millionaire.
If I saved £50 every month, **I'd have** enough for a new computer by the end of the year.

> **Tip** We use the phrase *if I were you* to give advice:
> **If I were you**, I **wouldn't** borrow so much money.

> **Tip** We can use *going to* instead of *will* in first conditional sentences:
> If I see her tomorrow, I'm **going to tell** her my news.

We often use other past/present tenses in the *if* clause:
If you**'ve finished** your test and you**'re waiting** to leave, you **should come** to my desk.

We can also use imperatives in the main clause:
If you've finished your test and you're waiting to leave, please **come** to my desk.

We can use modals other than *will/would* in the main clause (e.g., *might, could, should,* etc.):
If I weren't feeling so tired, I **might** go for a run.

Speech bubble 1: If I save a little every month, I'll be able to afford a new car soon.
Speech bubble 2: If I had £1 for every time I've heard that, I'd be a millionaire.

8B Third conditional; *should have* + past participle

▶ 08.05 **should have + past participle**
We can use the structure *should have* + past participle to criticise other people's past actions:
You **shouldn't have told** them about the party. I wanted it to be a surprise.

Third conditional
We use the third conditional to talk about imagined past events or states and their consequences:
If I'd arrived five minutes earlier, **I'd have seen** the robbery. (= But I arrived after the robbery, so I didn't see it.)

if clause	Main clause
If + past perfect	*would* + *have* + past participle
If you **hadn't told** me the answer,	**I'd have checked** on the Internet.
If there **had been** more time,	we **wouldn't have had** to hurry.

> **Tip** Be careful with *'d*. It's short for *had* in the *if* clause but *would* in the main clause. If **I'd known** earlier, **I'd have told** you.

We can use past perfect continuous in the *if* clause. We can also use *might* or *could* in the main clause:
It was a nasty accident. If I **hadn't been wearing** a helmet, I **might** have been very badly hurt. (= But I was wearing a helmet, so I wasn't badly hurt.)

▶ 08.06 **Mixed conditionals**
We combine clauses from the second and third conditional to talk about past conditions with a result in the present, or present conditions with a result in the past.

if clause	Main clause
If those burglars **hadn't damaged** that painting last year, … (Third conditional – unreal past)	… it **would be** worth a fortune now. (Second conditional – unreal present)
If I **didn't have** such a good relationship with my family, … (Second conditional – unreal present)	… I **would have left** the city years ago. (Third conditional – unreal past)

Grammar Focus

8A First and second conditionals

a Complete the sentences with a first or second conditional, using the prompts and the verbs in brackets.

1 [likely] Be careful with my phone! If you ___lose___ (lose) it, I ___'ll be___ (be) very angry.
2 [unlikely] If somebody ___spoke___ (speak) to me like that, I ___'d be___ (be) really angry.
3 [likely] It _____ (be) much cheaper if you _____ (come) by bus.
4 [likely] If you _____ (not spend) more money on advertising, your sales _____ (go) down.
5 [unlikely] I think you _____ (have) a great time if you _____ (study) abroad.
6 [likely] If Tony _____ (not finish) work soon, he _____ (not be) here on time.
7 [unreal] If you _____ (know) how to drive, I _____ (not have) to drive you everywhere.
8 [advice] If I _____ (be) you, I _____ (not say) anything about this to Ricky.
9 [likely] I'm sure they _____ (not be) angry if you _____ (tell) them the truth.
10 [unreal] She _____ (not have) a chance of getting that job if she _____ (not speak) English so well.
11 [likely] If it _____ (not rain) tomorrow morning, I _____ (walk) to work.
12 [advice] I _____ (not touch) that wire if I _____ (be) you.

b Look at the pictures. Write sentences using the prompts in brackets. Use the first or second conditional.

1 OK, so I promise ___I'll give you £1 if you wash my car.___ (give you £1 / wash / my car)

2 Sorry. _____ (love / go dancing tonight / not / have / so much work)

3 _____ (if / I / you / buy / new shoes)

4 Watch out! _____ (if / fall / might / hurt yourself)

5 Wow – just imagine! _____ (if / we / find / that gold / rich)

6 Of course it's not working! _____ (it / not / work / if / turn it on)

c ⟫ Now go back to p. 93.

8B Third conditional; *should have* + past participle

a Write sentences about each situation. Use the third conditional with the past perfect or past perfect continuous in the *if* clause.

1 I didn't take the exam because I didn't know about it.
I ___would have taken the exam if I'd known about it.___
2 They went to the same university, so they met and fell in love.
If _____
3 It was raining, so we took the metro.
If _____
4 We didn't buy the picture because it was so expensive.
We _____
5 You didn't hear the phone because you were listening to music.
You _____
6 My parents gave me some money, so I was able to buy a car.
If _____

b Write sentences about these situations using *should have* + past participle. Use the words in brackets.

1 Oh, no, they're going to be late again. (leave home earlier)
___They should have left home earlier.___
2 The customer was really rude. (he / not speak to me like that)
___He shouldn't have spoken to me like that___
3 You've made the alarm go off! (not press that button)
___You shouldn't have pressed that button___
4 I had no idea it was your birthday. (you / tell me)
___You should have told me it was your b'day.___
5 That car drove through the red light. (it / stop)
___It should have stopped at the red light___
6 She failed her driving test. (she / take / more driving lessons)
___She should've taken more driving lessons___

c Match the sentence halves.

1 ☐ If we'd had more time, …
2 ☐ I'm sure Walter would have lent you some money …
3 ☐ If you hadn't driven me home, …
4 ☐ They'd be a lot richer …
5 ☐ I wouldn't have bought so much food …
6 ☐ If Gloria wasn't so nice, …

a if they'd sold their flat when prices were still high.
b I'd still be at the station now.
c if you'd told me only four people were coming.
d we wouldn't have invited her to stay with us.
e we'd have done more sightseeing.
f if you'd asked him.

d ⟫ Now go back to p. 96.

149

9A Relative clauses

*Speech bubble: Did you know they've invented a car **that** stops people crashing?*

09.04 Defining relative clauses

Defining relative clauses give essential information about a noun:

They've invented a car. **The car** stops people crashing.
They've invented a car **that** stops people crashing!

- *who* describes a person and *which* describes a thing. In defining relative clauses, you can use *that* instead of both *who* and *which*:
This is the work **which/that** has to be finished today.
The man **who/that** I needed to talk to wasn't available.

When *who/which/that* replace **the object** of the clause, we can omit the relative pronoun:
You're applying for **the job**. (= object)
What's the job (**which/that**) you're applying for?

- *where* describes a place:
There's a new shop in town **where** you can buy furniture.
- *whose* is used to refer to people or things that belong to a noun:
The woman **whose flat** was burgled is called Mrs Plater.
- *when* describes times (e.g., *day/year/time*):
The days **when** I have to collect the children are stressful.

We sometimes use *who*, *which* and *that* with prepositions. The prepositions usually come at the end of the sentence:
There is a place nearby **which/that** we can stop at.

09.05 Non-defining relative clauses

Non-defining relative clauses give extra information about a noun. The clause is not necessary for the sentence to make sense. A non-defining clause has a comma before it and either another comma or a full stop after it:
My new doctor, **who I had my first appointment with on Thursday**, recommended the medicine to me.

In non-defining clauses, *which* can relate to a single noun or to the whole main clause:
I'm going to Thailand next week, **which** is very exciting.

There are two main differences between defining and non-defining clauses.

- we cannot use *that* in a non-defining clause:
Revolutionary technology, **which** is rare, usually costs a huge amount to develop. NOT ~~Revolutionary technology, that is rare…~~
- we can never omit the relative pronoun in a non-defining clause:
Jane, **who** I have always trusted, was the only person I told about the situation. NOT ~~Jane, I have always trusted…~~

> **Tip** Be careful when you describe places with *which* and *where*.
> - *which/that* replace a noun or pronoun:
> I grew up in the house (**which/that**) you're buying!
> (= you're buying **the house**)
> - *where* replaces *there* or preposition of place + noun:
> I still live in the house **where** I grew up.
> (= I grew up **in the house/there**)

9B Reported speech; reporting verbs

09.06

When we report what people said or thought in the past, we usually change the tenses, pronouns, possessives and references to time and place:
Anna: '*I **won't** go out **tomorrow**.*'
Anna **told** me she **would not** go out **on the following day.**

present tenses → past tenses
past tenses → past perfect tenses
will, *can* and *may* → *would*, *could* and *might*
Past perfect, *would*, *could* and *might* don't normally change.

When the reporting verb is in a present tense, we don't change the tenses:
'*I've never seen them in concert.*' → She **says** she**'s never seen** them in concert.

When we report questions, the word order is the same as in sentences. Use *whether* or *if* to report *Yes/No* questions. *Whether* is more formal than *if*.
'Where do you live?' → They asked me where **I lived**.
NOT ~~They asked me where did I live~~.
'Are you famous?' → They weren't sure **if/whether** I was famous.

Reporting verbs
After some reporting verbs there are different verb patterns:

Verb + (*that*) + clause	agree, assume, believe, complain, discover, find out, insist, promise, realise, say, state, …	He **stated that** he would stay with us.
Verb + sb + (*that*) clause	assure, inform, tell, warn, …	We **informed them that** it was ready.
Verb + *to* + infinitive	agree, promise, refuse, …	They **refused to speak** to us.
Verb + sb + *to* + infinitive	ask, order, remind, tell, …	She **ordered me to leave**.
Verb + gerund	admit, apologise for, deny, regret, suggest, …	He **admitted taking** the money.
Verb + (sb) + reported question	ask, discover, know, realise, wonder, …	I **wondered where they were**.

> **Tip** With negatives, use *not to* + infinitive or *not* + gerund.
> We agreed **not to go**.
> He apologised **for not stopping** at the red light.

Grammar Focus

9A Relative clauses

a Complete the sentences with the correct relative pronouns. If no word is needed, put (–).
1. This is my best friend, Kim, _____ I've known since we were little.
2. There are three things _____ I need to tell you about today's event.
3. Everybody congratulated the team, _____ hard work had won the contract.
4. The receptionist recommended the restaurant _____ we ate.
5. We never worried about money until the year _____ we bought our first house.
6. Who are the people _____ arrived late?
7. My job, _____ I love, is also really demanding.
8. They discovered a treatment _____ had no side effects.
9. I wish I could move to a seat _____ I could see out of the window.
10. The singer, _____ voice I have loved all my life, seemed to be singing directly to me.

b Correct one mistake in each sentence.
1. This is the book what I was telling you about.
2. There's a new machine at the gym I think you would really like it.
3. We're travelling to Dubai, where I've always wanted to visit.
4. I was worrying about my luggage, that I'd forgotten to weigh before we left.
5. Chris, who his father owns the company, always works really hard.
6. I've finally had to replace my old car, I've had since I passed my test.

c Rewrite the two sentences into one, making all necessary changes to punctuation and word order. Remember to cut unnecessary words.
1. The band didn't come on stage until nine o'clock. They were supposed to start at eight-thirty.
2. The rail company refunds passengers. The passengers' trains are delayed.
3. I looked in all the places. I thought I might have left my phone there.
4. The idea worked really well. We came up with the idea together.
5. Morocco is my favourite place for a holiday. We spent our honeymoon there.
6. The neighbours get back from holiday tomorrow. I'm looking after the neighbours' cat.

d >>> Now go back to p. 106.

9B Reported speech; reporting verbs

a Look at the direct speech in the left-hand column. Complete the reported speech or thoughts in the right-hand column.

1 'I don't understand what you want.'	He told me ___*that he didn't understand what I wanted.*___
2 'Harry can't ski.'	I didn't realise _____
3 'You may feel a little sleepy after you take the tablets.'	The doctor warned her that _____
4 'The exam will be really easy.'	I assumed _____
5 'No, I wasn't walking past the bank when I heard the alarm.'	The witness denied _____
6 'We've been trying to call you since we heard the news.'	They informed us that _____
7 'Margaret won't be happy when she finds out.'	I warned you _____
8 'I couldn't open the door because I'd forgotten my key.'	He discovered that _____

b Look at the questions from a job interview in the left-hand column. Complete the reported questions.

'What do you know about this company?' 'Do you have any experience with this sort of work?' 'How fast can you type?' 'Why did you leave your last job?' 'Are you good at dealing with customers?' 'Have you ever managed a team?' 'Why have you applied for this job?'	They started by asking me ¹___*what I knew*___ about the company. Then they wanted to know ²_____ any experience with that sort of work. They even asked me ³_____ type! Then I had to explain ⁴_____ my last job! The worst question was when they asked ⁵_____ good at dealing with customers. They also wanted to know ⁶_____ a team – I didn't know what to say! By the end, I wasn't sure ⁷_____ for the job!

c Complete the reported speech, thoughts and questions with **one** or **two** words in each gap. Contractions (e.g., *didn't*) count as one word.
1. 'I promise that I'll be really careful.' — I promised ___*to be*___ really careful.
2. 'You must explain what you're doing here.' — The guard ordered _____ explain what we were doing there.
3. 'Yes, OK. I told someone about the accident.' — Amanda admitted _____ someone about the accident.
4. 'How did they find out?' — I wondered how _____ found out.
5. 'I'll pay for the meal – no discussion!' — Robert insisted _____ for the meal.
6. 'I'll send you a postcard.' — Sam told _____ send me a postcard.
7. 'We're really sorry that we lost your order.' — They apologised _____ our order.
8. 'OK, I can give you the money.' — Patricia agreed _____ us the money.

d >>> Now go back to p. 108.

151

10A Past modals of deduction

We can use modal verbs to show that we are making a deduction, not stating a fact. We use the modal verbs *must, may, might, could* and *can't* + *have* + past participle to make deductions about the past.

▶ 10.02

Deduction	Meaning
They are late.	I know for certain that they are late.
They are never late. They **must have** got lost.	I believe they've got lost.
They **may / might / could have** gone the wrong way. They **might not have** found the right street.	I believe it's possible that they've got lost.
They **can't have** got lost. They have a satnav.	I believe they haven't got lost.
They haven't got lost. I can see them coming up the street now.	I know for a fact that they haven't got lost.

The opposite of *must* for deductions is *can't*.

We can also use *may not have* or *might not have* / *mightn't have*: Try calling them at home. They **might not have** gone out. (= It's possible that they haven't gone out.)

> **Tip** When we make the negative form, *not* combines with the modal verb and not with *have*.
> She may **not** have left home. (NOT ~~She may have **not** left home.~~)

10B Wishes and regrets

▶ 10.08 When we make a wish, we imagine an unreal situation in the past, present or future.

Wishes about the future	We use *would* to make wishes about the future. Don't use *would* to make a wish about yourself – use *could* instead.	I **wish** it **would** stop raining. I **wish** I **could** get a better job, but I haven't got enough experience. (= If I had more experience, I would be able to get a better job.)
Wishes about the present	We can use the past simple to make wishes about the present. We can also make wishes about the present with *could* + infinitive.	I **wish** I **had** more time. (= I would like to have more time.) I **wish** I **could speak** French – it's such a beautiful language. (= I would like to be able to speak French, but I'm not.)
Wishes about the past	We use the past perfect to make wishes about the past.	I **wish** I **hadn't been** so lazy at school. (I was lazy when I was at school, and now I regret it.)

> **Tip** To talk about something that we see as realistic, possible or likely in the future, use *hope*, not *wish*:
> I **hope** you get better soon. NOT ~~I **wish** you would get better soon.~~

I wish … / if only …
If only … means the same as *I wish …*, and we use it in the same way.

> **Tip** When making wishes about *I/he/she/it*, we can use *were* instead of *was*. *Were* is preferred in formal English, but in normal spoken English, both versions are common:
> If only it **were** that simple. (Or: … it **was** that simple.)

▶ 10.09 *should have* + past participle
We use *should have* + past participle to express regret about our own past actions:
It's my fault. I **should have locked** the door.
(= But I didn't lock it, so the burglars got in.)
I didn't know she was sleeping. I **shouldn't have turned** the music on. (= But I did turn it on, so I woke her up.)

Grammar Focus

10A Past modals of deduction

a Complete the sentences with one of the phrases in the box and the correct form of the verb in brackets. Use some of the phrases twice.

must have   may have   can't have   might not have

1 **A** We walked all the way home in the snow.
  B Wow – that ___must have been___ (be) cold!
2 **A** I think I saw Angela on the bus today.
  B No, it _____ (be) Angela – she's on holiday in the mountains this week.
3 **A** I saw a beautiful jumper in the shop, but I didn't buy it. It's probably too late now.
  B Maybe, but let's go back and check – they _____ (sell) it yet.
4 **A** That's strange. My bicycle tyre's flat. How did that happen?
  B I'm not sure. You _____ (ride) over some broken glass or something.
5 **A** Where have all the sandwiches gone? The plate's empty!
  B Tom _____ (eat) them. He was the only person who came into this room all day.
6 **A** I think I've broken my arm – it really hurts.
  B I don't know … you _____ (break) it. I'm not an expert, but it doesn't look broken.

b Tick (✓) the correct sentences. Correct the mistakes.

1 ☐ I said hello but he didn't reply. He ~~didn't have heard~~ me.   ___can't have heard___
2 ✓ Sorry, I may not have made myself clear.   _____
3 ☐ I can't find my purse. Someone might stolen it.   _____
4 ☐ I don't know who wrote the report – it could had been anybody.   _____
5 ☐ They can't have just disappeared! It's impossible!   _____
6 ☐ It might haven't been such a good idea to walk home alone.   _____
7 ☐ They look sad. They must lose the match.   _____
8 ☐ Wow! That's a nice car! It needs to cost a fortune!   _____

c ≫ Now go back to p. 117.

10B Wishes and regrets

a Match the sentence halves. Use the correct form of the verbs in brackets to complete each gap.

1 ☐ Hmm … I don't like the look of those dark clouds.
2 ☐ I really regret leaving my old job.
3 ☐ I was sure the bank would lend us the money if we filled in a few forms.
4 ☐ It's really annoying that you told me the match result.
5 ☐ I don't know why they're so late.
6 ☐ I really miss you.
7 ☐ You never do any cleaning around the house.
8 ☐ It looks like a lovely place for a holiday.

a If only it _____ that simple. (be)
b I hope nothing _____ to them. (happen)
c I wish you _____ quiet about it. (keep)
d I wish you _____ out a little more. (help)
e I hope it _____. (not rain)
f If only it _____ so expensive! (not be)
g I wish I _____ from it. (not resign)
h If only I _____ you again. (can see)

b Write wishes or hopes for each of these situations. Use *If only*, *I wish* or *I hope*.

1 Why didn't you remind us?   ___If only you'd reminded us.___
2 I don't know what to do.   _____
3 If I do this course, I might be able to speak Korean next year.   _____
4 They didn't warn us in advance, unfortunately.   _____
5 Maybe Ramón will help me.   _____
6 I'm angry that they cancelled the flight.   _____

c Write sentences about these situations using *should have* + past participle. Use the prompts in brackets.

1 Oh, no, we're going to be late. (leave home earlier)
  ___We should have left home earlier.___
2 I regret buying that new bag. It was too expensive. (not buy it)
  _____
3 I feel terrible after running so far. (stop earlier)
  _____
4 I really wanted to see that new film and now it's too late. (go to the cinema yesterday)
  _____
5 I went to a party yesterday. I didn't study. (not go to the party)
  _____

d ≫ Now go back to p. 120.

153

VOCABULARY FOCUS

1A Character adjectives

a Read the descriptions of people's characters. Which is personal and which is more formal?

Fred currently works as a researcher here at Bio-Tech. He's been a very **loyal** member of our staff and has worked here for over ten years now. He's **passionate** about alternative energies and this can be seen in the energy and enthusiasm he puts into his work. He's also **self-confident**, so he is never afraid to work independently or to work on difficult tasks. Finally, he's always **optimistic**, even when he comes across problems in his work.

We have this new colleague at work, Sheila. She's only been here for two weeks and already I don't like her very much. She's one of those **ambitious** people who has a lot of plans, but she's so **arrogant** about it all. She thinks she's better than everyone else. But if you try and suggest a different idea, she gets really upset. So she's a strange mix of being very sure of herself, but incredibly **sensitive** at the same time. She told me that she wants to be our team leader. If she thinks that's going to happen overnight, she's really **naive**!

b Match the **bold** character adjectives in **a** with the definitions.
1. when you don't have much experience of the world and believe things too easily
2. when you easily get upset by what people say about you
3. when you believe or behave as if you know more or are more important than other people
4. when you feel sure about yourself and your abilities
5. when you like something and have strong feelings about it
6. when you have a strong wish to be successful, powerful or rich
7. when you always support something or someone, even when other people don't
8. when you always think good things will happen

c ▶ 01.06 Complete the sentences with the adjectives from the texts in **a**. Listen and check.
1. He's very _____. If I give him any negative feedback, he gets angry and shouts at me.
2. I'm sure he won't be nervous when he gives the speech. He always seems very _____.
3. I feel quite _____ that this project will be successful – everything is going according to plan.
4. They both think they're fantastic and everyone else is stupid. I've never met a couple who are so _____.
5. She's helped and supported me since we were at school. She's a very _____ friend – I know I can always rely on her.
6. Phil is really _____ about being a doctor. He loves the job and looks forward to going to work every day.
7. She works really hard because she's _____ and wants to do well in her career.
8. Martin is a little _____ – he honestly thought his boss would listen to his suggestions, but of course in the end he didn't. He really is very young.

d 💬 Think of three family members or friends. Make notes on their character. Tell your partner.

> My father's very passionate, particularly about his work.

> I really like my aunt. She's a very successful lawyer. Some people think she's arrogant, but I don't.

PRONUNCIATION Word stress

a ▶ 01.07 Listen to these adjectives and underline the stressed syllable. Which syllable is stressed: the first, second, third or fourth?

optimistic   inspiring   arrogant   ambitious

b ▶ 01.08 Write these words in the table. Then listen and check your answers. Practise saying the words.

passionate   self-confident   sensitive   determined
determination   pessimistic   environment
environmental   influential   television

1st syllable stressed	2nd syllable stressed
3rd syllable stressed	**4th syllable stressed**

c 💬 Test each other. Student A: Choose a word in **b** and say a sentence.
Student B: Did Student A say the adjective correctly?

> I'm determined to become a millionaire.

d ≫ Now go back to p. 10.

154

Vocabulary Focus

2A Expressions with *get*

a Read what Emma and Martin say. Who do/did they have a problem with?

Emma:

Last year I decided to join the social club at work. I always thought the social club was boring, and I wanted to improve it. I talked to some other people in the club, and we tried to work out a way to **get rid of** the man running the club – the secretary – because we really thought he was the problem. Everyone liked this idea, and we all **got a bit carried away** and decided a direct approach would be best. At the next meeting, we were about to say something when all of a sudden he said, 'Look, I'll **get straight to the point**. I think the social club's getting too boring and we need some fresh ideas.' We couldn't believe his sudden change. Now the club is much more interesting and lots of new people have **got involved**.

Martin:

My brother's really **getting on my nerves** at the moment. He won't study at all. I can't **get across** to him the importance of doing well at school. He just won't listen and it's **getting me down**. The problem is he **got through** his exams very easily last year without studying. He thinks he can do the same thing this year, but I'm not so sure.

b Match the *get* expressions in **bold** in **a** with definitions 1–8.
1 to say something important immediately and in a direct way
2 to make someone understand something
3 to take part in an activity or organisation
4 to be successful in an examination or competition
5 when something annoys you
6 to become so excited about something that you are no longer careful
7 when something makes you feel sad or depressed
8 to send or throw someone or something away

c Pronunciation Notice the linking between *get* and the word after in this example.
Lots of new people have got‿involved.

▶ 02.02 Listen to these examples. In which sentences is there linking between *get* and the word after? What does that tell you about linking?
1 We tried to work out a way to get rid of the man running the club.
2 We all got a bit carried away.
3 I'll get straight to the point.
4 I can't get across to him the importance of doing well.

d Think of examples of these things.
1 a time that you got rid of something you didn't want
2 something that gets on your nerves
3 a time when you got through a presentation, test or interview
4 a situation where you got a bit carried away
5 a club or organisation you got involved in

e Tell each other about your examples in **d**.

PRONUNCIATION Sound and spelling: *g*

a ▶ 02.03 Listen to the words. In which words does *g* have … ?
1 a hard sound /g/
2 a soft sound /dʒ/

get   negative   manage

b ▶ 02.04 Decide which sound the *g* has in these words – /g/ or /dʒ/. Then listen and practise saying them.

guard   gymnastics   guide   generous
biology   together   religion   agree
dangerous   forget   bridge   gardener

c Look at your answers to **b**.
1 If *g* is followed by a consonant or *a*, *o* or *u*, is it hard or soft?
2 If *g* is followed by *e*, *i* or *y*, is it hard or soft? Are there exceptions to this rule?

d ⟫ Now go to p. 21.

155

3B Words connected with sport

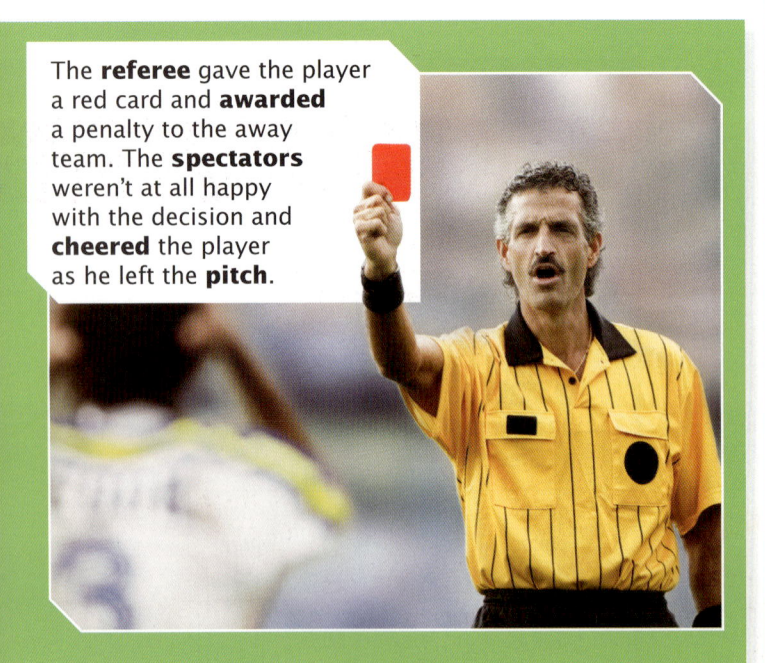

Pablo will once again **represent** Argentina at next year's championship. He already holds the **world record** for the fastest 800m. During that race in 2018, he **led** from the beginning.

The **referee** gave the player a red card and **awarded** a penalty to the away team. The **spectators** weren't at all happy with the decision and **cheered** the player as he left the **pitch**.

a Find words in the sports reports which mean:
1 play for your country or city
2 the people watching a match
3 be ahead during a game or competition
4 give (a prize or a point) for something you have done
5 shout to show you think someone is good
6 the best or fastest that has ever been achieved
7 the person who makes decisions during a sports game
8 the area where a football match is played.

b Underline the correct words.
1 Even though she holds the *world record / spectator* in the 1500m, Kirabo Sanaa probably won't *represent / award* her country at the next Olympic Games.
2 The spectators *cheered / represented* as the players walked onto the *pitch / referee*.
3 Mateo Amador *cheered / led* the race from the beginning and was *awarded / cheered* a gold medal.

c Write two short sports reports, using two of the sentence starters. Use the words in **bold** in the texts and your own ideas.
1 Ten minutes into the game, …
2 Eighteen-year-old Maria Ortiz from Uruguay …
3 Kenyan runner Pamela Abasi …

d 💬 Read your reports aloud. Who has the most interesting sports report?

PRONUNCIATION Word stress

a Add the words in the box to the table.

training ~~competition~~ victor competitor performance championship trainer athletic competitive athletics victorious performer professional

Verb	Noun (event or activity)	Noun (person)	Adjective
compete	competition		
		athlete	
	victory		
		champion	
train			
perform			
	profession		professional

b ▶ 03.04 Which syllable is stressed in each word in the table? Does the stress stay the same in all the word forms or does it change? Listen and check.

c ▶ 03.05 How does the vowel sound in **bold** change in each pair of words? Listen and check.
athl**e**te   athl**e**tics
vict**o**ry   vict**o**rious
comp**e**te   comp**e**titor

d 💬 Work in pairs. Cover the table and test each other.
Student A: Say a sentence with one of the words.
Student B: Make a follow-up sentence with a similar meaning, using a different word.

> He entered the championship.

> He wanted to be the champion.

e ⟫ Now go back to p. 36.

156

Vocabulary Focus

4B Talking about difficulty

a Underline a word or phrase in each sentence that means (*to be*) *difficult*.
1 Working as a waitress in a busy restaurant is one of the most <u>demanding</u> jobs I've ever had.
2 I find it a bit <u>awkward</u> when I have to speak to my staff about mistakes they've made.
3 Teaching a class on my own for the first time was a very <u>testing</u> experience.
4 Doing the outdoor survival training course really <u>challenged</u> me.
5 I have to talk to my teacher because I'm not happy with her lessons; it's a very <u>delicate</u> subject and I'm not sure what to say exactly. *= complicated*
6 Unfortunately, it's often <u>not very straightforward</u> for students here to find part-time work.
7 When I lived in Budapest, it was a <u>struggle</u> to learn Hungarian well.
8 I think I understand how computers work, but learning a programming language really <u>stretched</u> me.

b Which words in **a** do we use to describe situations that are embarrassing or need to be dealt with very carefully?

c Complete the sentences with words in **a**.
1 My final exams at university were really *demanding / testing* – I needed a long holiday after I finished!
2 I can't go to my best friend's wedding because I'm going on holiday. It's a(n) *awkward / delicate* situation and I'm not sure how to tell her.
3 I'm really busy at work at the moment and I'm finding it a *struggle* to get my work done by the end of the day.
4 I thought connecting my new printer to my computer would be easy, but actually it's not *straightforward* at all.
5 I'm not very confident, so giving a presentation at university last week in front of 50 people really *challenged / stretched* me.

d Think of an experience you've had for three of the things below.
1 an outdoor experience that stretched you
2 the most demanding thing about learning a language
3 a book you once read that wasn't straightforward
4 an awkward meeting you once had
5 a sport that was a struggle for you to learn
6 a delicate question that you had to ask someone
7 something you studied that really challenged you
8 a testing experience you had in a new place or country

e Now tell each other about the things you chose in **d**.

PRONUNCIATION Sound and spelling: *u*

a ▶ 04.07 Listen to the words.

| include | struggle | cushion | busy |

b Match the vowel sounds in the words in **a** with the sounds in words 1–4.
1 cup
2 put
3 true
4 thin

c ▶ 04.08 What sound does *u* have in these words? Listen to check and add them to the table.

subject	focus	punish
pullover	amusing	assume
unfortunately	super	pudding
business	supper	helpful

Sound 1 /ʌ/	Sound 2 /ʊ/	Sound 3 /uː/ or /juː/	Sound 4 /ɪ/	Sound 5 /ə/

d Write a sentence with two of the words in **a** or **b**. Read your sentence to other students and check if you pronounced *u* correctly.

e ≫ Now go back to p. 49.

5A Adjectives describing attitude

a Read about Tamara's family and add adjectives in the gaps.

> thoughtful   critical   disorganised   unreliable
> well-organised   irresponsible   sympathetic   competitive

My brother Nick is very ¹_____ – his desk is a mess and he can never find anything. But my sister Vera is a very ²_____ person. She plans her day carefully and she always knows exactly where everything is. She's also so ³_____. She wants to be the best – it's all she thinks about. I would say my grandmother is a very ⁴_____ person – you can go to her if you're in trouble and she'll always listen and make you feel better. My cousin Maude is very ⁵_____. She's always thinking about how she can help other people. She remembers everyone's birthday and always sends presents. I like my other cousin, Becky, but she can be quite ⁶_____. She never tells anyone where she's going when she goes out, and she sometimes leaves the front door open or doesn't lock her car. She's also terribly ⁷_____. If you arrange to meet her somewhere, she'll probably be late or she won't even show up. And what about me? Everyone in the family complains that I'm always commenting on what people are like. Some of them say I'm too ⁸_____ and I only see the bad things in them. I can't imagine why they would think that.

b Complete the table. Use prefixes or suffixes to make the opposites of the adjectives in **a**.

thoughtful	
well-organised	disorganised
	unreliable
	irresponsible
sympathetic	
competitive	
critical	

c Make a list of the prefixes and suffixes we can add to adjectives to make them negative.

d ▶ 05.01 Look at the sentences. Decide if the word in **bold** is correct or not. Then listen and check.
1 He often arrives late to meetings and doesn't bring everything he needs. He's very **disorganised**.
2 She always makes sensible decisions and she never does anything silly. She's very **irresponsible**.
3 She often expresses negative opinions about things and other people. She's very **critical**.
4 If he says he's going to do something, he always does it. He's very **reliable**.
5 He doesn't think about how the things he says might affect other people. He's totally **thoughtful**.
6 When you tell her your problems, she listens and tries to understand how you feel. She's **unsympathetic**.
7 He always wants to do better than everyone else. He's quite **competitive**.

e Look through the adjectives and their opposites and write down your own personality 'profile'.

f 💬 Tell your partner and mention a few examples of things you do.

> I think I'm fairly thoughtful and caring. For example, I call my grandmother once a week to ask how she is …

PRONUNCIATION Sound and spelling: *th*

a ▶ 05.02 Listen to *th* in these words. What two different sounds do you hear?

thoughtful	clothes
weather	seventh
sympathetic	

b ▶ 05.03 Which sound does *th* have in these words? Listen to check, then add them to the table.

leather	north
thumb	northern
month	Netherlands
together	healthy
something	enthusiastic
therefore	worth

Sound 1 /θ/ (*think*)	Sound 2 /ð/ (*the*)

c ⇒ Now go to p. 58.

158

Vocabulary Focus

6A Travel and tourism

a Put the correct words from the box in the gaps. The definition of each word is given in brackets.

feature   setting   structures   outskirts

1 … and there are waterfalls on the _____ of the city. (just before the city ends and the countryside begins)
2 However, the most amazing _____ you can see here is the nearby volcano, Parícutin. (an important thing that you notice)
3 … the whole island is like a museum of breathtaking wooden _____ that date from the 18th century. (things that you build)
4 In many ways it's the perfect _____ for them. (the position of a building)

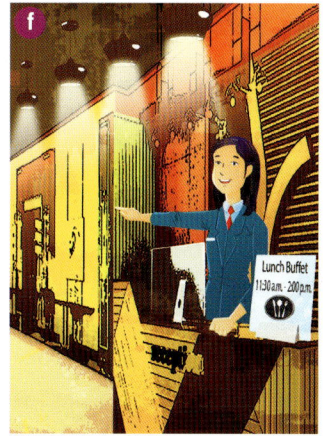

b Match pictures a–f to examples 1–6 from a tourist guide.
1 ☐ Remember to tell the taxi driver which **terminal** your flight's leaving from.
2 ☐ We also recommend a visit to the **studio** where he painted in the final years of his life.
3 ☐ We're both a hotel and a conference **venue**.
4 ☐ You can eat outside on our **terrace**.
5 ☐ The lunch buffet is served every day between 11:30 am. and 2:00 pm in the room next to this **lobby**.
6 ☐ If you would like to go **hiking**, there are trails of different levels of difficulty.

c ▶06.08 Listen to Annie's story about going to Malaysia. Write the correct words in the gaps.
Last year we wanted to ¹_____ away for a couple of weeks, so we decided to go trekking in the forests of Malaysia. We thought it would be cheaper to catch a train to the airport rather than go by taxi. But we were a bit upset to discover that the trains weren't ²_____ on time. We ³_____ at the check-in desk very late and just managed to catch our flight. The flight took 17 hours because we ⁴_____ over in Dubai for a couple of hours. By the time we got there, we were exhausted and not really in the mood for trekking.

d 💬 Think about answers to the following questions. Then ask and answer them with a partner.
1 When you go travelling, do you usually turn up at the station or airport early or on time?
2 Imagine you have to go on a long flight from your country to another one. Where would you like to stop over? How long would you like to stop over for?
3 Have you ever been trekking? If yes, where did you go? If not, would you like to try?

PRONUNCIATION Consonant clusters

a ▶06.09 Listen to the underlined sounds in these words. What do they have in common?

s<u>tu</u>dio   out<u>s</u>kirts   <u>s</u>tructure

b ▶06.10 Listen to these words. <u>Underline</u> where two or more consonants occur together in the same syllable.

approval   discussion   expensive   apply
hungry   transfer   contrast   destroy

c 💬 Write two sentences. Each sentence should contain at least two words from **b**. Read your sentences to each other.

d ⟫ Now go back to p. 70.

159

7B Films and TV

a Look at the words in **bold** in sentences 1–8. Find two:
- words that refer to people who work in film and TV
- verb forms that refer to when a film or TV programme is shown
- words that talk about the way TV programmes are divided
- verb forms that talk about what can happen during the making of a TV programme or film.

1 The longest-running science fiction TV **series** is the British production *Doctor Who*.

2 As she walked through the front door, her look of complete surprise **was captured** on camera.
3 The first *Star Wars* film **was released** in 1977.
4 After filming, the **editor** began the work of choosing the best shots and putting the film together.

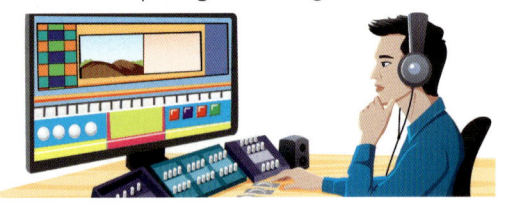

5 He appeared in only one short scene of the film, but it **was cut** after filming finished.
6 Any big international sports event **is broadcast** live all around the world.

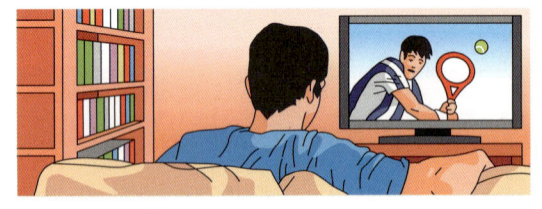

7 It's a really good news programme because the **presenter** is completely neutral and you never know what her opinion is.

8 There's an exciting crime show on TV at the moment. Tonight is the final **episode** and we'll find out who the murderer is.

b Answer the questions.
1 Does a TV series normally include more than one episode?
2 Viewers usually see a presenter on TV. Do they see the editor of a TV programme?
3 When a film is released, where do we usually see it, in a cinema or on TV? Are TV programmes normally released or broadcast?
4 Who usually captures something on camera, an editor or a camera operator? Who cuts something?

c Are the four verb forms in **a** in an active or passive form? Is this form more typical for these verbs?

d Write words in the gaps. Use a word in **a** or from p. 84.
1 The _____ of the new comedy programme is made up of actors who aren't famous.
2 The scene where he gets home has been _____. It's not necessary and it's a bit boring.
3 Every summer, a lot of big action films are _____ because studios think they'll do well and make money.
4 Some people think the way a film _____ puts together a film is just as skilful as the work of the director.
5 The film looked beautiful and was full of _____ of wonderful scenery, but the storyline and the _____ were terrible. I couldn't understand what was going on.
6 The UK soap opera *Coronation Street* has been running since 1960. My granddad maintains that he's seen every single _____.
7 Having talked to the director about his ideas for the film, the _____ felt enthusiastic and began thinking how he could get money to make it.
8 The accident was _____ on video by a member of the public using her phone.

e 💬 Discuss the questions.
1 What's a TV series that you've enjoyed recently? What's it about?
2 What kinds of things do you think shouldn't be broadcast live on TV?
3 What do you think is more important in a film – a good script or great shots? Why?
4 Which job do you think would be the most interesting: producer, director or editor? Why?

PRONUNCIATION Sound and spelling: *o*

a How many different pronunciations of the letter *o* are in the words below?

edit**o**r br**o**adcast epis**o**de direct**o**r c**o**mpany

b Which of the symbols and examples match the sounds in **a**?

Sound 1	Sound 2	Sound 3	Sound 4	Sound 5	Sound 6
/ɔː/	/uː/	/ə/	/ʌ/	/aʊ/	/əʊ/
f**ou**r	f**oo**d	pr**o**fess**o**r	m**o**ther	n**ow**	r**oa**d

c ▶ 07.07 Match the pronunciation of *o* in these words to the correct sound in **b**.
sh**o**w b**ou**ght p**o**lice supp**o**rt y**ou**ng
c**o**rrect ch**o**se thr**ow** n**o**thing c**o**rner

d 💬 Write two sentences. In each sentence try to use two *o* words that have a different sound. Read your sentences to each other.

e ≫ Now go back to p. 84.

8B Crime

a Read the two news reports. Match the pictures to the underlined words and phrases.

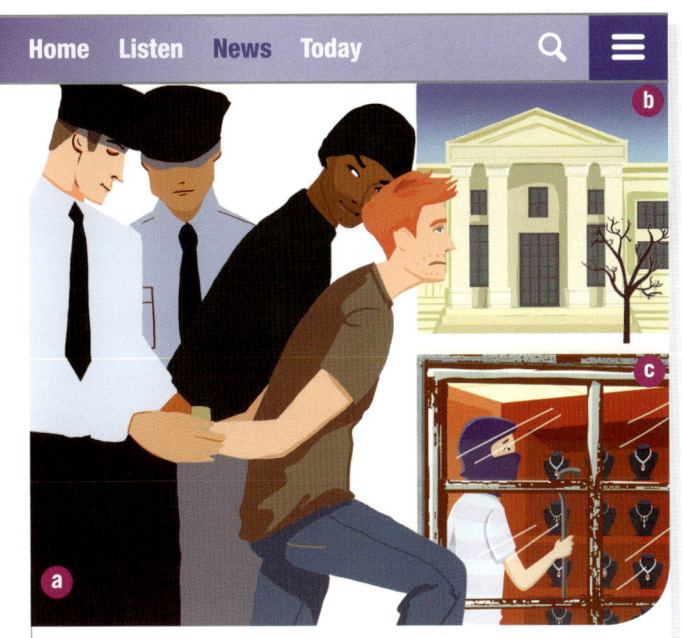

Home Listen News Today

Thieves ¹broke into a jeweller's shop and stole £5,000 worth of jewellery and watches. However, they were seen on CCTV, and ²two suspects were arrested yesterday. They will appear in ³court on Wednesday.

I saw her take money to the meeting.
We find her guilty.
We think you did it.

The ⁴trial of Rebecca Rivers, who ⁵was accused of theft, is finally over. It continued for over three weeks, and around 15 ⁶witnesses were called to give evidence. Yesterday the ⁷jury gave a verdict of guilty. The ⁸judge sentenced Ms Rivers to five years in prison.

b ▶ 08.07 Choose the correct words to complete the conversation. Then listen and check.

A Did you hear about the ¹*court / trial* of that company director?
B Oh, you mean the one who was ²*accused / arrested* of bribery. I knew he'd been ³*arrested / sentenced*. What happened?
A It was incredible. He appeared in ⁴*trial / court* yesterday and five ⁵*suspects / witnesses* all gave ⁶*evidence / verdicts*. They all said he had asked them for bribes.
B Wow. So, what was the ⁷*verdict / trial*? Was he found ⁸*accused / guilty*?
A No, the ⁹*jury / witnesses* said he was not guilty.
B Hmm. What did the ¹⁰*judge / jury* say?
A Nothing. She didn't ¹¹*arrest / sentence* him. She let him go free.
B Hmm. That's a bit odd, isn't it?

c Think of a famous court case from your country or from a film you've seen. Make notes on what happened. Think about:
- the crime and when it happened
- any suspects who were accused and/or arrested
- the trial and the witnesses who gave evidence
- the jury's verdict
- the judge's sentence.

d 💬 Discuss the court cases. Which one is the most interesting?

PRONUNCIATION Sound and spelling: *l*

a ▶ 08.08 Listen to the words. Is the letter *l* pronounced in all of them?

stole	talk
will	trial

b ▶ 08.09 Underline the word in each group where *l* is not pronounced.

1 called   could   cold
2 milk   incredible walk
3 should   guilty   told
4 film   gold   calm

c 💬 Practise saying all the words in **a** and **b** with and without the /l/ sound.

d ≫ Now go back to p. 97.

161

9A Health

a Match the texts to the pictures.

1 'Last night I **bumped** my head against the kitchen cupboard door so hard that I collapsed on the ground and **lost consciousness**. I didn't cut myself badly, so I won't have a **scar**, but this morning there's a large **bruise** on my forehead.'

2 'A few months ago I woke up feeling very ill. My face was very **pale** and my head was **aching**. I also felt really **dizzy**. I went to the doctor and he said it was probably just an **infection**, so I stayed at home until I felt better.'

b Match the words in **bold** in the texts to the definitions 1–8.
1 a temporary dark mark on your skin
2 to hurt part of your body by hitting it against something hard
3 when your face has less colour than normal because you are ill
4 when you feel the world is spinning around
5 a more formal way of saying 'pass out'
6 to have a continuous pain in a part of your body
7 a disease in a part of your body that is caused by bacteria or a virus
8 a permanent mark on the skin after you cut yourself

c Complete the sentences using the correct form of the words in **a**.
1 When I sit at my desk behind my computer all day, my back often starts to _____.
2 I almost _____ _____, so he poured cold water on my face to keep me awake.
3 I hardly slept last night, so now I feel exhausted and my face is _____.
4 I have a small car and I often _____ my head when I get in.
5 The _____ on my stomach is from an operation I had when I was a child.
6 He fell down and hit his leg on a chair yesterday. Now he has a big _____ on his knee.
7 My throat is very sore today. I probably have an _____.
8 I always eat breakfast because if I don't, I usually start to feel _____ with hunger at about 11 o'clock.

d Choose five of the words in **a** and **b** and tell a partner something that happened to you or someone you know, using the words. Ask and answer questions.

> I had an infection last month after I had a cold. I was off work for a week.

PRONUNCIATION Sound and spelling: *ui*

a ▶ 09.01 Put the words in pairs of the same vowel sound. Listen and check.

br**ui**se q**ui**et
w**i**re g**ui**tar
d**i**zzy sh**oe**s

b ▶ 09.02 What sound does *ui* have? Put the words in the correct box.

fr**ui**t req**ui**re
inq**ui**re g**ui**lt
s**ui**t n**ui**sance
b**ui**ld circ**ui**t
bisc**ui**t acq**ui**re

Sound 1 /ɪ/	Sound 2 /uː/	Sound 3 /waɪ/
guitar	bruise	quiet

c Write three sentences. Each sentence should contain a *ui* word with a different sound. Read your sentences to other students. Check each other's pronunciation.

d ≫ Now go back to p. 106.

Vocabulary Focus

10A Adjectives with prefixes

a Read about William and his change of lifestyle. What part of his life does he change?

> William was working as a **legal** adviser. He was an **experienced** and **responsible** employee with **regular** working hours. But he was bored. He was not a **patient** man either, and wanted to change his life before it was too late. So he handed in his notice and explained in a **formal** and **polite** manner that he was not **satisfied** with his situation.
>
> He then started working for himself as a gardener and discovered that it was even better than **expected**. He enjoyed working outdoors, he loved seeing all the wildlife around him and he felt like a very **fortunate** man. He was happy that he had been **honest** with himself and followed his heart.

b Look at the adjectives in **bold** in the text. Add the opposite of the adjectives in the correct place in the table. Use a dictionary to help you.

un-	in-	im-
ir-	il-	dis-

c Look again at the adjectives in the blog on p. 118. Add them to the correct places.

d Complete these rules:

> We use *im-* instead of *in-* before adjectives beginning with the letter _____.
> We use *il-* instead of *in-* before adjectives beginning with the letter _____.
> We use *ir-* instead of *in-* before adjectives beginning with the letter _____.

e Use adjectives in the table to complete the sentences.
1. Karen left top-secret documents in her car with the window open. It was very _____.
2. I inherited my grandmother's jewellery when she died. I had no idea she wanted me to have it, so it was completely _____.
3. Be careful of Alex. He may try to cheat you! He's a bit _____.
4. My sister always reads the last chapter first because she wants to find out what happens in the end. She's so _____.
5. I stayed in a hotel with terrible service. My friend recommended it to me, but I was very _____.

f 💬 Choose two of these questions and discuss them with a partner.
1. Do you ever get impatient? When?
2. What is the most unbelievable piece of news you've heard recently?
3. What's the most unexpected thing that's ever happened to you?

PRONUNCIATION Word stress

a ▶ 10.04 How many syllables do these words have? Put them in the correct place in the table. Listen and check.

impatient	illegal
unfortunate	irregular
dishonest	inexperienced
irresponsible	dissatisfied

3 syllables	4 syllables	5 syllables

b ▶ 10.04 Listen again and mark the main stress in each word. Which two words also have a secondary stress?

c Where is the stress in all the 3- and 4-syllable words? What's different about the 5-syllable words?

d 💬 Choose three words with a different number of syllables. Say the word in a sentence to your partner. Check that your partner's stress is correct.

e ⟫ Now go back to p. 118.

Phonemic Symbols

Vowel sounds

Short

/ə/	/æ/	/ʊ/	/ɑ/
teach**er**	m**a**n	p**u**t	g**o**t
/ɪ/	/i/	/e/	/ʌ/
ch**i**p	happ**y**	m**e**n	b**u**t

Long

/ɜː/	/ɑː/	/uː/	/ɔː/	/iː/
sh**ir**t	p**ar**t	wh**o**	w**al**k	ch**ea**p

Diphthongs (two vowel sounds)

/eə/	/ɪə/	/ʊə/	/ɔɪ/	/aɪ/	/eɪ/	/oʊ/	/aʊ/
h**air**	n**ear**	t**our**	b**oy**	f**i**ne	l**a**te	c**oa**t	n**ow**

Consonants

/p/	/b/	/f/	/v/	/t/	/d/	/k/	/g/	/θ/	/ð/	/tʃ/	/dʒ/
pill	**b**ook	**f**ace	**v**an	**t**ime	**d**og	**c**old	**g**o	**th**irty	**th**ey	**ch**oose	**j**eans
/s/	/z/	/ʃ/	/ʒ/	/m/	/n/	/ŋ/	/h/	/l/	/r/	/w/	/j/
say	**z**ero	**sh**oe	u**s**ually	**m**e	**n**ow	si**ng**	**h**ot	**l**ate	**r**ed	**w**ent	**y**es

Irregular verbs

Infinitive	Past simple	Past participle
be	was /wɒz/ / were /wɜː/	been
become	became	become
blow	blew /bluː/	blown /bləʊn/
break /breɪk/	broke /brəʊk/	broken /ˈbrəʊkən/
bring /brɪŋ/	brought /brɔːt/	brought /brɔːt/
build /bɪld/	built /bɪlt/	built /bɪlt/
buy /baɪ/	bought /bɔːt/	bought /bɔːt/
catch /kætʃ/	caught /kɔːt/	caught /kɔːt/
choose /tʃuːz/	chose /tʃəʊz/	chosen /ˈtʃəʊzən/
come	came	come
cost	cost	cost
cut	cut	cut
deal /dɪəl/	dealt /delt/	dealt /delt/
do	did	done /dʌn/
draw /drɔː/	drew /druː/	drawn /drɔːn/
drink	drank	drunk
drive /draɪv/	drove /drəʊv/	driven /ˈdrɪvən/
eat /iːt/	ate /et/	eaten /ˈiːtən/
fall	fell	fallen
feel	felt	felt
find /faɪnd/	found /faʊnd/	found /faʊnd/
fly /flaɪ/	flew /fluː/	flown /fləʊn/
forget	forgot	forgotten
get	got	got
give /gɪv/	gave /geɪv/	given /ˈgɪvən/
go	went	gone /gɒn/
grow /grəʊ/	grew /gruː/	grown /grəʊn/
have /hæv/	had /hæd/	had /hæd/
hear /hɪə/	heard /hɜːd/	heard /hɜːd/
hide /haɪd/	hid /hɪd/	hidden /ˈhɪdn/
hit	hit	hit
hold /həʊld/	held	held
keep	kept	kept
know /nəʊ/	knew /njuː/	known /nəʊn/
lead /liːd/	led /led/	led /led/

Infinitive	Past simple	Past participle
learn /lɜːn/	learned learnt /lɜːnt/	learned learnt /lɜːnt/
leave /liːv/	left	left
lend	lent	lent
let	let	let
lose /luːz/	lost	lost
make	made	made
meet	met	met
pay /peɪ/	paid /peɪd/	paid /peɪd/
put	put	put
read /riːd/	read /red/	read /red/
ride /raɪd/	rode /rəʊd/	ridden /ˈrɪdən/
ring	rang	rung
run	ran	run
sink /sɪŋk/	sank /sæŋk/	sunk /sʌŋk/
say /seɪ/	said /sed/	said /sed/
see	saw /sɔː/	seen
sell	sold /səʊld/	sold /səʊld/
set	set	set
sing	sang	sung
sleep	slept	slept
speak /spiːk/	spoke /spəʊk/	spoken /ˈspəʊkən/
spend	spent	spent
stand	stood /stʊd/	stood /stʊd/
steal /stiːl/	stole /stəʊl/	stolen /ˈstəʊlən/
swim /swɪm/	swam /swæm/	swum /swʌm/
take /teɪk/	took /tʊk/	taken /ˈteɪkən/
teach /tiːtʃ/	taught /tɔːt/	taught /tɔːt/
tell	told /təʊld/	told /təʊld/
think	thought /θɔːt/	thought /θɔːt/
throw /θrəʊ/	threw /θruː/	thrown /θrəʊn/
understand	understood /ʌndəˈstʊd/	understood /ʌndəˈstʊd/
wake /weɪk/	woke /wəʊk/	woken /ˈwəʊkən/
wear /weə/	wore /wɔː/	worn /wɔːn/
win	won	won
write /raɪt/	wrote /rəʊt/	written /ˈrɪtən/

Acknowledgements

The authors and publishers acknowledge the following sources of copyright material and are grateful for the permissions granted. While every effort has been made, it has not always been possible to identify the sources of all the material used, or to trace all copyright holders. If any omissions are brought to our notice, we will be happy to include the appropriate acknowledgements on reprinting and in the next update to the digital edition, as applicable.

Key:
U = Unit, C = Communication Plus, V = Vocabulary Focus

Text
U2: The New Zealand Herald for the extract from 'Robert Hewitt's story of survival', by Leah Haines, *The New Zealand Herald, 19/03/2006*. Reproduced with permission; **U6:** Guardian News & Media Ltd for the adapted text from 'Ancient tribal language becomes extinct as last speaker dies', by Jonathan Watts, *The Guardian, 10/02/2010*. Reproduced with permission; **C:** Extract from 'Separated twin boys with almost identical lives', *Reader's Digest*. Copyright 1980 Reader's Digest magazine. Reproduced with kind permission.

Photography
The following photographs are sourced from Getty Images.
U1: Ullstein bild; MaFelipe/iStock/Getty Images Plus; Damocean/iStock/Getty Images Plus; Sebnem Coskun/Anadolu Agency; Patrick McMullan; Bloomberg; Daily Herald Archive/SSPL; Handout/Getty Images News; Thomas Barwick/DigitalVision; Westend61; PixelsEffect/E+; GlobalStock/E+; Tim Robberts/Stone; Tim Robberts/DigitalVision; FG Trade/E+; Filadendron/E+; Lilly Roadstones/Stone; **U2:** JUSTIN TALLIS/Stringer/AFP; Jeff Rotman/Photolibrary/Getty Images Plus; Zac Macaulay/The Image Bank/Getty Images Plus; Frederic Pacorel/Photolibrary/Getty Images Plus; Praphan Sanstongngam/EyeEm; LILLIAN SUWANRUMPHA/AFP; Lori Adamski Peek/Photolibrary/Getty Images Plus; Martin Harvey/DigitalVision; ePhotocorp/iStock/Getty Images Plus; Zdenek Maly/EyeEm; Maxime Riendeau/500px Prime; Martin Mecnarowski/500Px Plus; Andy2673/iStock/Getty Images Plus; Christopher Pillitz/Hulton Archive; ULTRA.F/The Image Bank/Getty Images Plus; Tetra Images; Witold Skrypczak/Lonely Planet Images/Getty Images Plus; Marco Livolsi/EyeEm; Yasuhide Fumoto/Photodisc; **U3:** Thomas_EyeDesign/E+; Hill Street Studios/DigitalVision; Luis Alvarez/DigitalVision; Kimberrywood/iStock/Getty Images Plus; Drbouz/E+; Cecilie_Arcurs/E+; Kasto80/iStock/Getty Images Plus; Vgajic/E+; Paul Kane/Stringer/Getty Images Sport; Laurence Griffiths/Staff/Getty Images Sport; Tim Clayton/Corbis Sport; STAFF/AFP; John Dorton/ISI Photos/Getty Images Sport; OLAF KRAAK/Staff/AFP; PhotoAlto/Sandro Di Carlo Darsa/PhotoAlto Agency RF Collections; Michael Steele/Staff/Getty Images Sport; Tim de Waele/Staff/Velo; VCG/Visual China Group; Matt Sullivan/Stringer/Getty Images Sport; Sportstock/E+; Tom Werner/DigitalVision; Dean Mouhtaropoulos/Getty Images Sport; **U4:** Marko Geber/DigitalVision; Vstock LLC; Ariel Skelley/DigitalVision; Andresr/E+; Ty Downing/Photolibrary/Getty Images Plus; FG Trade/E+; Fairfax Media; Education Images/Universal Images Group; EXTREME-PHOTOGRAPHER/iStock/Getty Images Plus; Ade_Deployed/E+; Sam Edwards/OJO Images; Sisoje/E+; Mariusz_prusaczyk/iStock Editorial/Getty Images Plus; Tuul & Bruno Morandi/The Image Bank; Westend61; Alexander Spatari/Moment; Michaeljung/iStock/Getty Images Plus; **U5:** Frans Lemmens/The Image Bank Unreleased; Hinterhaus Productions/DigitalVision; Meredith Heil/iStock/Getty Images Plus; Charlie Waite/The Image Bank/Getty Images Plus; JohnnyGreig/E+; Brett Phibbs/Image Source; DigitalGlobe/ScapeWare3d/DigitalGlobe; Paul Souders/Stone; Joseph Van Os/The Image Bank/Getty Images Plus; Andresr/E+; William King/Taxi/Getty Images Plus; Juanmonino/E+; Chasing Light - Photography by James Stone james-stone.com/Moment; Simon Bottomley/DigitalVision; Jens Kuhfs/The Image Bank/Getty Images Plus; Spondylolithesis/iStock Unreleased; Richard Clark/The Image Bank; Andrew Merry/Moment; Damir Khabirov/iStock/Getty Images Plus; **U6:** Fuse/Corbis; Museimage/Moment/Getty Images Plus; Westend61; PeopleImages/iStock/Getty Images Plus; Maskot; Salvator Barki/Moment/Getty Images Plus; Jose Fuste Raga/Corbis Documentary/Getty Images Plus; JORGE MURGUIA/500Px Plus; 12ee12/iStock/Getty Images Plus; Tsepova_Ekaterina/iStock/Getty Images Plus; Dinodia Photo/Corbis Documentary; MUJAHID SAFODIEN/Stringer/AFP; Boston Globe; Gallo Images - Emil von Maltitz/Riser/Getty Images Plus; www.sierralara.com/Moment/Getty Images Plus; Edb3_16/iStock/Getty Images Plus; GCShutter/E+; Mark Newman/The Image Bank; Prasit photo/Moment; Jane Khomi/Moment; RebeccaAng/RooM; Grant Faint/The Image Bank; **U7:** Philip Gould/Corbis Documentary; Grant Faint/The Image Bank Unreleased; Kevin Clogstoun/Lonely Planet Images/Getty Images Plus; BEN STANSALL/AFP; View Pictures/Universal Images Group; Copyright Michael Mellinger/Moment; Peter Unger/The Image Bank; Lorado/E+; Caspar Benson; RuslanDashinsky/E+; M-gucci/iStock/Getty Images Plus; Claire Doherty/In Pictures; Xuanyu Han/Moment; Ajr_images/iStock/Getty Images Plus; Marvin Fox/Moment Open; Yellow Dog Productions/DigitalVision; JohnnyGreig/E+; Jetta Productions Inc/DigitalVision; Luis Alvarez/DigitalVision; Zorazhuang/E+; **U8:** Tristan Fewings/Getty Images Entertainment; LightFieldStudios/iStock/Getty Images Plus; Maskot; Annabelle Breakey/Stone/Getty Images Plus; Rattanakun Thongbun/EyeEm; Laurence Mouton/Canopy/Getty Images Plus; Funstock/E+; Deborah Feingold/Corbis Entertainment; **U9:** Jonas Gratzer/LightRocket; THOMAS SAMSON/AFP; Westend61; Massimo Ravera/Moment; Natthawut Nungsanther/EyeEm; Berlise De Jager/EyeEm; Wingmar/iStock/Getty Images Plus; GlobalStock/E+; Underwood Archives/Archive Photos; Stevica Mrdja/EyeEm; Patrickheagney/iStock/Getty Images Plus; PNC/DigitalVision; **U10:** Michael I I/Stone; Hulton Archive/Stringer/Hulton Archive; SEAN GLADWELL/Moment; Max Dannenbaum/The Image Bank; 104kelly/iStock/Getty Images Plus; Andrew_Howe/iStock/Getty Images Plus; Lillian SUWANRUMPHA/AFP; Johnny Nunez/Getty Images Entertainment; Warrengoldswain/iStock/Getty Images Plus; Hill Street Studios/DigitalVision; Bokan76/iStock/Getty Images Plus; Tadamasa Taniguchi/Digital Vision; **C:** SebastiaanKroes/Moment; GUILLERMO LEGARIA/Stringer/AFP; Devasahayam Chandra Dhas/iStock Unreleased; George Mathew/Moment; Sergei Bobylev/TASS; Anton Novoderezhkin/TASS; Justin Paget/The Image Bank/Getty Images Plus; Westend61; Sonatali/iStock/Getty Images Plus; DouglasPearson/Photolibrary/Getty Images Plus; Asbe/iStock/Getty Images Plus; DeAgostini/L.Romano/DeAgostiniPictureLibrary/Getty Images Plus; PATSTOCK/Moment; **V:** Hendrik Sulaiman/EyeEm; David Madison/Stone; Commercial Eye/The Image Bank.

The following photographs are sourced from other sources/libraries.
U1: Swietenia Puspa Lestari Photo by Divers Clean Action 2021; **U2:** © Mauro Prosperi; **U4:** Tuk Tuk Chai; Image courtesy Mark Pearson; Jannarong/Shutterstock; Derek Meijer/Alamy Stock Photo; **U6:** © FMGB Guggenheim Bilbao Museoa, 2020.

Cover photography by Stanislaw Pytel/Stone/Getty Images.

Illustrations
QBS Learning; David Semple; Dusan Lakicevic; Gavin Reece; Jerome Mireault; Jo Goodberry; John (KJA Artists); Marie-Eve Tremblay; Mark Bird; Mark Duffin; Martin Sanders; Paul Williams; Roger Penwill; Sean (KJA Artists); Sean Sims.

Video stills
Commissioned by Rob Maidment and Sharp Focus Productions for Cambridge University Press: U1–U10.

Audio Production by Leon Chambers and by Creative Listening.

Typeset by QBS Learning.

Corpus

Development of this publication has made use of the Cambridge English Corpus (CEC). The CEC is a computer database of contemporary spoken and written English, which currently stands at over one billion words. It includes British English, American English and other varieties of English. It also includes the Cambridge Learner Corpus, developed in collaboration with the University of Cambridge ESOL Examinations. Cambridge University Press has built up the CEC to provide evidence about language use that helps us to produce better language teaching materials.

English Profile

This product is informed by English Vocabulary Profile, built as part of English Profile, a collaborative programme designed to enhance the learning, teaching and assessment of English worldwide. Its main funding partners are Cambridge University Press and Cambridge Assessment English and its aim is to create a 'profile' for English, linked to the Common European Framework of Reference for Languages (CEFR). English Profile outcomes, such as the English Vocabulary Profile, will provide detailed information about the language that learners can be expected to demonstrate at each CEFR level, offering a clear benchmark for learners' proficiency. For more information, please visit www.englishprofile.org.

CALD

The Cambridge Advanced Learner's Dictionary is the world's most widely used dictionary for learners of English. Including all the words and phrases that learners are likely to come across, it also has easy to understand definitions and example sentences to show how the word is used in context. The Cambridge Advanced Learner's Dictionary is available online at dictionary.cambridge.org.

CAMBRIDGE
UNIVERSITY PRESS & ASSESSMENT

Shaftesbury Road, Cambridge CB2 8EA, United Kingdom

One Liberty Plaza, 20th Floor, New York, NY 10006, USA

477 Williamstown Road, Port Melbourne, VIC 3207, Australia

314–321, 3rd Floor, Plot 3, Splendor Forum, Jasola District Centre, New Delhi – 110025, India

103 Penang Road, #05–06/07, Visioncrest Commercial, Singapore 238467

Cambridge University Press & Assessment is a department of the University of Cambridge.

We share the University's mission to contribute to society through the pursuit of education, learning and research at the highest international levels of excellence.

www.cambridge.org
Information on this title: www.cambridge.org/9781108958080

© Cambridge University Press & Assessment 2022

This publication is in copyright. Subject to statutory exception and to the provisions of relevant collective licensing agreements, no reproduction of any part may take place without the written permission of Cambridge University Press & Assessment.

First published 2022

20 19 18 17 16 15 14 13 12 11 10 9 8

Printed in Poland by Opolgraf

A catalogue record for this publication is available from the British Library

ISBN	978-1-108-95808-0	Upper Intermediate Student's Book with eBook
ISBN	978-1-108-96131-8	Upper Intermediate Student's Book with Digital Pack
ISBN	978-1-108-96135-6	Upper Intermediate Workbook with Answers
ISBN	978-1-108-96136-3	Upper Intermediate Workbook without Answers
ISBN	978-1-108-96133-2	Upper Intermediate Combo A with Digital Pack
ISBN	978-1-108-96134-9	Upper Intermediate Combo B with Digital Pack
ISBN	978-1-108-96137-0	Upper Intermediate Teacher's Book with Digital Pack
ISBN	978-1-108-95951-3	Upper Intermediate Presentation Plus
ISBN	978-1-108-96132-5	Upper Intermediate Student's Book with Digital Pack, Academic Skills and Reading Plus

Additional resources for this publication at www.cambridge.org/empower

Cambridge University Press & Assessment has no responsibility for the persistence or accuracy of URLs for external or third-party internet websites referred to in this publication, and does not guarantee that any content on such websites is, or will remain, accurate or appropriate. Information regarding prices, travel timetables, and other factual information given in this work is correct at the time of first printing but Cambridge University Press & Assessment does not guarantee the accuracy of such information thereafter.

This page is intentionally left blank.

This page is intentionally left blank.

1-b   6-a
2-a   7-c
3-c   8-c
4-a   9-a
5-d   10-d

1- If you had done
2- We wouldn't ~~have to stand~~ be standing / If we had brought
3- If I hadn't stayed up / I wouldn't be feeling
4- I wouldn't be / hadn't helped
5- I would have recorded
6- I would have asked / I hadn't had a boyf already

This page is intentionally left blank.